WILD
SEX

WILD SEX

Way Beyond the Birds
and the Bees

Susan Windybank

St. Martin's Press

NEW YORK

Library of Congress Cataloging-in-Publication Data

Windybank, Susan.
    Wild sex : way beyond the birds and the bees / Susan Windybank.
      p.   cm.
    ISBN 0-312-08336-X (pb)
    1. Sexual behavior in animals.   I. Title.
    QL761.w54   1992
    591.56—dc20   92-9747
                                                                    CIP

First published in Australia by Reed Books Pty Ltd.

First U.S. Edition: September 1992

10 9 8 7 6 5 4 3 2 1

Contents

Mating Styles

Introduction

There are over a million known species in the world and maybe another million, predominantly insects, yet to be discovered. With such a wide range of animals it is no wonder that sexual habits vary greatly from species to species. Some creatures mate in mid-flight, others underwater, on land or underground. Once they have found each other and copulated some stay together for the rest of their lives, others part company and never meet again.

Some mating styles found in the wild are considered abhorrent by human society. These include group sex, rape, homosexuality, bondage, sadomasochism and polyandry. On the other hand, there are many creatures who favour monogamy and display considerable tenderness and beauty.

However, animal reproduction does not merely consist of copulation and like humans there are certain behavioural codes and activities associated with the physical act including courtship and caring for the offspring.

How animals find each other and prepare for sex is a fascinating study which is referred to scientifically as courtship and is similar to that of humans. We have devised countless ways of attracting a mate, from catching the eye of someone across a crowded room to blatant propositioning. The mating game is much the same for animals. In fact, the loud and elaborate sounds, the display of colours and patterns and the dancing rituals that animals employ to catch the eye of a mate frequently attract humans too.

The most important function of courtship is to ensure that sex takes place in the most favourable conditions; that fertilisation occurs and that the maximum number of offspring survive. Higher animals have developed complex systems of parental care to nurture their young while less sophisticated marine animals simply produce copious quantities of eggs.

In this way sex provides the foundation stone for all life on this planet. If animals and plants did not reproduce, life on Earth would be stagnant. Fortunately, there is an ineradicable instinct in all living things which drives them to come together and mate. Thus, the offspring that are constantly being produced balance out the numbers that die of old age, illness or are killed. Sex is the great force which sustains life. Moreover, every creature seems to exist solely for the purpose of reproduction and there are few animals that outlive their period of sexual usefulness.

In fact, humans are the only animals that survive after their reproductive days are over and are the only species with an unlimited capacity to enjoy sex at any time of the year. Having greater imagination and communicative skills, humans use hundreds of different sexual positions whereas most wild creatures enjoy just one. So when someone tells you you are behaving like an animal having sex they are actually wrong. Contrary to popular myth, animals cannot fornicate at the drop of a hat but are subject to very strict laws. Thus, it is only when humans begin restricting their sexuality with moral codes that they do in fact behave like animals.

The only creatures to defy all laws of nature are the protozoans and they are the living proof that perpetuation of the species is by no means always linked to sex instinct. Lower plants and unicellular animals reproduce asexually which means they do not have any sex organs but instead employ a number of other methods to produce offspring. By closely examining these primitive organisms it is possible to discover the beginnings of sex in the animal world and to trace the path of evolution right up to modern methods of reproduction.

Section 1

THE EVOLUTION OF SEX

In the beginning...

Sex and hunger are the two great instincts that dominate all living things. Hunger compels animals to look for food so that their individual survival is guaranteed; sex compels them to come together and mate so as to ensure the survival of the species. With over one million known species of animal life existing on this planet it is no wonder that there is an incredible variety of ways in which animals procreate. Some go to extraordinary lengths to couple and multiply; take the edible Roman Snails as a case in point. These creatures add new meaning to the old adage 'there's a fine line between pleasure and pain'. When mating they shoot love darts at each other before copulation to determine if they are both members of the same species.

In addition to the vital part sex plays in the perpetuation of species, it has also played and continues to play a major role in the gradual evolution of new species. Indeed, the history of evolution is inextricably linked with the development of sex as Charles Darwin's theory of evolution by natural selection rests on the development of sexual reproduction. Without the variation in species that results from the sexual cycle evolution would not be possible.

Darwin's theory of the origin of species by natural selection, otherwise known as survival of the fittest, excited considerable controversy on its release. It dealt a severe blow to the creationist belief that the incredible diversity in the natural world had been created by a higher force as documented in Genesis, the first chapter of the Bible. It is still possible that the Garden of Eden existed but in the light of evolution and modern genetics it does not seem probable that God created Adam and Eve but rather that humans evolved from other forms of life. Today it is generally accepted among scientific and non-scientific communities alike that the world's animals and plants developed in the course of evolution and that the human race evolved from the ancestors of these animals.

Natural selection occurs when a member of a species possesses a characteristic which is favoured by environmental change. While those without the particular characteristic die ,the animals with the feature survive and reproduce, passing on the quality that helped them to survive to some of their offspring. Darwin could not explain how the attributes favoured by environmental change came about. However, modern genetics and the discovery of genes have shed light on this dilemma. Genes are carriers of information that are passed on from parents to offspring. Each individual receives half of his genes from one parent and half from the other. Sometimes a parent gene may undergo a mutant change which is inherited by the offspring. If environmental change occurs which favours this mutation then those carrying it will generally live longer and produce more offspring, thus evolution will gradually occur.

In this way important changes in the reproductive behaviour and sex organs of animals have taken place, allowing some creatures to conquer new habitats. Indeed, life would still be condemned to the sea if animals did not have the ability to gradually adapt their way of life to a new habitat. The transition from aquatic to terrestrial ways of life, for example, could not have happened without the development of internal fertilisation. Yet life on land constitutes only 5% of the total number of known species; terrestrial creatures include spiders, insects, birds, mammals and reptiles. The rest live and love in the murky depths of the planet's oceans, lakes and rivers which cover more than 70% of the Earth's surface. In fact, it was in the ocean that life first originated as fossil evidence indicates.

Fossil records shed a great deal of light on the evolution of species. By examining fossils in conjunction with living species, it is possible to start putting the pieces of the evolutionary jigsaw puzzle together. Other records of past life are the embryos of the present; the study of embryos in order to trace the path of evolution is known as biogenesis.

A human embryo is formed when a sperm and ovum meet and fertilisation takes place. First, cell replication occurs by binary fission in the same way protozoans reproduce, forming a shapeless clump of cells. Next a worm-like shape develops, then gill slits, a tail and a digestive system emerge before the embryo finally takes on a human form.

In the beginning, however, sex between animals was not nearly as complex as human reproduction. At first animals reproduced without any male or female sex organs and differentiation between the sexes did not emerge for some time. For this reason their reproductive cycle is not linked to the sex instinct as this sexual practice, known as asexual reproduction, does not require the male and female to find each other and mate. The absence of a sexual cycle means that courtship rituals and sexual behaviour are not evident as such. However, the beginnings of courtship behaviour can be seen in some protozoans, those most primitive animals belonging to the Phylum *Protozoa* meaning 'first living things'. Chemical reactions involving pheromones do take place among unicellular animals that favour a combination of asexual and sexual reproduction.

The protozoans form part of a large group known as the *Invertebrata* or animals without backbones; the other main group is the Sub-Phylum *Chordata* or animals with backbones. The chordates are probably the most well- known division within the Animal Kingdom, which consists of 25 major subdivisions or *phyla*. Those belonging to a particular phylum are placed there because of certain common features; in this way classification of animals into groups is essential in identifying species. It is also important in revealing the evolutionary associations between various phyla.

Humans belong to the chordates which is one reason why this group is often studied more closely than the invertebrates. It is natural that humans are curious about their ancestry but this imbalance in knowledge does not suggest that invertebrates are less worthy of study than chordates.

However, the sheer size of the category is an obstacle to close examination. Invertebrates actually outnumber chordates many times over as well as dominating the animal world in terms of the numbers of species. For instance, almost 300,000 varieties of beetles, from the insect class, are known to scientists; thus these tiny creatures outnumber the living species of vertebrates by over 7 to 1.

Inadequate fossil records are another reason for the comparative lack of knowledge on invertebrates. The soft bodies of these animals do not preserve well as fossils and so the links between the many phyla are often tenuous. The chordates on the other hand are more readily fossilised due to their hard body parts and skeletal structure and they show a much clearer evolutionary progression: fishes, amphibians, reptiles, birds and mammals. The gradual evolution of the invertebrates is less clear and patchy fossil records are not the only obstacle to study. Difficulties associated with observing invertebrates like the protozoans in their natural habitat have also contributed to the relatively thin volume of information available on their bodily functions.

The protozoans are generally the starting point for studying the history of evolution. They are the modern representatives of the common ancestors shared by all living things including humans. How these early creatures originated, however, is still a matter of speculation. One recent idea suggests that four thousand million years ago, when the Earth was a swirling mass of gases, liquids and solid particles, a series of chemical reactions took place from which some simple chemical compounds were formed. These became the basic building blocks of life. Vegetation then gradually appeared, followed by the first unicellular animals.

For the purposes of this book we will follow the development of life from the primitive protozoans through to the more advanced animals. One of the dangers in tracing evolution in this way, however, is that it can suggest a ladder-like progression from 'lower' to 'higher' animals. If

A male Wolf Spider semaphores his love signals during courtship.

this was the case then the course of evolution would be very easy to trace. But evolution cannot be conceptualised as a ladder with a bottom and a top rung; humans being at the top and protozoans at the bottom; all other creatures supposedly following after each other in a neat progression. It is more useful to envisage evolution as the tree of life with branches spreading out in every direction. Thus the use of the labels 'lower' and 'higher' are somewhat misleading. The term 'higher' is generally used to describe an animal whose body structure and behaviour are comparatively complex. A 'lower' animal is usually one of simple structure. This ignores the fact that the unicellular organisms, for example, are very efficient and successful within their habitat, as proven by the number of different species that exist today.

Sexual Origins

The protozoa or unicell first introduced reproduction into the animal world by splitting in two about three billion years ago. These microscopic creatures are the most simple form of life on earth, consisting of a single living cell with a central nucleus that controls all its functions. The rest of the Animal Kingdom is made up of multicellular animals called metazoans. The term protozoa comes from the Greek *protos* meaning 'first' and *zoa* meaning 'animals' and it is thought that life ultimately originated from these uncomplicated animals. Yet despite their basic structure the protozoans are a highly successful phylum and it is estimated that over 80,000 species exist today. They have the ability to live in environments inaccessible to other animals and are found in fresh and salt water, as well as moist soil. In the case of parasitic varieties, they also thrive in the bodies of multicellular hosts.

Reproduction is a straightforward and loveless process for these tiny creatures; the parent cell simply divides into two new identical daughter cells. This quick and efficient form of multiplying is known as asexual reproduction by binary fission and it is widespread among the protozoans. The textbook unicellular animal, *Amoeba proteus*, reproduces asexually and may do so in less than an hour up to eight times a day, resulting in a rapid rise in numbers. Parasitic protozoans have developed an even faster procreative process; moving from host to host is risky but prolific reproduction increases the chances of success. The malarial parasite, for instance, divides repeatedly to produce eight, 16 or more offspring by a cellular process known as multiple fission.

Budding is another more complex method of asexual reproduction found in some protozoans, although it is normally associated with plants. It is also widely used by the sponges and coelenterates. Budding occurs when the parent grows a wart-like bud on the outside of its body, which breaks off and develops into a new individual. Like the evolution of multiple fission from binary fission, budding too has developed into speedier methods favoured by parasites. Schizogony or multiple budding involves the growth of between four to 1000 new individuals which develop as buds on the parent's body.

The advantages of asexual reproduction lie in its great simplicity. Unlike sexual species where the male and female have to find each other and copulate, the animal just divides in two and thus populations can build up very quickly. Sometimes numbers increase so dramatically that these microscopic creatures can be seen by the naked eye. In California and the Carribean the protozoan population of *Gonyaulax* can swell to such a degree that they create a glow in the sea at night. By day they form red tides that produce toxic waste material deadly to all other marine life.

The main disadvantage of reproducing asexually is that there is no blending of genetic characteristics during fertilisation. Asexual offspring are clones of their parents, resulting in a more or less homogeneous population. This makes it difficult for species to adapt to environmental change because there is no variation among the offspring and so the forces of evolution cannot really work. When each individual is different some will be better equipped to survive in the face of change and will pass on their useful qualities. Those not so well suited will die.

Despite favouring asexual reproduction over the sexual cycle protozoans have been observed reproducing sexually, albeit at a primitive level. The *Paramecium*, for example, generally reproduces asexually by binary fission but sometimes it will resort to a sexual process called conjugation when the surrounding environment deteriorates or when another colony of *Paramecium* enter its habitat. Conjugation occurs when two individual cells align side by side, their cell membranes break down and they exchange parts of their nuclei. Then they separate and divide into four daughter cells. This process foreshadows sexual union and the differentiation of the sexes. In fact, it is not unlike copulation except that the two sexes are equal.

While it has been established that sex first began with the protozoans little is known about how it originated. This is because mating in many unicellular animals is rare and it is difficult for scientists to observe their sexual cycle. For this reason, far too little is known about sexual reproduction in its primitive forms. In addition, the incredible diversity of species within the phylum makes the study of the life cycle of every variety virtually impossible.

There is no doubt that the development of reproduction at the protozoan level helped speed up the evolutionary process. In species multiplying by asexual means, evolution is very slow because only one mutation, or the offspring of one individual, can be selected at any given time. But in species with a sexual cycle many different mutations can combine in one individual and then be subjected to natural selection simultaneously.

The way in which multicellular animals developed from the protozoans is still not entirely clear. Animals that could have given clues to the relationship between the two have long since been extinct and fossil evidence is sketchy. Existing animals such as the *Pandorina* only point to a possible path of development. Classed as a plant-animal because it

FATAL LOVE

For the queen bee sex is a once in a lifetime experience. One night of passion is all it takes to keep her producing eggs to her dying day. However for the lucky male, who wins over stiff competition, it is all over in a matter of seconds. After copulating in mid-air his penis snaps off inside the queen, acting as a plug to prevent the loss of any sperm. He has now played his final hand and falls to the ground where he bleeds to death.

makes its own food by photosynthesis but has retained its animal characteristic of being able to move about, *Pandorina* lives in cell colonies made up of 16 to 32 cells. When reproducing, the colony breaks down and conjugates with individuals from another colony. These conjugated cells then divide by binary fission to form new colonies. It is possible that the cell colonies in animals like the *Pandorina* could have failed to separate during reproduction and thus become permanent. Division of labour between cells, which is the basic difference between multicellular and unicellular animals, could then have occurred.

Some of the earliest multicellular animals can be found today in all the oceans and seas of the world; they are the Phylum *Porifera* (sponges) and the Phylum *Echinodermata*. Most scientists believe that the echinoderms are the ancestors of the chordates. Sponges can still be found in their original form, thus representing an independent line of evolution. Both phyla evolved roughly around the same time and have a number of features in common. Structurally they are the only two phyla, apart from the coelenterates, to have radial instead of bilateral symmetry. Their body consists of arms that radiate from a central point instead of having two sides that mirror each other. The larvae of the echinoderms, however, are structured on the bilateral symmetry plan, like the chordates, but this is lost as the animal matures and assumes the radial form.

Sexual simularities are also apparent between the two phyla. Firstly some species within both phyla interchange between reproducing asexually and sexually. This usually occurs in an alternating sequence. One generation reproduces asexually to produce a second generation that reproduces sexually to give rise to one more generation that multiplies asexually again. In addition, sponges and echinoderms also carry out a unique method of asexual reproduction known as regeneration. For example, if the body of a sponge splits or fragments, each little piece is capable of forming a new individual. Sponges may also reproduce asexually by budding. Although not all echinoderms can reproduce by regenerating as effectively as sponges, starfish are the exception. If a starfish loses an arm, it can replace it or the lost arm will grow into a new starfish.

Despite their primitive form sponges have also developed an advanced way of reproducing sexually in that they practice both external and internal fertilisation. With internal fertilisation the ova are fertilised within the parent sponge body. External fertilisation involves the release of the ova into the water where they are fertilised by sperm. Sponges are also hermaphrodites; this means they produce male and female eggs although at different times so that self-fertilisation does not occur. The term actually derives from Greek mythology. Hermaphroditos, son of Hermes the Greek messenger of the gods and Ahprodite, the love goddess, was the love object of the nymph in the fountain of Salmacis. She prayed to the gods that they never be parted as she clung to him. The gods took pity on her and made them into one.

Echinoderms reproduce sexually by external fertilisation. This is sex at its most impersonal; the two sexes never touch each other but reproduce at a distance. The males discharge their sperm into the water and the females follow suit with their ova. If and when the two meet, fertilisation occurs. To boost the chances of successful fertilisation both the male and female release a staggering number of ova and sperm. At the same time they secrete chemicals known as pheromones, the love drug of the animal world, which spark off a chain reaction among others of the same species and mass spawning begins. Spawning is concentrated into a short period of time to reduce wastage by increasing the odds of the ova and sperm meeting up. Yet despite the lack of contact between the sexes some echinoderms, like the Sea Urchins and Sea Cucumbers, show the first signs of parental care in the Animal Kingdom. They protect their young in special brood pouches on the upper part of their body. Parental care is an important part of ensuring reproductive success and is seen in its most advanced forms amongst the birds, mammals and primates. However, life in the sea and sex by external fertilisation does not call for more sophisticated forms of parenting and so care of the young remains at this rudimentary level for some time.

Apart from echinoderms and sponges, coelenterates are the only other animals to be built on the radial symmetry plan. The jellyfish, coral polyps and sea anemones which make up the Phylum *Coelenterata* also have tentacles with stinging cells. These are used to paralyse food before drawing it into their 'mouths', a single opening leading to a digestive cavity. Although they are still relatively simple animals, the beginnings of specialisation can be seen in the coelenterates. The Portuguese Man-Of-War, for example, is a group of polyps attached to a floating bladder; each polyp has a different role. Some catch food, others eat and digest it, some excrete it and of course there are others strictly concerned with reproduction.

The coelenterates' sex life is a varied one. Most species reproduce sexually by external fertilisation and show the same degree of parental care as the echinoderms. Their offspring are kept in special brood pouches until they are young adults ready to lead a life independent of their parents. Other species alternate between sexual and asexual reproduction; the *Hydra* is a textbook example. The only coelenterate to live in freshwater, it is hermaphrodite but releases ova and sperm at different times so that self-fertilisation does not occur. It can also reproduce asexually by its remarkable regenerative powers. For this reason it was named after the monster, Hydra, from Greek mythology, that kept growing heads as quickly as Hercules could cut them off.

Flatworms and roundworms are not regarded as particularly complex animals but they do have some structural advances over the coelenterates. They have three distinct cell layers and although they are hermaphrodites, their sex organs are much more advanced. These worms have a muscular penis which is kept in a sac and only brought out in the heat of the moment. Copulation begins in earnest when the two individuals assume a sexual position where their undersides touch. Then the penis protrudes through a genital pore and deposits the sperm in a copulatory sac, after which the two pull apart and withdraw their penes. The sperm travel down an oviduct and at the same time the ova are released into the oviduct where they meet up with the sperm for fertilisation. Eggs are then laid which attach themselves to plants and rocks. The parasitic varieties, such as the Liver Fluke and Hairworms, are also hermaphrodites but they tend to favour self-fertilisation. Hermaphrodites are an important step in the evolution of the male organ for they were the first real advance towards the penis seen today in the reptiles, mammals and the human race. Despite the relatively simple structure of creatures like the flatworms and roundworms they have at least managed to develop a tool for introducing sperm directly into the female's body.

These worms have also pioneered some of the first visual methods of courtship. The sea-dwelling fireworms, for example, light up the surface of the sea with their lovemaking. The females radiate a glow that attracts the males, who flash their love lights on and off to indicate their readiness to procreate. This spectacular display involves mass numbers and serves to bring the two sexes together so that the release of sperm and ova is synchronised and fertilisation assured.

Despite the fact that many varieties of worms are parasites and live on and cause death to plants, animals and people, some worms gradually evolved that were not harmful to humans. About 500 million years ago the segmented worms emerged, heralding a giant step in evolution. All higher animals including humans have evolved from the worm. There are about 15,000 freshwater, marine and land species of the segmented worm or *Annelida* including earthworms, freshwater worms, marine worms and leeches. *Annelida* are distinct from all other worms as they were the world's first animal to have an eating and digestive tube, sex parts and excretory organs. Although some varieties will occasionally reproduce asexually, most have a sexual cycle.

The *Lumbricus terrestis*, or Common Earthworm for example, is a hermaphrodite. When mating earthworms lie next to each other with their sex organs held together by mucus and then exchange sperm. This is stored in special receptacles called spermathacae and used later for fertilisation when the eggs are being laid. After discharging the eggs into a hiding place, the earthworm secretes a liquid that makes a closed cocoon which gradually hardens around its eggs. Other annelids also show concern for their young. Leeches make similar cocoons to earthworms, although the jawed leech takes the parent/child relationship one step further by actually wrapping itself around the cocoon or carrying it until the eggs hatch.

From the segmented worms developed the joint-legged animals known as the Phylum *Arthropoda*, the first group to include both land and sea animals. This phylum is the largest in the Animal Kingdom and includes the crustaceans, arachnids and insects; young insects in their grub-like form show a clear link with the annelids. The first arthropod, the now extinct trilobite, lived in water like crustaceans. It was the development of the exoskeleton which allowed arthropods to colonise land without losing too much water from their bodies.

Internal fertilisation is largely practised by the terrestrial varieties of *Arthropoda*. Once fertilisation has occurred each egg is laid in a protective shell that prevents dessication. In marine species, external fertilisation is widespread but instead of leaving their young to fend for themselves crabs, for example, will carry the eggs attached to their undersides until they hatch. Some crabs have also come very close to developing internal fertilisation. When mating, the male places a packet of sperm known as a spermatophore inside the female. This is later released with the ova and fertilisation occurs outside the female.

Around the same time as the evolution of the arthropods, the Phylum *Mollusca* was developing. This consists of snails, slugs, oysters, mussels, clams, cockels, scallops, squid, cuttlefish and many more. Molluscs have hard shells which cover the soft parts of their bodies in the same way that arthropods' exoskeletons protect their bodies, although molluscs' shells are more cumbersome. Thus most varieties of molluscs are found in water while most arthropods are found on land. The few terrestrial species of molluscs, such as snails, move very slowly on land.

As most molluscs are water creatures they tend to favour external fertilisation. One exception is the Periwinkle, or Marine Snail, which lives on the shoreline and is often used to demonstrate the link between internal fertilisation and life on land. Each variety of periwinkle is able to mate out of water by internal fertilisation. Those lower down on the shore must release their larvae into the water while those higher up in the splash zone, where water may not reach them for many days, omit the larvae stage by laying eggs in seaweed.

The evolution of the arthropods and molluscs also led to a significant advance in the structure of the sex organs. In these animals the penis and vagina, seen in their most advanced form in humans, begin to take shape. Most species carry out internal fertilisation by depositing a spermatophore in the female cavity by way of an artificial penis; even the water bound *Cephalopoda* (squids, cuttlefish, octopuses) use this method. In *Cephalopoda* this artificial penis is known as a hectocotylus and it is usually a specially modified tentacle. Some species have even developed a detachable penis which they leave behind in the the female body. Arachnids also have an artificial penis. In their case it is a leg that doubles as a penis and is known scientifically as a maxillary palp.

That courtship and mating techniques have become more sophisticated in these two phyla is easy to see at a glance. The spider has developed elaborate courting rituals to discourage hunting behaviour in the female and make her receptive to his sexual overtures. He may do this by plucking the strands of her web in a series of vibrations that announce his intentions. Spiders with keen eyesight use visual displays to attract a female while others woo their sexual partners with an aphrodisiac such as an insect wrapped up in silk. *Cephalopoda* also display sophisticated courtship signals. For example male squids court females with a display of colour changes while cuttlefish adopt a bright striped courtship dress. The use of colour and patterns in courtship displays are also seen later in the fish, the other major inhabitants of the world's oceans and seas.

By far the largest and most successful land animals are the insects. Being the biggest existing group of animals, the sex life of the insects is an incredibly varied one. It would be impossible to look at the complex sex lives of vertebrates without first saluting the amazing procreative activities of these tiny animals. Insects may mate on land or in the air and this has given rise to an incredible range of copulatory positions, the most common being the end to end position. Courtship behaviour is quite complex and there are many different visual and aural displays used by insects to attract a mate; some even release a scent which stimulates the female. In some fireflies, males are attracted by the female's light while in crickets it is the female who is attracted by the song of the male.

Sex between insects occurs when the male ejaculates sperm into the female, where it is kept in a special organ, the spermatheca, also found in some worms. Fertilisation involves the release of the ova which travel through the oviduct to be laid. Next the sperm leaves the spermatheca and enters the egg through a special opening, the micropyle, and fuses with the egg's nucleus. In rare cases a spermatophore is used instead of free flowing semen to inseminate the female. The young insect then develops inside the egg and hatches in a grub-like form known as the pupal stage. Although the insects' body structure is based on the arthropod

Amati moths mating end to end, the most common sexual position for insects.

plan, they have a number of additional features that have helped them adapt to land so well. Firstly, they have a waterproof layer on the outside of their exoskeletons so they do not dry up in the sun. Most insects also have a pair of wings and the development of flight has led to the conquest of a variety of habitats and thus great biological diversity. The growing complexity in sexual behaviour at this level is due in part to the refinement of sensory organs and to sex by internal fertilisation. Not only has it made life on land possible, it has also given the terrestrial varieties more independence and control of their environment through increased mobility. Unlike external fertilisation where ova and sperm are scattered into the sea and often meet up by chance, the male and female that employ internal fertilisation must find each other first - as the old saying goes it takes two to tango. For this reason sensory organs are more acute and courtship displays are more elaborate.

Eye catching displays are usually used by animals that have to look over a considerable distance for another member of their species with which to mate. In general it is the male that is the more attractive of the species as he must compete for the female who has the exceptional luck of being able to pick and choose. Male birds, for example, sport brilliant plumage and feathers while the females tend to be dull and plain looking. Other birds serenade their potential partners with intricate song patterns. In higher animals such as mammals and primates, the males fill the air with their mating calls or use pheromones and other sexual scents to attract a mate. Caring for the young also becomes more intricate in higher animals. As they produce fewer offspring they must take special care to ensure their survival. Parental care can be seen at its most complex in the primates where social organisation and customs mimic those of humans, albeit at a very primitive level.

Sex becomes increasingly specialised in the vertebrates, in conjunction with a growing complexity in all the bodily organs and functions. As a result pregnancy periods, or gestation, become longer and less offspring are produced, leading to a rapid development in care of the young. Differentiation between the sexes gives rise to secondary sexual characteristics or sexual dimorphism, accouting for the physical differences between males and females. This in turn sparks off social structures totally unlike those of insects, leading to territorial behaviour and the beginnings of a society structure. Also, reproduction between vertebrates always involves separate sexes. Even when the animals are hermaphrodites they will perform their sexual duties as either male or female. Asexual reproduction simply does not occur in the vertebrates.

The vertebrates are a Sub-Phylum of the lesser known Phylum *Chordata*. The most notable feature of animals within this phylum is that they have a skeletal rod called a notochord around which the backbone develops, thus supporting the body. The Phylum *Chordata* also includes three groups of animals without backbones, the protochordates; they are the hemichordates, tunicates and lancelets. These are primitive marine animals that are often used to demonstrate the evolutionary link between invertebrates and vertebrates as they display a mixture of invertebrate and vertebrate characteristics. However, there are still far too many gaps between them and the most primitive of modern vertebrates. All they can do is hint at some of the stages vertebrate animals passed through when they evolved from their invertebrate form. One well-known example of these three subphyla is the Sea Squirt or *Ascidiacea* from the Sub-Phylum *Tunicata*. These tubular shaped animals are hermaphrodites and reproduce by internal fertilisation. In their tadpole-like form chordate characteristics like the notochord are clearly evident. It gradually disappears as the Sea Squirt adopts its mature sedentary form and is replaced by a cartilaginous skeleton.

From the protochordates developed the fishes which are the oldest vertebrates. All other vertebrates including humans evolved from the fishes. There are over 20,000 species of fishes which account for over 40% of all existing vertebrates. They are cold-blooded animals that have adapted to life in water with fins and gills. The ancestors of modern fishes had no jaws. Their living descendants, *cyclostomes*, consist of the hagfish and the lampreys. Most are parasites and will latch on to a host fish with their teeth before sucking out their blood and muscle. They breed by external fertilisation. The male fertilises the eggs while the female spawns. Then the eggs are buried in the sand in simple nests made by moving stones with their mouths.

Cartilaginous fishes, which include the sharks, dogfish, skates, and rays, have as their name indicates, skeletons made up of cartilage rather than hard bone. They are covered in pointed scales. The much feared teeth of the shark are simply specially adapted scales; mammals including humans have inherited these teeth which are the only scales that we retain. One of the few fishes to practise internal fertilisation, sharks and rays use their pelvic fins to place sperm inside the female cloaca. Most females keep their eggs within their oviducts while they develop and usually give birth to large litters. Blue sharks and hammerheads even have a placenta, a characteristic unique to mammals. It forms when the walls of the abdomen and oviduct combine.

The other important type of fishes are the bony fishes which dominate the seas and freshwater through their sheer numbers and variety of species. In some varieties, such as the *Amia calva* or Bowfin, role reversal takes place when the male takes care of the young instead of the female. The male Seahorse, or *Hippocampus* takes this one step further; he boasts a brood pouch where the young stay for about three months. Sturgeons such as salmon and Sea Lampreys live in the sea but return to rivers to spawn. Salmon, *Salmo salar*, are well known for their ability to jump up waterfalls and weirs on their journey to clean shallow water where they bury their eggs in the gravel bed.

One particular fish which shows an important evolutionary link between fishes and amphibians is the lungfish. Today these fish are almost extinct. Lungfish, so called because the air bladder usually found in fishes is replaced by a lung-like structure, are found in slow moving water. They show their closest resemblance to amphibians during reproduction when large eggs surrounded by jelly are laid by the female on the river bed or among water plants. When they hatch the young have external gills and suckers under their heads and look a lot like the tadpoles of amphibians.

Amphibians represent one of the most important stages in evolution. These land/water animals bridge the gap between aquatic and terrestrial life, giving rise to reptiles, birds, mammals and humans. To be able to survive on land the young amphibian undergoes quite a transformation; indeed it is the reproductive cycle of the amphibians that has tied them to water. As their eggs have no protective covering like that found around reptiles' eggs, they must be laid in water so that they do not dry up. The eggs are usually fertilised externally and hatch in tadpole form with gills and a fish-like tail. After several months, lungs replace their gills, two pairs of limbs develop, blood vessels appear at the skin's surface, and in frogs and toads the tail is completely lost.

Those amphibians that do not breed in water, such as the newts, place a spermatophore in the female's cloaca. When laying the eggs, the female wraps each up in the leaf of a water plant and from this a tadpole emerges. A similar sexual pattern occurs in the salamanders except that the fertilised eggs develop within the female's oviduct. When the eggs hatch into tadpoles the female finds some clear running water and stands at the edge with her hind legs submerged and the tadpoles pass out into the water.

Unlike amphibians, reptiles have severed all links with their watery past. They have successfully adapted to terrestrial life in a number of ways. The development of a waterproof layer over their skin solved the problem of dessication that so plagued the amphibians, confining them to moist and dark habitats. Their skin is also covered in scales which offer some protection against predators; turtles, tortoises and crocodilians have modified these scales into a hard shell. Lungs are more sophisticated in the reptiles and their limbs are also more advanced allowing them greater mobility on land. Once their ancestors the dinosaurs were the most dominant form of life on earth but today only four main groups of descendants remain: the crocodilians (crocodiles, alligators); the chelonians (turtles and tortoises); squamatines (snakes and lizards); and the rhynchocephalians. These modern reptiles are a vital link between the lower vertebrates (fishes and amphibians) and higher vertebrates (birds and mammals).

They also represent an important advance in reproduction. Reptiles developed the first genitals as we know them, the penis and vagina. Snakes and lizards have not one but two penes, known as hemipenes, which may be used together or separately. They are located in the tail and when they are not being used they are stored in the cloaca. The only amphibians to have sex in this manner are the primitive caecilians whose temporary penis is found in the tip of their tail; it is possible that many extinct reptiles used this method. Modern lizards and snakes practice this type of copulation but with two sex organs. These two penes are horrifying to look at as they are covered with tiny spines or hooks that stick inside the female so that the two sexes cannot be separated during copulation. This variation on the penis explains why two dogs often appear to be 'stuck' together. Although the male dog only has one penis, it swells up once inside the female. He cannot remove it for up to half an hour, which often causes the female dog great distress and discomfort. However, it ensures that no precious sperm is wasted.

Most reptiles are egg laying animals, although some varieties of lizards retain their eggs in the oviduct, foreshadowing the more complex development of the young inside female mammals. Lizards are also the only reptiles to defend their territory during the breeding season; this territorial behaviour is seen at a more complex level in birds and mammals. The spectacular displays by male lizards during this time were thought to be designed to attract females. Now it seems more likely that they are to ward off other males from their territory simultaneously. Although concern for their offspring is not strong amongst the reptiles, most species do build nests for their young and incubate the eggs until they hatch. Some bury them in leaf mould or in the case of the pythons, wrap them in the coils of their body.

There is no concrete proof that birds, or Class *Aves*, evolved from reptiles except perhaps the fossil *Archaeopteryx*. This extinct animal that ruled the skies during the Age of the Dinosaurs combined features from both birds and reptiles. It had feathers and the ability to fly as well as keeping reptilian characteristics such as teeth, a long tail and three digits on the fore limbs. Modern birds no longer retain these although reptilian scales can still be found on their feet and legs. Although their sexual practices remain similar to reptiles in that they are also egg laying animals, birds boast a number of unique characteristics. They have feathers, wings and beaks; they are warm blooded with two legs and generally have good eyesight, especially birds of prey. Almost all species are able to fly and those that cannot have powerful legs and can move very quickly when in danger.

Sex for the majority of birds is a simple matter of rubbing the male and female cloacae and turning them inside out so that sperm can pass from one to the other. Most male birds do not possess a penis, except for ducks, swans and ostriches. For this reason birds appear to have fallen behind penis pioneers the reptiles at first glance. However, birds have left their scaly ancestors for dead in the courtship and parental care stakes. Although there are a few exceptions, reptilian parents do not generally

A male kingfisher hopping onto a female's back for sex.

stay around to watch their children grow up. However, birds are model parents and the sight of them feeding their hungry chicks or teaching them to fly strikes a sentimental chord in many humans.

Courtship becomes more complex as sexual dimorphism is very evident in birds; the cock is usually the larger one with the fine feathers. This brilliant plumage makes the male an eye catching sight for a female some distance away. Other birds serenade their potential partners with shrill love songs that put the females 'in the mood'. Courtship displays may also involve feeding rituals, dancing, preening and flying shows. Concern for the young has also increased and all birds will construct some sort of nest. The function of the nest is to act as an insulator for the eggs and hairless young, as baby birds hatch in a near embryonic state and must be nurtured in order to survive those first few weeks. The nest also acts as a hiding place and shelter for the eggs, the young chicks and the brooding bird. When the chicks hatch, they are fed by their parents and taught to fly, at which point they leave the nest to lead independent lives.

Those birds that do not build nests are the flightless species such as the penguins, cuckoos, brush turkeys, ostriches, emus, rheas, cassowaries and kiwis. Most lay unusually large eggs, often prized by humans. The chicks hatch fully feathered and active, eliminating the helpless stage that flying birds go through as well as the need for a well-built nest. Those that live in cold climates, such as the penguins that inhabit Antarctica, have a unique way of protecting the egg from the harsh elements. In yet another instance of role reversal first seen in the fishes, the males incubate the eggs against the cold by carrying them on the top of their feet, where each egg is covered by a fold of abdominal skin.

Like birds, mammals have also descended from the reptiles. They too are warm blooded but in addition are characterised by body hair and the production of milk with which they suckle their young. Sex between mammals is a very specialised process. In the monotremes, which are some of the earliest mammals, egg laying still occurs as it does in reptiles and birds, although the eggs are bigger and have a larger food supply. The difference is that when they hatch the young are then suckled by the female who has special mammary glands or teats that produce milk; suckling thus helps to form a bond between the mother and her young. Marsupials keep their eggs in their oviducts until hatched. The foetus then develops in a special pouch where it latches on to a teat and is fed with its mother's milk.

Then the placental mammals developed a way of keeping eggs at a constant temperature and since then they have not looked back. They retain the embryo in the uterus or womb where it is fed through a special connection from embryo to oviduct wall, known as the placenta - hence the name placental mammals. Development takes place inside the uterus. This period of pregnancy is known as the gestation period and will vary according to the size of the animal. The average gestation period for an elephant, for example, is 21 months.

Most mammals also have a definite breeding season. For females this is known as the oestrous cycle and for males the rutting season. This seasonal activity of the reproductive organs is controlled by hormones which stimulate the production of milk in the female's mammary glands and sperm in the male. These hormones also give rise to secondary sexual

JUMPING JOEY-SOPHAT

The kangaroo is less than three centimetres long at birth but grows to a height of over two metres as an adult in some species. This amazing discrepancy in size is common among all marsupials. Their young are born in an embryo-like state, completely naked, blind and helpless. At birth the tiny creature must grope its way to its mother's pouch and hang on to a teat for dear life, or else die of starvation. Usually the mother licks a path through her fur for the infant. Once in the pouch the young kangaroo, now known as a joey, continues its development. It stays there for up to nine months, often enjoying rides of up to 40kph as its mother moves around.

characteristics; in males hormones are released from the testes and in females from the ovaries. Male mammals may be bigger in size than females, have a stronger voice, or more hair in the form of manes and beards.

Mammals have also developed the penis and vagina, first seen in their primitive forms in the reptiles. In some mammals the testes are found internally in the pelvis and only come out during the rutting season. These animals are called *Cryptorchidia* and include elephants, edentates (armadillos, sloths, South American Anteaters), and cetaceans (whales, dolphins, porpoises etc). In many other mammals, especially carnivores, there is a penial bone. Others have a penis with spikes on the end of it, making it difficult for the male to withdraw quickly and thus lose valuable sperm. Several important developments can also be seen in the development of the vagina. In the monotremes and marsupials there are two vaginas and uteri; in placental mammals the two vaginas become one, although the two uteri remain. The vagina has glands, protective lips and a sensitive clitoris. By having an organ devoted to sex the female was introduced to new heights of sexual pleasure.

Care for the young can take a variety of forms in mammals. Small animals build nests which protect their babies. Others keep their young beside them as they travel around and teach them some of the skills needed for survival. Among mammals social structures become more obvious and animals will often live together in herds for protection. Within the herd there is usually a pecking order or social hierarchy which keeps the group stable. Herds often live in territories which are marked by the scent of the male whose job it is to protect the herd from outsiders.

Primates are not restricted to a breeding season like other mammals. Female monkeys have a menstrual cycle not unlike humans and are receptive to males at certain times during the cycle when conception is most likely. In some species the female initiates the lovemaking; the female chimpanzee presents her external genitalia, which are pink and swollen, to the male. This stimulates the male and copulation occurs. Other female monkeys secrete pheromones from their vagina to attract a mate; this is why primates are often seen sniffing the genitalia of the female. The role of pheromones in primate sex is not as significant as it is in other mammals, where the release of these sexual chemicals begins the breeding season.

Visual displays have become just as important for initial attraction as they are in humans because primates have developed keen eyesight through the evolution of forward facing eyes. Another human-like characteristic is the gestation period of primates, which varies slightly between species but it is usually about eight months. As a mother, the female primate is one of the most devoted parents in the animal world; when born the offspring is helpless and must learn to how to feed itself and survive in the jungle. Because primates live in small groups or communities known as troops, baby primates are protected from predators. Smaller primates tend to live in large groups whereas the larger varieties, such as the gibbons and orang-utans of dense forests, live in small groups. The males defend the troop's females and offspring against danger; for this reason they are usually larger than the female. Some primate societies, such as that of baboons, have a very rigid social hierarchy. Others like the chimpanzees have a more relaxed social structure which accounts for their promiscuous nature. Although there is competition between males in a number of social situations like receiving the most food, the mating system allows all the males to take turns in copulating with a female in oestrous; in more common parlance, a 'gang bang' takes place.

The largest of the primates, the gorillas, live in a small family with one dominant male, three or more sexually mature females and their offspring. All these primates have a number of social tasks of which grooming is among the most important. Not only does it rid the animals of lice but it also serves as a reminder of social positions with those at the top receive the most grooming. Such attentions help to form a bond between individuals in the community. Sexual opportunities for the male gorilla are less frequent compared to the male chimpanzee. Although he may have sex every two to three hours when the female is in oestrous, he must often wait two or three years for a female to become sexually receptive as she can only give birth every four years.

Monkeys, apes and humans are also mammals with the unique characteristics of primates: a large, complex brain and a flexible hand with an opposable thumb. The supple hand is thought to have evolved from the arboreal life led by some monkeys as they needed a better hand to grip with as they swung from branch to branch. Larger varieties of monkeys were less agile and found life on the ground much more suited to their size. Some monkeys are monogamous while most apes tend towards promiscuity. Sex organs, in the male at least, are also very similar to male humans

Many would argue that the promiscuity favoured by some primates has carried over into the sexual habits of the male human. However, this is a rather frivolous notion given the human being's capacity for thought, complex civilisation and social conditioning.

It would not be fitting to finish a discussion of the evolution of sex without looking at the unique sexual equipment of human men and women. They are similar to mammals, especially primates in that the penis in human men hangs freely when flaccid and is not attached to the abdomen as it is in some mammals. The human penis is also one of the few among the mammals to lack the small penile bone found in gorillas as well as among creatures such as the whales, bats and hedgehogs. The female sex organ has a number of unique features as well. Firstly, the vaginal opening in female humans is closer to the front of the body, a position clearly influenced by the development of the upright stance. Humans are also the first primates to have a real hymen, a thin skin that covers part of the external opening to the vagina. When this is broken by a penis it is said that a woman has lost her virginity; an event that has taken on far too much cultural significance in some countries.

Basic Urges

Sex is an inescapable instinct in all living things which drives them to come together and mate. Yet there is much more to animal reproduction than the mere physical act. Nature has preordained certain patterns of behaviour before and after sex to ensure reproductive success. Most scientists agree that this innate sexual behaviour is a mixture of an animal's genetic composition which is then simultaneously influenced by the surrounding environment during the formative years. The extent to which these two influences, nature and nurture, affect the animal varies from species to species.

Some sexual behaviour will develop independently of any experience while other behavioural patterns will be established early on in the young animal's life by a process known as sexual imprinting. In birds and mammals, for example, the basic framework of sexual behaviour is innate, although experience also plays an important role in selecting a mate and the subsequent success of the union. A male songbird may be born with the ability to sing basic song patterns but in order to ward off other males from his territory and attract a female he must learn how to improve the song during his early development.

Evolution has modified the act of sex in each species according to body structure and the habitat in which they live. Sexual behaviour is subject to the same evolutionary pressures and several factors have evolved in every species which influence the success of reproduction. They include timing, selecting a mate, cooperation and caring for the offspring. The only animals to fall outside the laws laid down by nature are the protozoans and other primitive creatures that reproduce by asexual means. They retain the only living form of immortality and so obey a slightly different set of rules than animals with a sexual cycle, as sexual reproduction brings with the it certainty of death. Yet despite being blessed with the secret of everlasting life, a quest that still eludes humans, the reproductive practices of asexual species are influenced by their habitat. If conditions are favourable they can build up their numbers very quickly; if not the population remains stagnant or drops in size until the right conditions return.

Mating times are largely determined by the habitat in which an animal lives. Certain environmental factors, such as a change in day length, temperature or season, trigger the release of hormones which stimulate the testes and ovaries; these organs then produce the sex hormones which characterise sexual behaviour. For many animals the longer days and warmer weather introduced by spring spark off hormonal changes in their bodies and the breeding season begins. A drive through the countryside at this time is a delightful experience for most people as they can watch new born lambs bounding across the landscape and long legged foals chasing each other around paddocks. In fact, it is not an unusual sight to see a car parked at a bend in the road with its occupants gazing out the window in wonder as they watch a cow giving birth to her calf. Most plants also produce new growth during spring, making it one of the most pleasant and prettiest of the four seasons. New flowers come into bloom and green leaves appear on the trees, especially in the northern hemisphere where spring heralds the end of the big freeze and the beginning of the thaw. New life can be seen everywhere.

As a general rule, animals that reproduce by external fertilisation have internal clocks which determine the time of the mating season. This inbuilt sense of time is particularly important in synchronising sexual activity between male and female individuals, especially those belonging to marine species. For them the chances of fertilisation are much greater if the sperm and ova are released at the same time into the water. Mussels, for example, engage in mass spawning in spring. One individual spawning sparks a general release of sex cells from neighbouring mussels; sometimes mass spawning occurs on such a scale that the water may turn cloudy. Another marine animal famous for the precision of its internal clock mechanism is the Palolo worm, found in the Atlantic Ocean (*Eunice Fucata*) and the Pacific Ocean (*Eunice Viridis*). It would be no exaggeration to say that these animals have narrowed sex down to almost split second timing. They only reproduce twice a year during the neap tides of the last quarter moon in October and November.

Animals that reproduce by internal fertilisation usually have less rigid breeding seasons as this sexual practice is more efficient and reduces the wastage of ova and sperm. Amphibians such as frogs and toads, for example, place less emphasis on timing and instead have a traditional meeting place such as a pond or creek where females and males gather for the breeding season. Instinct guides them on their migratory trip but once they have all congregated in the one spot the male and female still have to find each other. As mating usually occurs at night, frogs and toads have developed a system of croak signals to distinguish male from female. The male belts out a different series of croaks to attract a female and she follows them until she is practically on top of him which, of course, is exactly what he wants.

Reptiles such as snakes, lizards and crocodiles are solitary creatures by nature that come together only for sex and part company soon afterward. The eggs laid by the female are sometimes incubated by her until they hatch but once the young are born she shows little or no interest in them. The reptiles' more sophisticated relatives, the birds, are just the opposite. They take great care of their young, building nests to keep them safe from predators and feeding them until they are old enough to fly away and collect food on their own.

Birds generally mate in spring when there is an abundance of food and the warm, spring air is filled with the joyous songs and calls of males singing for females or defending their territory. The male bird's song is triggered by sex hormones released from the testes. Sea birds such as penguins, petrels, gulls and cormorants also breed during spring although at much colder temperatures than their cousins. These birds form crowded breeding colonies on rocky outcrops, cliff faces and in caves as they have no natural predators on land and their chicks can hatch in safety.

THE MORE THE MERRIER

The Apostlebird of Eastern Australia does everything in a group of twelve individuals, hence its name. During the mating season a communal nest is built on a horizontal branch. The females lay eggs in each other's nests and all members share the task of incubating the eggs and rearing the young.

Sexual activity in mammals is also seasonal with some species having a shorter period where they are 'on heat', known as the oestrous cycle. During this cycle, which is strictly controlled by hormones, the females are sexually receptive for only a short time. Some mammals, such as the Red Fox, *Vulpes vulpes*, only have one period of sexual heat a year. Other mammals have a series of cycles at regular breaks throughout the mating season. Then, of course, there are those animals whose ability to have sex is not restricted by time. Some primates, humans included, are sexually active all year round. For this reason the oestrous cycle has been replaced by the menstrual cycle. Changes in hormone levels result in periodic bleeding from the uterus and vagina in sexually mature females as well as giving rise to sexual behaviour. Once the breeding season is underway the search for the perfect mate begins in earnest. For animals with a sexual cycle finding the right partner is of prime importance in determining reproductive success, i.e. healthy offspring that will survive to sexual maturity and begin the breeding cycle again. Thus, finding the right mate serves a number of important functions. Firstly it prevents inter-breeding. Most species have behavioural patterns or characteristic physical features which distinguish them from similar varieties. Some species of fish, for example, have developed a small dance ritual to which only a female from the same species will know the steps. This safety net provided by nature is known as reproductive isolation. Occasionally interbreeding can produce healthy offspring but they are always sterile; for instance, when a female horse and a male donkey mate the resulting mule is infertile.

Attracting a mate involves an incredible variety of courtship rituals which may include bright colours and patterns, repetitive dancing, loud and elaborate songs and other conspicuous behaviour; this is especially evident in the higher animals. For others sex may be a planned meeting at a particular spot along with members of other species or it may be a chance encounter. Certainly, sex is low-key to the point of being non-existent for animals that reproduce asexually although some species do secrete the sexual chemicals pheromones.

Mate selection has one other important function; it allows animals to select the best possible mate from a number of potential suitors. The sexual partner should provide the best possible benefits for the offspring in terms of genetic contribution and parental care. Generally it is the female who chooses a male with high potential so that the maximum number of offspring are produced. In order to be chosen, the male must court the female; this is why the female of a species is usually the plain one while the male is the more attractive. The next step after the male and female meet is to sexually stimulate each other so that copulation can occur. This is not unlike human foreplay, which apart from being very pleasurable, serves its purpose in bringing both parties to a point of mutual sexual motivation.

In many species it is the courtship of the male which brings the female into a state of sexual desire. The brilliant plumage of some male birds, for example, is thought to bring the female into a state of sexual excitement so that she will participate in copulation when the male is ready to ejaculate. Other species use less spectacular ways of creating a sexual mood. The land tortoise is a case in point; this large and slow animal has an extremely blunt approach to lovemaking. The male simply lumbers up to the female and headbutts her. He may do this several times to drive the message home as the female is often slow to take the point. If she remains unresponsive to the headbutting technique he begins biting her on the legs for further stimulation; he also bites to stop himself sliding off the dome of her shell. Having swept her off her feet with this brief but effective courtship the male then rears up and slides in his penis.

Not all animals have to go through the rigmarole of finding a mate each breeding season. Some return to their former mates and in many

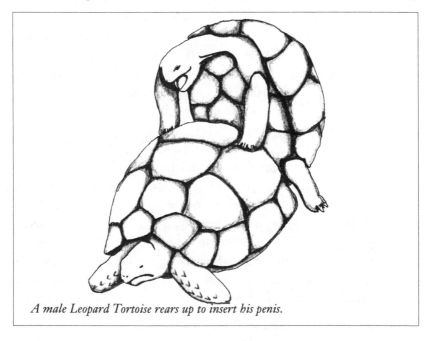

A male Leopard Tortoise rears up to insert his penis.

cases they continue to do so for the rest of their lives. These monogamous pairings are particularly common among songbirds and some primates. Lifelong attachments usually make the male aggressive to all other females except his mate and he reserves all his courtship displays for her as well as offering her protection. In return she continues to produce his offspring and her sudden death or disappearance may result in symptoms of stress in the male. There are many advantages in a monogamous lifestyle. Having a lifelong mate or one that can be recognised each breeding season saves a lot of time and effort usually spent searching for a mate and distinguishing if they are from the same species. This is especially useful in species whose breeding times are short due to climatic changes and who must produce their offspring quickly so that they will be strong enough to survive the oncoming change in weather.

Once copulation and fertilisation have occurred animals enter into the final stage of a successful reproductive process. This is known as parental care, behaviour which assumes top priority in some species and very little or none in others. A common misconception surrounding parental care is that it only includes behaviour after the birth of the young but this is not strictly true. Parental care behaviour usually begins at the very moment of fertilisation and includes such activities as nest-building and nourishment of the developing embryo.

Very few marine species that practice external fertilisation look after their eggs beyond the point of fertilising them; this is why such large quantities are produced. However, some fish, although they also practice external fertilisation, build tiny nests for the eggs. In the case of the stickleback, the males even protect their young until they are old enough to swim away for an independent life. In other varieties of fish the female carries the eggs around in her mouth or the male takes care of them in a tiny pouch on the outer layer of his skin. These fish are typical of most invertebrates in that they have developed very basic forms of caring for their young by building crude shelters for the eggs.

More advanced forms of life not only provide shelter for the developing young but also enough food to keep them going until they hatch. The female Digger Wasp, *Bembex rostrata*, lays her egg in a burrow along with the decaying carcass of an insect she has paralysed. Amphibians do not generally take much notice of their eggs after they hatch but there are exceptions to the rule. In one species of toad, for example, the young remain in the female's reproductive cavity and are fed through blood vessels found in the toad's tail; this method is not unlike the function of the mammalian placenta.

Reptiles, despite their often offputting appearance and poisonous nature, can actually be quite tender parents. Most snakes and lizards guard their eggs which are deposited in a nest and in some cases actually incubate them. For instance, the female Cobra, *Naja*, wraps her coils around the eggs to keep them warm. Incubative behaviour foreshadows the parental care of the birds who invest a lot of time and energy in feeding their chicks and teaching them to fly, among other survival tips.

Indeed, caring for the young reaches a complex level in birds. Firstly the eggs are laid in a nest constructed by the parents. The egg white and yolk give the embryos all the food and water they need until they hatch, at which point the parents fly away for short periods of time in search of tasty morsels for their young chicks. While the embryos are developing inside the egg, the male or female depending on the species, incubates the egg and keeps it at a constant temperature by sitting on it. Some birds share the task of incubation. In ostriches, the male sits on the eggs during the day while the female incubates at night. For the male half of the Button Quails, Jacanas and perching birds the task of looking after the children falls almost universally on him. In ducks, geese and other poultry it is the female who spends most of her time incubating and feeding the young.

In some ways the development of the placenta in mammals reversed this trend to share or place parental responsibility with the male. Unlike the birds, where it is often the female's task to simply lay the eggs, the female mammal must bear the burden of pregnancy, live birth and feeding of the offspring. Very often the male need not do any more than simply fertilise the female, after which she is left 'holding the baby' as the old adage goes. The female mammal, who is equipped with special mammary glands that produce milk for her young, forms a special bond with her offspring by feeding them in this way. This maternal behaviour allows the mother to pass on essential survival tips later on. Animal lovers

A LABOUR OF LOVE

The nesting habits of the Silvery-Cheeked Hornbill add new meaning to the term confinement. When the time comes to roost the female finds a suitable hole in a tree and goes inside. The male then brings mud to his wife who plasters herself inside for over three months. She leaves a narrow slit so that the male can pass through food for her and the chicks.

rarely see a more touching sight than new born foals, still unsteady on their long legs, running with their mothers or baby lambs taking those first, few, uncertain steps under their mother's watchful eye. Although the males usually have very little to do with child rearing, they do play an important role in protecting the offspring and the mother, still weak from childbirth, from predators.

Male primates fulfil a similar role as the protector of their small family or group, offering not only protection from predators but also a territory abundant in food and water. Humans have built many cultures and societies on the premise the male is the protector and breadwinner while the female rears the children. As we head towards the 21st century these ideas are changing but in nature, it remains a tried and tested blueprint for survival in the wild among many animals.

Section 2

THE MATING GAME

In the human world the search for a partner has become a multi-million dollar business. Romance sells and newspaper phones run hot with people wishing to advertise in the personal columns for the perfect mate. Introduction agencies have also mushroomed with hopeful singles being matched with potential mates from data stored in computers. Meanwhile television stations have also recognised the lucrative possibilities of the mating game and dating shows and have turned the process (the initial rites only, so far) into public entertainment. What all this tells us is that either civilisation has stunted the human ability to communicate mating desires or else there are just so many of us that a number of the shy, ugly and the less desirable, for whatever reason, risk being left out.

But while humans have civilised themselves and in the process learnt to suppress their natural urges, the Animal Kingdom has no such inhibitions. For them courtship and mating have usually evolved with one goal in mind; successful reproduction. Natural selection has many ways of ensuring that the best possible offspring are produced and courtship rituals are just one of the ways in which the process works. But before any of this can occur the male and female first have to find each other. To facilitate this, nature has worked out many different ways in which the two sexes of almost every species can meet. Indeed, finding a partner in the natural world is essential for perpetuation of the species. Thus animals advertise their single status in a variety of ways to ensure they meet up with a member of the opposite sex. It is this behaviour which often attracts human attention as striking patterns, brilliant colours or wild love dances are frequently employed to impress potential lovers. The behaviour that precedes the physical act of sex and leads to conception is scientifically known as courtship and it is this essential step in the sexual process that creates circumstances conducive to successful mating. The methods used by animals to attract a mate are as varied as the total number of species that exist on the planet. In fact, each species has developed a courtship ritual that is slightly different from any other so that members from the same species can identify each other and will not mate with a member of a different species. Indeed, any offspring that is produced from such a liaison is usually sterile. Some courtship procedures are designed to attract a mate over a long distance and for this reason they are usually the most conspicuous. Other animals such as the frogs have gradually developed special meeting places and times strictly designated for sexual pleasure. At certain times of the year some species of frogs aggregate in a pond or creek and sex *en masse* takes place. However, although they come together in large numbers, individual frogs still have to find a member of the opposite sex but at least they do not have to look far. It should be remembered that the way animals attract each other and mate depends much upon their environment and the development of their sensory organs. Insects and mammals for example have highly developed senses of smell and so they use pheromones to attract each other. Birds, on the other hand, have highly developed senses of vision and hearing but a poor sense of smell and they generally attract their mates by visual displays and/or by songs and calls. More primitive lifeforms such as the protozoans reproduce with very little or no interaction. In some protozoan species male and female do not exist. Thus, there is no sexual dimorphism and no sex as we know it. When protozoans wish to reproduce they simply multiply by dividing.

Sex signals

It is often revealing to observe how animals go about attracting a mate in the wild since many of their behavioural rituals give us clues to our own sexuality and courtship customs. Among some hunting spiders, for example, the male woos the female with a gift such as a fly wrapped up in silk, reminding us of an eager young lad giving the female object of his desires a bunch of flowers or a box of chocolates (well known aphrodisiacs). Of course, in the case of the spider, he offers the gift to make his intentions clear and to discourage the female's hunting behaviour but the process of softening up the female is still obvious in both spiders and humans. Birds that preen themselves with their beaks and fluff up their feathers to attract a mate resemble the elaborate grooming of men and women who wish to catch the eye of the opposite sex. In fact everywhere you look in the animal world there are examples of animals behaving like humans during courtship and vice versa. Even the display of beautiful clothes, cars or other expensive material possessions that are often used to impress in the human world is mirrored in nature by many species of birds, fish and amphibians. Some of these animals actually change their surrounding environments to make themselves more attractive to a potential mate. The Egyptian Ghost Crab, *Ocypode saratan* for example, digs a burrow in the sand and lies in wait for the female. It has earned its name because the excavated sand is built into a pyramid which can be seen by female crabs from quite a distance.

This habit of modifying the environment so that sexual display is more noticeable over long distances is most common among birds. It is a similar process to nest building except that the task is performed by the males and the structure is used solely for the purpose of courtship. The male bowerbird, *Ptilonorhynchus* for example, goes to extraordinary lengths to attract a female. These birds are related to the beautiful birds of paradise but they do not rely solely on their good looks to attract a mate. The males build veritable love bowers to entice the female. Firstly they collect twigs and build the outside structure so that it resembles a tiny hut, then they begin the task of decorating it with pretty flowers and other colourful plants and objects. The Atlas Bowerbirds and other species too, even spruce up the walls of their love nests with a little paint, made by the male dipping bark or leaves into the blue or dark-green saliva they secrete. Those that live near human civilisation make good use of the things we throw away and pieces of coloured glass and paper can often be found in their nests. The males may spend weeks, and even months, building the bowers and sometimes change the decor scheme every day by adding or taking away little ornaments they have collected. Yet this is not the extent of their talents. Not only have the bowerbirds been blessed with good looks and decorating flair, but they are also dancers and singers. The female is attracted to the bower by the whistles and calls of the male as he performs an energetic love dance outside the front of his palatial bower. Sometimes a male bowerbird will offer a female a pretty coloured item from his collection to impress her. She in turn often joins in the dance with him and a game of encouraging and then discouraging the male ensues until she finally submits to his amorous advances. As they say it takes two to tango. Although the building of this elaborate nest and the complex courtship that follows may seem unnecessary it is thought that the weeks or months spent in its construction may actually sexually stimulate the male. Certainly the female is bowled over by the colour and intricacy of the design and is sexually aroused.

The lovenest of the bowerbird serves a similar purpose to the display mounds used by the Australian Lyrebird. Most commonly found in the south-eastern part of Australia, the lyrebird is so called because of its two tail feathers shaped like a lyre. The male is famous not only for his beautiful plumage but also for his remarkable ability to imitate sounds which he then incorporates into his courtship song. Lyrebirds are able to mimic almost anything including the ring of a bicycle bell or the giggling of children as well as a whole range of sounds that they hear in the natural world. When the male is ready to mate he clears a space among the surrounding vegetation and builds a small mound of dirt which he later uses as a dance floor. These small dirt hills are known as display mounds and serve to make the creature as conspicuous as possible from a distance. When trying to attract a female the male will begin an intricate courtship dance on his display mound to show off his fan of tail feathers. At the same time he produces a continuous song of which many notes are copied from the sounds around him.

Other birds choose a small stretch of land which becomes a communal mating ground. This is called a lek. All the males congregate at the one spot and all courting takes place within this restricted area. Indeed, this is the major difference between leks and display mounds since display mounds are usually a territory held by only one male whereas leks are the meeting place for many members of both sexes. Within the lek males compete fiercely with one another for their own territory within the small area. The more central territories are the most strongly contested as the females show a distinct preference for males in the centre. This is thought to be because the females are looking for the best possible genes and as the males in the centre are obviously the dominant males they tend to favour them. The Sage Grouse, *Centrocercus urophasianus*, is a lek species found on the plains of North America. As is the case with most animals in the natural world, the female is the plainer of the two sexes, being a brownish colour, while the male Sage Grouse is larger with yellow air sacs, a white front and showy tail feathers. During the breeding season large numbers of males come together of which one male is usually dominant, although a few subordinates may occasionally challenge him. The female Sage

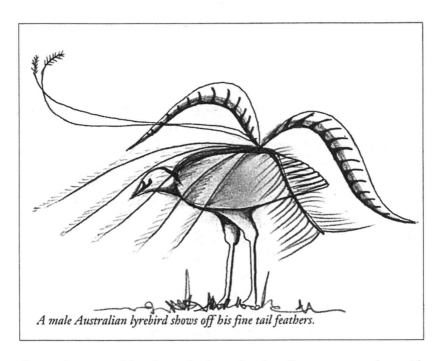

A male Australian lyrebird shows off his fine tail feathers.

Grouse is attracted by the gathering of males all eager to copulate with her. Natural selection is clearly at work here since the female has a greater choice of partners and tends to gravitate towards the centre of the lek where the stronger individuals are holding their own against the competition.

Another species that uses the lek during the breeding season is the Ruff, *Philomachus pugnax*. There are two types of Ruff males. Dominant males are aggressive, defend a small central territory and have quite an unremarkable appearance, being dark in colour. Subordinate males are comparatively passive by nature, do not defend a mating territory but are striking to look at as they boast magnificent white plumage that forms a ruff around their neck. These birds attach themselves to the dominant males who tolerate them because their white ruff attracts females to the lek. The females copulate with the dominant males as they tend to gravitate towards the central territory these males have fought for. This is because the males that have won this prime mating territory are older and more experienced and demonstrate the perfect balance between charm and threat. Only an older male with some experience in courting knows the right balance and the younger male often has no idea of the right strings to pull to get his sexual partner 'in the mood' and must learn by trial and error and by watching his elders. In the meantime, however, the subordinate or satellite males are also able to sneak sex behind the back of the male while he is busy defending his territory. Thus both types of males are perpetuated. An indication of how strong the instinct is to move to the traditional mating ground was illustrated by a population of Ruffs in Britain who continued to visit their old communal mating ground even after a road had been built through it.

Lek behaviour appears to be the most common among birds that do not have great powers of flight and hence cannot call their mates from

Male Ruffs gather to display their magnificent plumage.

long distances like songbirds. Also, the territory that is so vigorously contested and defended by lek species is usually of poor quality when compared to other bird species. This is especially so with the polygamous varieties who must offer their partners abundant food supplies and safety from predators. Leks on the other hand are often just small bare areas of ground which the females visit when breeding time comes around. Lek behaviour, as this fight for dominance over a display area is called, is also favoured by some species of grouse, pheasant and manikins as well as the Village Weaverbird. The kob, a species of antelope found in Central Africa, gives a fascinating example of lek behaviour because it is so rare in the mammalian world. At the onset of the breeding season a large herd of approximately 1,000 kobs select an area roughly the size of two football fields. This comparatively small piece of land will be used exclusively for mating. The kob never tries to copulate anywhere but within the boundaries of the lek and the females follow suit. Like the communal mating grounds of the Sage Grouse discussed earlier, the centre of the lek is the most valuable piece of real estate. The females always make a beeline towards the fiercely contested middle ground where the dominant males must constantly fend of potential usurpers. The value of land gradually falls towards the perimeter and this off-Broadway area is occupied by the less dominant males. Even so they must face constant battles with other males who do not own any mating land. Once the males are in position the females descend upon them eager to be fertilised. These graceful ladies are in the extremely fortunate position of being able to pick and choose but usually begin by heading towards the dominant males in the centre to ensure the best genes for their offspring. When the female approaches the buck shows no signs of the aggressive territorial behaviour he displayed at the beginning of the rutting season. Instead, he affects a cool and disinterested stance as does the female who, once she has wandered into his territory, pretends to graze on the cropped grass.

Eventually the buck tires of the game and moves up to the doe, placing his two front legs behind her hind legs. If she does not move the buck proceeds to mount her and copulation occurs, but quite often the doe suddenly wriggles out of his embrace at the last minute and walks off, leaving her suitor sexually frustrated. Sometimes he tries wooing her again but often the doe walks off into another buck's territory at which point he forgets he ever laid eyes on her and patiently awaits the arrival of another female.

African Waterbucks, another species of antelope that live on the plains, are also lek animals. Although they live in monosexual groups for most of the year, these break up at the onset of the breeding season. The males head off in search of mating territory, often fighting each other for an area no bigger than 50 square metres. The stronger males win the best territory, which lies right in the middle of the females' path, while the lesser males must content themselves with territories on the fringe, often too far away from the action. Unlike other species where the dominant males are constantly defending their land, once the male Waterbucks have settled down in their territories there are no challenges to their superiority. Instead they wait happily for the females who stroll around from territory to territory before making their choice. The minute a female steps into a buck's territory he does everything he can to please her but will not fight for her if she rejects him and walks off to another patch. It is the perfect example of ladies' choice. The females choose who they mate with and will often copulate with several of the biggest males who occupy the best territories.

A less aggressive form of lek behaviour is found in the Green Tree Frog, *Hyla cinerea*, who adopts a sneakier method of finding a mate similar to the satellite males in the Ruff birds. While the dominant male frogs are defending their tiny mating territory and calling out loudly to attract a female, others sit on the edge of the territory and wait for the females to appear. At this point they try to intercept and mate with them before they reach the territorial male who has attracted them in the first place. The same sort of sneaky behaviour can be seen in the Live-Bearing Fish, *Poeciliopsis occidentalis*. Some males are black in colour, aggressive and territorial and attract females swimming by with their complex courtship displays. The other males are a dull brown like the females and are non territorial. They simply circle the perimeters of the black male's territory and when a female comes into view they rush up and attempt to copulate with her.

It is difficult to measure the reproductive success of the dominant males against the passive males. The latter male may copulate less than his rival but on the other hand he probably lives longer because he is not fighting off challengers to his territory. In the case of the Sage Grouse it is thought that the subordinate males are young and inexperienced and will eventually grow up and emerge victors in the battle for the central territory. If however he is simply a weaker individual then stealing sex when the dominant male is busy fighting is about the best he will ever do. Other lek species such as the Ruff, the Green Tree Frog and the Live Bearing Fish appear to have struck up quite harmonious arrangements where both males benefit equally. In this type of situation the best strategy for a male is obviously to take advantage of the behaviour of his brothers. If all the Green Tree Frogs called out at once, for example, then it would be more sensible to adopt the sneaky approach and intercept the female as she arrives or vice versa. Thus different sexual behaviour may still result in roughly the same reproductive success. The balance of passive males and dominant males is maintained and there is no need for either to change his sex strategy.

The glow of love
In old Hollywood movies sex scenes between the two romantic leads used

to be indicated by a gradual blacking out of the screen as the couple drew together and kissed. What happened after that was left to the imagination. Although this rather coy practice has been replaced in modern films by graphic sex scenes that leave nothing to the imagination, there are some animals in the wild that opt for the more old fashioned approach. One such species is the *Syllis*, a Marine Bristle Worm found in the warm waters of the West Indies. Females who are ready to reproduce swim close to the surface of the sea and give off a steady light to attract a male, who will swim around her blinking his lights! As soon as mating is complete their lights go out. Often referred to as Fireworms, the lights of each sex bring the two together and synchronise the release of sperm and ova so that minimal wastage occurs. The male releases a cloud of sperm first which is thought to contain hormones that trigger off the subsequent dispersal of ova by the female. The initial spurt of sexual activity is sparked off by an internal clock causing the Bristleworms to swim up to the surface for mass spawning. Timing is crucial and for about 20 minutes, beginning just after sunset on the third quarter of the moon, spawning starts in earnest as large numbers of glowing worms light up the surface of the sea. Indeed, Christopher Columbus is believed to have been the first European to witness this illumination and brought back glowing reports to the King of Spain.

Many other marine animals of different shapes and sizes glow with love during the mating season as they seek out sexual partners. The Common American Squid, for example, woos the female with a kaleidoscope of colour changes. Coloured spots appear on his arms and a rosy flush slowly suffuses his whole body rather like the embarrassed blush that spreads across a human face. This squid also favours mass courtship and mating and so during the breeding season the colourful courtship in the ocean depths may often resemble a psychedelic nightclub. Deep-Sea Shrimp, fish, crustaceans and worms all beam out lights for the same reason: to attract a mate. One especially intriguing variety is the Deep-Sea Angler Fish. This fish, whose strange sex life is described later in the book, glows steadily in the dark and murky ocean depths, where very little vegetation grows except for the non-photosynthetic varieties and where very few creatures choose to live. In fact, many deep-sea creatures sport luminous organs which glow in the permanent darkness of the ocean bottom. These include some worms, crustaceans, squid and other varieties of fish.

The Cookiecutter Shark, *Isistius brasiliensis*, is another small but very conspicuous deep-sea dweller that emits a steady light when navigating the ocean depths. It is thought that this light attracts both its prey as well as sex partners, and although this shark only grows to a length of about 50 centimetres it is an extremely efficient carnivore. Of all sharks the feeding habits of the Cookiecutter are the most amazing. With its razor sharp, triangular teeth in the lower jaw and small and narrow cusps in the upper jaw it is able to remove chunks of meat from large fish, dolphins or even whales. When it encounters its prey it locks on with its lips, then drives its lower teeth into the victim while twisting its body like a screwdriver. The reward is a neat circle of flesh for which the shark gained its name. When it comes to attracting a mate the male is hardly a wallflower. His entire underbelly is covered with luminous organs which shine with a green phosphorescent glow.

Fireflies are probably the best known love lamps of the wild. They are especially numerous in tropical countries where they put on illuminating shows. The male flashes at the female to introduce himself and she flashes back to identify herself. Despite the brightness of these flashing signals, they do not in fact give out much heat as they are produced by luciferin. This unique and energy efficient substance uses up to 98% of the firefly's energy to make the light and yet loses only 2% of the heat. Each firefly is capable of emitting about 1/40 candlepower at a wavelength to which human eyes are particularly sensitive. In fact, the glow from a firefly is enough to read by and firefly lanterns were once common in Asian countries during summer months.

Apart from being surprisingly bright and energy efficient, flashing fireflies are also remarkably accurate. In North America, where they are known as 'lightning bugs', the male flashes his light every 5.8 seconds exactly. The female must respond precisely two seconds later so that the male will approach her.

The females of some species of fireflies are wingless and these are commonly known as 'Glowworms'. During the day they lie in the grass with their glowing bands or spots hidden from view but as soon as the sun sets they turn over and shine a red or green light from their abdomen. This attracts the winged males who dart through the air and touch down on the females. When this happens *en masse* the illumination is spectacular.

Mating calls

The natural world is a constant symphony of sounds and is never silent. Some sounds are incidental to the movement of an animal through its habitat or are merely the result of the wind in the trees or rain pounding the ground. Others are the intentional noises of animals such as birds singing from the treetops, frogs croaking in ponds, pack animals braying in the distance or merely a fly buzzing around on a summer day. Indeed, there is an incredible diversity of sounds that animals make when they wish to communicate with each other. They may do this to warn, inform or attract and the sounds are usually explicit and carefully used so that they do not catch the unwanted attention of predators. For this reason the sound patterns developed by each species are usually instantly recognisable among the veritable din of other creatures both great and small. Animal languages may also vary depending on where they live, just as human languages change slightly within the one race of people. French people living in France all speak the same common language, French, although many different dialects exist throughout the country. The same thing occurs in the natural world. Many birds, for example, have local dialects that are refashioned from the general song of the species.

Of all the various means of communication open to animals, sound is surpassed only by visual displays. Sound travels well over long distances, it is quick, and can carry a wealth of information about a number of different things. Animals can vary the volume, pitch and frequency of sound as well as the time between notes which is known as a sound pattern. The type of sound produced relates to the structure of the animal. Arthropods such as lobsters, crabs, spiders and insects, play their bodies like an instrument by tapping their exoskeletons while terrestrial varieties create songs powered by the air rushing through their respiratory systems. The most sophisticated sounds are those with variations in pitch, volume and pattern, like whale songs, human speech and the exquisite calls of the birds which can impart much more information than simple sounds.

The first communication by sound, however, was not these glorious songs but the instrumental noise of crustaceans, insects and spiders. These creatures produce sounds by clicking, tapping and scraping parts of their carapaces. Among the loudest and most musical of these animals are the insects. Some insect songs can be quite deafening for humans, particularly when cicadas and crickets raise their voices in unison. Fish too have acoustic systems of communication, making sounds by grinding their teeth, plucking special spines, or by vibrating the swim bladder. These sounds often carry for several kilometres as they are acoustically reflected by the top and bottom of the ocean. Then, about 200 million years ago one of the most significant advances in animal communication occurred with the rise of the amphibians. These half-water, half-land animals produced the first voice or song by using their vocal chords. This development paved the way for the birds that have to the human ear at least, developed some of the most beautiful songs and calls in the natural world. Birds sing by breathing out air and can vary their songs by changing the way in which the air is expired, altering the position of the neck and head and by opening and closing their beaks. Mammals too make sound by breathing out air through their mouths. They can also vary it according to the shape of the lips and the position of the tongue.

Nevertheless, it is humans who have developed the ultimate system of vocal communication by combining several words to produce a sentence. Human language is incredibly complex with hundreds if not thousands of different languages in daily use. The evolution of a sophisticated language is thought to have come about due to the politics of living in a group. This competitive way of life, once followed by primitive humans, can still be observed today in our distant relatives the primates. Communication is always paramount in a group and it is possible that those who had the ability to use a vocal signal held a distinct advantage over other members. Yet despite the superiority of humans in communicating, our sense of hearing is not nearly as acute as some species of dogs, for example, which are able to detect sound at a much higher frequency than humans.

Many other sounds also fall outside the human's range of hearing. For this reason we cannot hear the sounds of fish and crustaceans which form part of the ocean orchestra yet sound is a very important means of communication for ocean animals. Deep water sound systems range from the simple snapping of shrimps to the complex songs of whales and dolphins. Indeed, whales are famous for their underwater songs which rival the songs of birds in their beauty. Some scientists believe that whale song even resembles bird song when speeded up. In fact, interest in whale song became so great at one point during the 1950s that a recording of the sounds of the Humpback Whale, *Songs of the Humpback Whale*, topped the music charts worldwide. Dolphins share the same degree of popularity. These mammals are intelligent creatures with a brain the same size as a human's and are soon able to learn tricks and play games that amuse us. Yet despite the complexity of the sounds made by these cetaceans, some smaller and more primitive marine creatures are actually capable of producing even more powerful sounds as we shall see later on.

The ocean orchestra

Crustaceans, a group which includes crabs, lobsters and shrimps, make their instrumental sounds by tapping or scraping their exoskeletons. One particular species, the Spiny Lobster or *Palinurus elephas* found off the Atlantic coast, produces a sound rather like running a finger along the teeth of a comb. To make this rasping noise the lobster has a sharp edged pad on the end of each antennae which it rubs on the shell between its eyes.

As lobsters do not have ears they receive the sound through tiny hairs on the antennae and other body parts. This noise is used with great success by the female during courtship and it is strong enough to be clearly received over distances by some lucky male. The female lobster's love call may well attract up to a dozen eager suitors who, as they approach, begin to fight for her hand until a single male manages to win her over. After this she stops producing her hypnotic sound and the rest of the group lose interest. Rasping, which is also commonly known as stridulation, is also the preferred mating call of the crab. When ready to mate, the male crab lifts his large claw with special ridges on the underside and rubs it against his shell, producing a rasping sound irresistible to female crabs. This noise even has regional dialects as it varies from one ocean to another. However, by far the loudest crustaceans are the shrimps. The Pistol Shrimp produces noise by lifting its giant claw, which is usually half the size of its body, and raising it in front where it aims it like a gun and fires. The sound is so intense that it usually stuns its prey and a Pistol Shrimp will will often follow small fish around and fire when close to them.

Water music

The more advanced marine creatures, namely the whales and dolphins, have much more sophisticated systems of underwater communication. The Humpback Whale, found in the Pacific and Atlantic Oceans, has been the subject of prolonged study as its song is the longest and most complex animal song known to humans. These whales sing mainly during the breeding season but occasionally they can be heard singing during migration. Once whales begin to sing they may continue for many hours and one whale was recorded singing in the Caribbean non-stop for 22 hours. The intensity of the whale's song increases the deeper the whales go and so too does the distance the sound is able to travel. As a whale comes closer to the surface the sound tends to become softer, although scientists recording whale song from a boat have reported that their vessel was literally rocked by the vibrations from the song as the whale approached them. Despite the huge public interest and time and money spent on research about whales, scientists still do not know how the whale produces its unique sound.

The same amount of interest has also been expressed in dolphins. These delightful creatures have a close affinity with humans and their playful personalities have has made them extremely popular. Their brains are about the same size as a human brain which has led many people to overestimate their intelligence. Certainly dolphins are quick to learn new tricks but then so are dogs. Dolphins are able to produce a variety of sounds, the most well-known probably being the chuckles made famous by the television dolphin Flipper. Other sounds include whistles, groans, clicks, barks, chirps and moans. Various interpretations have been put on them with whistling being thought to be associated with feeding while clicking is used mainly for navigation by echolocation.

The instrumentalists

Another group of animals whose courtship calls and instrumental noises are not usually heard by humans is the spiders. Like the crustaceans, many spiders have stridulatory organs which make a rasping sound when rubbed against the two leg-like organs below the spider's mouth. These are known as the pedipalps. Some males use an intermediary to transmit love messages to a female. Male Wolf Spiders, for example, stridulate to produce vibrations which are passed through a leaf to a chosen female. These love vibrations are picked up by the female through tiny, sensitive hairs located on her legs. Once she hears the call of the male, the sound acts as a love potion and she immediately becomes sexually receptive. That the female should hear and act on the mating calls of the male spider is of vital importance. Frequently this can be a matter of life or death. If a female spider fails to switch off her hunting instincts and the male arrives unannounced, it is possible that she will eat him. In the world of spiders, the female is usually larger than the male and invariably cannibalistic. A male spiders would be well advised to watch his step!

The sounds of many other spiders are often produced in the same way that humans evoke sounds from musical instruments of the string and woodwind families. Some varieties of spider actually pluck the silky strands of the female's web, playing it like a harp. By flexing their legs against their abdomen the male spiders can produce vibrations that ripple across the web and induce the female to lessen her aggression and prepare herself for mating. Other species make drum-like sounds by tapping their pedipalps against their exoskeleton while some large tropical spiders throw themselves wholeheartedly into the act of winning over a female by vibrating their entire body to produce an almost hypnotic humming sound. Although it is rare for the human ear to detect the sounds spiders produce, some noises made by the Wolf Spider are just audible. One species, *Schizocosa ocreata*, produces a purring sound by stridulating with its pedipalps and tapping the ground with its front legs at the same time.

The loudest instrumentalists in the animal world, however, would have to be the insects. Insects do not have proper voices because their sounds are not produced by the passing of air over the vocal chords. Nor do they have ears but rather hearing organs. Yet despite this, some species have developed remarkably efficient ways of producing sound and also receiving it. It is nearly always the male that is equipped with the sound making equipment and thus he must make the first move in the mating game. On the other hand, the female is usually the sexual aggressor in species that use visual displays to attract a mate. The human ear has no trouble detecting the sounds of the most common insects. The synchronised screeching of cicadas can fill the air on a hot summer's day and is often painfully clear. The cicada song is so loud that it can sometimes be heard up to one kilometre away. When ready to mate, the male cicada positions himself high up in a tree and begins calling loudly to attract a mate. His song sparks off a chain reaction and suddenly all the males in the area will also burst into song. The sound of so many males vying for her attention quite overwhelms the female who flies right into the middle of this boisterous singing group. Needless to say copulation occurs soon afterwards.

The cicadas, along with crickets and grasshoppers, are the loudest and most musical in the insect world and have remarkably complex ways of producing their unique sound. Cicadas make their noise by contracting hard plates known as tymbals on either side of their thorax. Each contraction produces a click and when the muscles are relaxed another click is heard; thus there is an 'in' click and an 'out' click. On average a cicada will produce between 200 and 600 clicks per second, although one species of cicada has been known to make up to 1,000 clicks per second. Those with a higher click rate often have a series of ridges on the tymbal which each make a click, so the more ridges there are the more clicks per second. This is essential in differentiating between the species and those cicadas able to produce more clicks per second can vary their songs to make them distinct from other varieties. In addition to this cicadas can, by raising and lowering a cover over the tymbal, make their song louder or quieter.

As already stated crickets and grasshoppers also produce strident love songs. Cricket choirs often fill the air on summer nights with their continuous chirping. This complex song is made simply by rubbing their two wings together. On the underside are veins with tiny teeth which scrape along the opposite wing as they are closed. The length of the chirps is controlled by the speed at which the wings are closed and the silence between the chirps is modified by the speed of opening. In this way, crickets can produce a range of sound patterns by changing the speed at

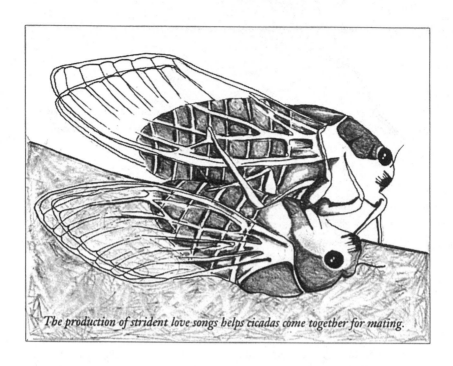

The production of strident love songs helps cicadas come together for mating.

which they open and close their wings. Grasshoppers use a more complicated method. They have large hind legs with a serrated edge which they rub against the folded wing. This gives grasshoppers two sources of sounds and so their songs can vary enormously in harmony and length.

The song of crickets can be heard at all times of the day and night but only if they are ready for sex. Their song signals to the female that the male has produced a spermatophore and is eager to copulate. Indeed, sound plays a vital and almost exclusive role in the attraction of a mate. Most male crickets have a basic calling song but this will switch to a more romantic melody once they have attracted a female. When she comes within sight of the male the first strains of the courtship song can be heard but as soon as copulation begins he falls silent and concentrates all his energy on the task at hand. The songs of grasshoppers work in a similar fashion to those of the crickets but with one important difference. The females are able to answer back. In one particular species, the *Syrbula*, the female can weave a spell over an entire male community simply by her answering call. By responding to the male call she lets him know that she is ready to copulate and they begin to court. At the same time all the other males in the vicinity gather around the loving couple in the hope that they can tempt her away from her chosen lover. They chirp madly but often to no avail.

Many smaller insects are also talented instrumentalists. Flies and mosquitoes for example, flap their wings at close range to produce a low frequency sound signal. This is not the buzzing of flies and mosquitoes hovering around that humans find so irritating but rather more discreet sounds that can only be heard with the help of amplifiers. Three sounds produced by mosquitoes have been identified by scientists in this way, although it is only the third which plays a part in their sex life. This is the call of the male to the female and it is believed to be similar to the wolf whistle that some men in the human world use when an attractive woman strolls by. It apparently also has the same effect with the female mosquito usually ignoring the whistle and scurrying off. However, if she makes a gentle cooing sound the male immediately follows her and carries her away to some bushes where copulation usually occurs. The female cooing is a very powerful lure and has been used successfully as a mosquito trap in many countries.

Flies produce their courting repertoire in a similar way to mosquitoes by vibrating their wings when close to a female. This sound cannot be heard by the ordinary human ear and needs considerable amplification to be detected. The female fly cannot hear her suitor's plaintive love song either unless he flies very close to her. If he is further than a centimetre from the female, the sound becomes inaudible. Ants too possess stridulatory organs which produce a rasping sound that is carried through the air although they can also detect vibrations as they have very sensitive hairs on all their legs. Bugs and beetles are other insects who communicate by sound vibrations, often using an intermediary such as a leaf, to transmit the vibrations from one sex to the other.

The stridulatory method of producing sound favoured by insects works particularly well underwater where the acoustics of the ocean often carry sound a lot further than on land. Stridulation is one of the three main ways that fishes communicate their love to each other. The other two are hydrodynamic sounds produced by lightning quick changes in direction and swim bladder sounds caused by the flexing of muscles attached to this resonant chamber. In the same way as insects use parts of their body to make stridulatory sounds, fish too strike different body parts against each other to produce a noise. They may do this by rubbing together teeth, fin spines or bones. Sea Catfish produce high squeaks when they flex their pectoral spines. Trigger fish emit a low frequency vibration when they move their dorsal fins. When fish use the swim bladder method of making noise they often reveal their presence to fishermen as tiny bubbles of expelled air which are used to make the squeaky sound rise to the surface of the water.

Some of the best known fish in terms of the amount of noise they make are the Drum and Croaker family. The males of these species possess muscles near the swim bladder especially for producing loud sonic booms similar to a drum roll. Catfish too make drum-like sounds, by contracting and relaxing a thin springy piece of bone that lies over the swim bladder. Toadfish produce a short low frequency grunt and then a blast of pure tone, by vibrating sonic muscles attached to their swim bladder. The sounds are usually heard just before the mating season. These noises are generally made in pulses, that is a grunt or squeal followed by a measured period of silence before the next noise. When pulses are produced at different rates various sound patterns are formed which are important in distinguishing species from species. The haddock, for example, courts the female by swimming around her in a close circle making knocking sounds that gradually become faster until he sounds like he is purring. As soon as the female spawns he becomes silent.

A voice in the wilderness

At the same time that fishes and crustaceans were calling to each other in the murky depths of the ocean and insects and spiders were colonising dry land, the amphibians were slowly evolving. The rise of these half-land, half-water animals was significant as they were the first vertebrates to be able to survive on land. They also developed the first voice in the animal world as they possess vocal chords which produce a loud croak or grunt when air passes over them. The croak of a toad or a frog may not mean much to the human world when compared to the operatic singing of the canary, but for the frog it is the only way he can attract a mate. Visual displays are rarely used because frogs and toads mate at night to avoid predators. Therefore the male frog or toad must serenade his sweetheart in his characteristic deep voice, using balloon-like air sacs on either side of his mouth to help amplify the sound. Some toads can be heard up to two kilometers away while the Common Toad, *Bufo bufo*, is only audible for about 150 metres. Not all amphibians possess as fine a voice as the frogs and toads however. The newts and salamanders do not have a love song so the male and female usually find each other by smell. Not all species are entirely mute either as some produce a small squeak or peep when they are alarmed. However, sound is not an integral part of courtship as it is with frogs and toads.

Generally speaking, frogs and toads will congregate for mating in spring as described later in the book. They meet at special breeding ponds and the resulting croaking chorus fills the night air. The sounds that each species make are specially modified to suit their chosen environment. Some sound frequencies or call patterns carry better under particular conditions and frogs and toads have developed some of the most effective long distance love songs in the animal world. The song pattern of each species is also quite specific as it must be distinguished by the female from the thousands of calls of males from other species that breed in the same area. To ensure that she mates with a member of her own species the female will often sit and listen for several hours before she makes her move towards a male. It is possible that she may also be trying to discern the age of the male as this is a good indicator of the ability of the frog or toad to survive for several years. Hence age can be an indicator of good genes! To distinguish a mature male from a younger male is not a difficult task since as with humans, the voice of the male frog or toad deepens and becomes louder with age.

Once the female has made physical contact with the male frog or toad she may not be released for several hours. During this time she must endure the ardour of the male before her eggs are finally fertilised. Hav-

Inflated sacs on either side of a male frog's mouth help amplify his mating call.

ing mated, a female is unable to copulate again until the next breeding season. However, as she makes her way back from the love match she may often be grabbed by another eager suitor. At this point she gently rejects him by making what is known as a release call which may last for several minutes so that the message is loud and clear. The release call is an important step in the courtship of frogs and toads. If the male grabs a female who is ready to mate she will remain silent and copulation usually occurs later that night; if not the release call is produced to let him know he has the wrong partner. The release call evolved because the male is not very adept at establishing the sex of a silent frog or toad in the middle of the night and may grab an already mated female or even another male. Frogs and toads have also been observed keeping a firm grip on small animals and objects in the hope that they are females. Some even rush into amplexus which prevents their captives from making the release call. In some instances this may amount to rape or sodomy but to the male frog or toad the silence of their captive is taken as assent.

Bird song

Like the croaking of frogs and toads at night, the joyous songs of birds announce the arrival of spring each year. Generally it is the male who is blessed with the ability to sing, just as male birds usually boast the most brilliant plumage while the hens are usually plain or downright dull looking. The sounds birds make range from simple and brief calls to complex songs consisting of a series of notes. For birds that live in dense forests or marshes, sound is often their only means of communication while those that live in more open areas use a mixture of sound and visual displays to communicate. Some unfortunate species are mute and among these are the cormorants and pelicans while others, like canaries and nightingales, sing gloriously. True songbirds come from the Suborder *Oscines* which is a division of Perching Birds usually described as *Passeriformes*.

In addition to the songs and calls that birds produce, there is also a variety of instrumental sounds that are used by some species. The Swiftlets of South-east Asia, whose nests are used to make bird's nest soup, produce a clicking sound that vibrates off their surroundings to help guide them through the dark caves in which they breed. This form of navigation, or seeing by sound, is called echolocation and is also used by dolphins and bats. Some birds emit very low frequency sounds that carry over long distances; for this reason they are known as 'boomers'. Others are referred as 'drummers' like the Woodpeckers who, although they possess a voice, also make a drum-like sound by hammering the trees with their beaks. This 'pecking' is used to proclaim territory and attract females at the same time. Sound patterns vary according to the speed of the hammering and the tree trunks used; in this way males and females can recognise each other by sound. There are also the imitators or mocking birds that mimic the sounds of other animals or noises from their surrounding environment and then incorporate it into their own elaborate song. The Australian Lyrebird, *Menura novae-hollandiae* is famous for its unique ability to copy almost any sound and then use it in its courtship song. Even human speech is not beyond the power of the imitators as the owner of a pet budgerigar or parrot would know.

One surprising instrumentalist among a family of well-known singers is Loddiges' Racket-Tailed Hummingbird, *Loddigesia mirabilis* ,This strange bird is found in a valley 7,000-9,000 feet above sea level in Peru. Its distinctive feature is a long and brightly coloured tail which the male rattles during courtship. Instead of the usual ten tail feathers it only has four. The long and slender outer pair of tail feathers cross over and end in purple racket shapes. During courtship the male 'shakes that tailfeather', as the popular song goes, in front of the female. First he will make one undulate and then the other or he may strike them against each other. The result is a rattling sound to which he adds the noise of his primary wing feathers shaking. By contrast the female has no claims to beauty and talent. She is, however, renowned for being a doting mother and a female hummingbird seldom abandons her eggs or chicks.

Despite the pleasure that bird songs and calls give to humans, birds do not sing just to hear their own voices. Each species has developed its own range of songs or calls which convey messages to other members of the species. They may warn others of impending danger or broadcast the location of food sources; also they can attract a mate or be used in defence of territory. Proclamation songs, for example, play a crucial role in breeding and defending territory. Often the one song may have a twofold purpose; to attract a female and at the same time ward off other males from the singer's territory. For this reason proclamation songs are usually very specific to avoid confusion with the songs of other species.

The ability to sing is innate in birds although the song or call must be learned when the bird is young. For this reason one single species may evolve several different dialects which all vary slightly from the general song. The experiences of a young bird and the amount of practice time he has, play a significant role in the development of song. Incidentally, the sounds that do emerge from birds at this time are often referred to as subsong. Mature males will also practice new tunes before the breeding season in a similar fashion to the warm-up of an orchestra before the first strains of the overture. Subsong therefore is usually longer and less re-fined. The transition from subsong to full song occurs when the notes become more pure and the bird is happy with this composition. Songs also tend to differ from one individual to another; the song of the Blackbird consists of a series of melodious phrases which are not likely to be repeated in exactly the same order next time. However, the same notes will be repeated over and over again. This repetition ensures that the message is eventually heard above the sounds of other animals and the noises of the environment. Birds also have a repertoire of different calls or songs for different situations. When courting the song is usually unbroken so that the female will eventually notice and fly towards the male while territorial songs tend to be loud with long breaks in between patterns.

The ability to produce such an amazing variety of tones is due to a highly developed singing instrument which evolved in birds known as the syrinx. Made of muscle fibres, the syrinx protects the vocal chords and is found at the bottom of the windpipe before it divides into two bronchi. Although birds can change their song using the syrinx whenever they want to, cranes, geese and swans possess an additional feature with which to modify sound. This comes in the form of lengthened windpipes which produce a deeper call or honking sound. For most birds the control of the syrinx is usually sufficient to modify and control song. The Gouldian Finch, which is often kept as a cage bird, can sing two songs at the same time accompanied by a pleasing drone.

For centuries courtship songs and calls of birds have delighted humans, even inspiring poetry. These songs are not loud and harsh like the territorial screeching of the Australian Magpie or the European Crow but rather they are softer and more melodious. After all if humans prefer tender tones to screeching voices, female birds are quite likely to have similar tastes. Thus, the soft cooing of doves and pigeons has been considered a symbol of romance by a succession of poets and writers while the song of the Capercailzie or Cock-in-the-Woods has been described by Europeans in glowing romantic terms as it is supposed to inspire the hunter. Any song heard outside the breeding season is usually associated with defence of territory and is different to the courtship song. Some species, however, only sing during the breeding season. One such bird is the Sedge Warbler, *Acrocephalus schoenobaenus*, that lives in thick marshes and swamps. Their courtship song is particularly elaborate as it is their only hope of attracting a female. For this reason they can often be heard singing throughout the day and well into the night until a female settles with a male for the breeding season. After this the little bird falls silent and relies on threatening visual poses to scare off other warblers.

Like most forms of courtship, the love song of a bird not only advertises the fact that the male is ready and looking for sex but it also acts as a stimulant. Around the beginning of the breeding season the testes become active and release the sex hormones that trigger off the sometimes relentless love song of the male. When the female hears these tender tunes she too will begin to prepare herself for breeding. The female canary, for example, must hear her male partner's song in order for her ovaries to develop. The more he warbles the quicker the ovaries ripen and the eggs develop. Although females do not generally sing, some do join in a duet with their male partner during the mating season. The Eastern Whipbird, for instance, has an unusually long song that starts as a pure note and gradually increases in volume before ending suddenly in a loud bang. The female then replies in a similar fashion. It is thought that this duet helps reinforce bonding and keeps the pair together as the Whipbird is a monogamous species. Other species of tropical birds that live in forests where visibility is severely restricted also sing together to maintain contact. One of the pair initiates the song and the other responds almost immediately; they are also both able to sing the partner's part in their absence despite the complex pattern that has developed by this stage. The length and complexity of bird song will often depend on their mating preferences. Monogamous birds like the Whipbird compose relatively simple songs that last for long periods of time as their female partner is not impressed by show. She is looking for a healthy male who is able to fly long distances to look for food and pass on the best possible genes to her offspring. Thus, monogamous species tend to have relatively poor and small territories. On the other hand, a female from a polygamous species usually picks out the male with the best possible territory as she is quite likely to be deserted by her mate when the next female comes along and left to bring up the chicks on her own. The territory must therefore be large and abundant in food.

Mammalian mating calls

Mammals have evolved a highly complex way of producing sound through an organ known as the larynx or 'voice box'. Found at the end of the trachea nearest the mouth it is supported by a network of cartilage which can be moved by muscles to change the shape of the voice box. There is also an outer opening that can be covered by a muscular film known as the *epiglottis*. The vocal chords run along the inside of the larynx and can be relaxed or tensed by the movement of muscles. Sound is produced when air is exhaled through the voice box. The vocal chords tense up and vibrate producing a tone which depends on the tension. Air sacs located in the larynx act as resonators and help the sound to carry; these air sacs are particularly well developed in the primates. In humans modification of sound can also occur by moving the tongue or changing the shape of the lips. Different sounds can also be made by breathing in and then breathing out; the characteristic bray of the donkey is produced by an 'Ee' when breathing in and an 'Aw' on expulsion of the breath. There is one mammal that does not use its larnyx to produce sound; the elephant's distinctive trumpeting is made through its trunk instead. When an elephant becomes excited, whether sexually or otherwise, it lifts up its trunk and lets the world know. This multi-purpose tool resonates the sound so that it reverberates through the jungle. However, the elephant is an exception in the somewhat subdued sexual world of the mammals.

Unlike birds, where sound plays an integral part in bringing the two sexes together for copulation, mammals tend to favour scent and visual displays in their courtship rituals. This is due to the fact that most lower mammals live in wide open spaces where visibility is high. The primates that live a largely arboreal life in the jungle tend to use their vocal chords when attracting a mate. The evolution of group life among mammals, seen earlier with schooling in fish and flocking in birds, also means that the dominant males simply have to turn around and fertilise the females within the herd at breeding time instead of searching for a partner. Thus, elaborate visual and auditory courtship rituals are unnecessary. In fact, compared to the complex courtship rituals of birds and even fishes, most mammals appear to have a very casual approach to sex; if you blink you can miss it in some species. Although pheromones are widely favoured as a means of sexual communication, the observer is unable to appreciate this and as a result, courtship often seems entirely lacking.

THE SEX SERENADE

Sing me a song and watch my love grow! The female canary must hear her male partner's song in order for her ovaries to develop. The more he sings the quicker the ovaries ripen and the eggs develop.

However, mammals do have one important biological advance over every other form of life which explains this apparent casualness. Females have a built-in food supply and so they do not have to rely on the male to find food for their offspring. As a result, the males waste little time and energy on sex, yet the female's offspring still receive the best possible genes because the dominant male in the herd has fought his way to the top by possessing qualities of strength and endurance. However, this does not mean the mammalian world is silent during the breeding season. On the contrary the air is usually filled with the cries of males for it is during the mating season that the authority of dominant males is often challenged. The Red Deer that live in Scotland, for example, engage in noisy battles for most of October which is their breeding or rutting season. These battles are fought firstly by a lengthy exchange of loud roars. Then, if the challenger does not back down the two circle each other menacingly before a physical fight takes place. This involves engaging and locking antlers and when the joust is over the victorious stag chases away the rival. The initial roaring more often than not stops the battle from progressing to the physical stage; thus the winner of the fight is decided without actually staging the battle. Stags may roar up to three times a minute for nearly an hour; the best fighters are usually able to roar the loudest and most frequently which is why a challenge does not often progress beyond this point. Roaring, like fighting, is tiring and the quality of the roar will be best if the stag is at his peak of physical fitness. The pitch of the roar is also important. Young stags, like young human males, have a thinner and higher roar from which the mature stags can ascertain their fighting ability. Not all mammals, however, enjoy group life. Many predators lead a solitary life and only come together for the express purpose of mating, after which they resume their former lifestyles. The Red Fox, *Vulpes vulpes*, has only a maximum of six days in which to find a mate and copulate as the females are only 'on heat' once a year. No wonder then that the still of the night is broken by the frantic screams of the dog foxes and vixens as they call to each other in short shouts. The vixen's shriek is particularly piercing as it must carry over long distances to other foxes in the area. Other calls usually follow which are softer and more subtle and these continue, gradually increasing in volume, until the two come together.

Even domesticated animals such as dogs and cats hear the call of the wild at breeding time. Around spring and early summer suburban backyards can be filled at night with the wild cries of female cats 'on heat' and the howling responses of tomcats. These calls are used initially so that the two can locate each other and are the most efficient way of advertising their whereabouts. During the mating season tomcats also release a sex scent in their urine which they spray on nearby objects at every opportunity; this powerful smell is deplored by householders as it tends to linger and often pervades the whole house. When the male and female felines finally come together they engage in a rough tussle. Indeed, there is nothing gentle about the sex life of a cat, despite the deceptively lazy appearance of most household pets. During copulation the tomcat often seizes the female's neck with his teeth in a love bite common to both domestic cats and their larger cousins in the wild.

Monkey chatter

A significant number of the lower primates live in dense forests where visibility is reduced and, like birds, they must use sound to find each other and keep in contact. The noise made by these species is particularly evident around dawn when the jungle comes alive with the chattering of monkeys and the calls of larger primates such as the gibbons. Next to birdsong the sounds made by primates, an order of the Animal Kingdom that includes man, are among the loudest noises in the animal world. Yet despite this ability to produce long distance sound, primates do not generally use it as a means of courtship. Instead it is used as a way of keeping their tight social groups together and warning group members of danger. The use of pheromones during courtship, favoured widely by mammals, is not as common in the primates although some of the higher primates still use sex scents as a principal means of attracting a mate. Most primates, however, use visual signals to attract a mate as they have developed keen eyesight through the evolution of a flattened face with forward looking eyes.

Like other mammals the courtship rituals of the primates often seem very casual to an observer; monkeys are a prime example of this. Although female monkeys have a menstrual cycle like humans they are not able to have sex whenever they wish but rather only during their oestrous cycle. That the female is 'on heat' is obvious to all and sundry by the display of her enlarged and coloured external genitalia; the female chimpanzee signals her readiness to mate by a huge pink swelling which attracts and stimulates the male chimpanzee. Others like the female Rhesus Monkey release a pheromone called copulin from their vagina which arouses the sexual interest of males, who sniff around the female's genitalia before mounting her. The sex life of the chimpanzee would horrify the moral majority who have condemned so many sexual practices between humans. To begin with chimpanzees live in small groups with very few rules and individuals are free to come and go as they please. Their courtship is crude and casual as indeed are their morals. Chimpanzees are among the most promiscuous of all the primates and when the mating season comes around the female simply strolls up to the nearest male and presents her inflamed pudenda for his pleasure. After he has had his way she moves on to the dominant male in the group who ignores her until she is in the middle of her oestrous cycle when fertilisation is most successful. In the meantime she contents herself with some of the lesser males in the group until the dominant male is ready.

Some of the loudest of the primates are those species that are monogamous, such as the Indris and the gibbons. The wail of the Indris, for example, can be heard up to three kilometres away. The male Indris lets out a low howl while the females tend to bark. Most of these species have evolved special sound production mechanisms such as the aptly named Howler Monkeys of South America who start their characteristic noise as soon as the sun comes up. In the Indris, for example, the loudness of both sounds is due to modified bones around the throat which form a resonating chamber; the male's resonating chamber is so large that it looks like an enormous double chin. These sounds are usually produced by a male and female who have formed a monogamous team. Noises made by primates usually form a sound pattern and in the case of monogamous species a duet is generally developed between a male and female soon after they meet, mate and decide to pair up for life. It is thought by scientists that this form of auditory communication helps reinforce bonding between two individuals who have formed a lifelong partnership. It is also a useful tactic when defending their territory against intruders as they are usually deterred by the fact that there are two working together instead of a solitary occupant and defender. The loudest call, known as the great call of the gibbon and the Indris, comes surprisingly from the female. This long and loud song is thought by scientists to be the gibbons way of avoiding a fight as any wound would severely hamper their mobility in the tree tops. However, out of all birds and mammals, Ring-Tailed Lemurs have one of the largest repertoires of sound and gesture.

Gibbons are particularly interesting primates in terms of the sound they produce. Unlike all other higher primates, their song occupies a very limited frequency specially suited to their dense rainforest habitat. They succeed in compressing their sound signal so that it will travel a lot further. Most also call around dawn as this is a time when sound carries well. When the sun comes up the air above the canopy of trees becomes heated while the air below is still cool. The animals climb to the top of the trees where the sounds they make carry because they are not absorbed by ground litter. The noises that filter up through the canopy are reflected back down by the warm layer of air and so travel a longer distance. The Siamang, which is the largest of the gibbons and has the most complex call, gives out a deep boom from two resonating vocal throat pouches that help the sound to travel. This species also sing in pairs so the effect is double. Like other gibbons this duet is important in promoting bonding between a pair although grooming each other and occasional play are equally important.

However, it is the highest of all primates, humans or *Homo erectus* that have developed the most sophisticated methods of communication by the evolution of language. Although animals have not formed words, phrases and sentences from their noises and sounds, they nevertheless manage to convey specific messages as efficiently as possible. The vervet monkeys, for example, have a different alarm call for leopards, eagles, pythons, baboons and humans. In this way it could be argued that animals have developed languages which perform the same functions as those in the human world, the only difference being that human languages are more complex.

Water colours

Some of the most colourful examples of sexual dimorphism in the natural world can be found underwater among the fishes. At mating time many male fishes adopt brilliant colours to attract a female and the sea becomes a kaleidoscope of changing colours. In the Three-Spined Stickleback, *Geasterosteus aculetus*, the male adopts a distinctive nuptial dress that lights up the murky depths. He is distinguished by his flashing red belly and blue eyes which only appear during courtship.

Sticklebacks mate in spring and the gradual warming of the water triggers the onset of these brilliant colours. Once a male is in breeding condition he claims a territory and begins making a nest within its confines, gluing it together with liquid secreted from his kidneys. If another Stickleback with a red belly enters his territory he immediately becomes aggressive and chases him off; sometimes a fight may begin. The female, on the other hand, plays the minor role in breeding. Instead of developing a red belly she has an abdomen swollen with eggs. When she swims by the male's territory he darts out and performs a zig-zag dance in front of her and tries to lure her to his underwater love nest. If she is interested she assumes an upright position and turns and follows the male to his nest. The nest itself is relatively small and the head of the female will protrude at one end and her tail the other. The male will then induce her to lay her eggs by prodding her tail with his snout. Having done this, the female swims away leaving the male to fertilise the eggs and keep watch over them until they hatch. When the young Sticklebacks emerge the father acts as a guardian for some time afterward as well. This complicated ritual serves several purposes. It not only differentiates male from female, but also ensures they are of the same species and that they are both ready for mating. The building of a nest guarantees that the eggs

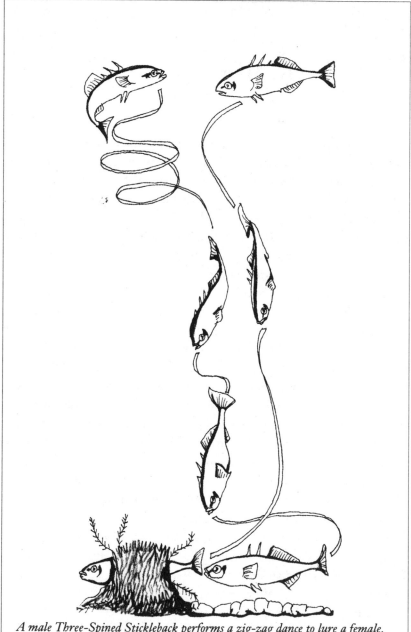

A male Three-Spined Stickleback performs a zig-zag dance to lure a female.

and sperm are deposited at the same time in the same place in a similar fashion to the more sophisticated mechanisms of internal fertilisation.

That colour plays an essential role in the successful breeding of Sticklebacks cannot be denied. The red belly is the only signal to a resident male that another male has invaded his territory. Experiments conducted by leading behavioural scientist Niko Tinbergen showed that the resident male would not attack a model of the Stickleback unless the belly was painted red. Even a crudely shaped model with a red underside was attacked. A red mail truck that passed the laboratory windows would also arouse an aggressive reaction from the Sticklebacks. However, colour is not the key to winning over the female and in most species the male fish is more than just a pretty face. He may well be beautiful to look at but this is rarely enough to melt the heart of his cold-blooded partner. He must also carry out a courtship dance or perform a small series of ritualized movements to which the female responds with her own gavotte. This courtship dance is common in many species as some fish are unable to distinguish whether the individuals they meet are male or female and only discover this in the ensuing ritual.

Cichlids are another fish that, like sticklebacks, are popular with aquarium owners because of their colour and the ease with which they breed in captivity. These small fish are black with orange and white stripes. During the breeding season the males adopt a coloured throat which they display by opening their mouths to every member of the species they encounter. They will also spread their fins and raise the covers on their gills in a threatening gesture. If two males in breeding condition meet each other there is usually a battle of wills before one decides to bow out of the contest. In this way the males are able to recognise each other's sex. The losing fish sneaks off, closing his mouth as he goes and his colour soon fades away. The victor, on the other hand, glows with even brighter colours and the females who are ready for spawning follow him. However, if a female cichlid sees the male's threat-ening pose she holds her ground and dodges his attacks until he realises she is not a rival male and changes his tune and begins to woo her.

Sexual relations between the bitterlings are similar to those of the sticklebacks and the cichlids. However, these fish add another dimension to breeding by associating with a species of freshwater mussel. During the breeding season the male appears in his bright colours while the female develops a 4cm long tube. Once they meet up, the two bitterlings set off together to search for a suitable mussel. Having found one, the female takes her place over its siphon (the tube through which the mussel draws in water), sticks her tube in and lays her eggs in the mussel's body cavity. The male then disperses his sperm over the mussel. Fertilisation occurs and the young bitterlings spend a month in their mussel incubator before swimming out into the underwater world. Of course, the mussel does not simply accept these baby bitterlings without good reason; it too benefits from the arrangement. While the female bitterling is laying her eggs, the mussel releases its own larvae which cling to the bitterling. The fish's skin eventually grows over them and they are fed by its juices until they are big enough to break away as a perfectly formed mussel. Another colourful fish is the African Mouthbrooder, *Haplochromis burtoni*, so called because the female swallows her eggs as she sheds them and then carries them around in her mouth. The male swims by her in his courtship colours, a series of bright spots on his anal fin, and releases his sperm. The female, mistaking the spots for more of her eggs, attempts to swallow them and instead takes sperm into her mouth and fertilises her eggs. Almost a case of fellation!

The salmon has long been a favourite of the literary world because of the migratory trip it embarks on at the beginning of each breeding sea-son. Many writers, such as the Irish poet William Yeats, have written about the salmon. Yeats wrote scornfully of the salmon's fertility and upstream spawning in one of his most famous poems *Sailing to Byzantium*, rejecting the transient world of the sensual in the search for something more permanent. However, the upriver spawning of the salmon is a truly amazing feat. After spending years out sea, where it eats enormous amounts to put on weight, the male salmon returns to his birthplace as a mature adult. It is certainly an uphill struggle with some salmon having to literally leap over waterfalls to reach their shallow breeding grounds. Their silvery skin turns to pink and is flecked with black and it is at this stage of their development that salmon are considered a great delicacy by humans. Their remarkable sex life does not just stop with a change of colour at the end of their journey. Now it is the female's turn to have a little fun as she usually has the choice of two males. Her breeding behaviour begins when she starts scraping out a nest in the river gravel by lashing her tail and sweeping pebbles aside so that a shallow pit is formed. When the male swims by he spreads his fins which is the signal for the female to start spawning. She lays her eggs in the nest and the male quickly sprays sperm over them. Fertilisation must take place very quickly as the sperm only has a life span of a minute and risks being swept away by the river current. For this reason one of the golden rules of nature is often broken and parenthood may not always be certain. It is a wise salmon indeed that

ABSENCE MAKES THE HEART GROW FONDER

Family is so important to eels that they actually return to their birthplace when adults to have sex. Their migration from the ocean depths to the spawning ground of their parents is an amazing feat of navigation. Like salmon, eels are able to push through seemingly insurmountable obstacles to reach their homeland. They may not be able to jump up waterfalls but eels can be found wriggling across land to reach their breeding areas.

knows its own father! Cuckoldry may occur when a young salmon that has not yet matured sneaks in and fertilises the eggs. Thus the young male sometimes functions as a kind of safety net in cases where the mature male's sperm is swept away.

Although it is generally the males in the animal world that are blessed with great looks there are exceptions to the rule. In the pipefish, which belong to the same family as the popular sea horses, the female is by far the more attractive of the two sexes. This species is quite unusual in appearance, being shaped like snakes but with long noses fashioned into a tube. When the breeding season begins the female assumes her bright courtship colours and darts coquettishly around the male, flirting outrageously. She then lures him to the surface where she swims around him circles, slowly weaving her seductive spell. Totally captivated by her charm, the male pipefish allows the seductress to wrap herself around his body, stimulating him into releasing his sperm at the same time as she disperses her eggs.

Yet fish are not the only creatures in the underwater world to show spectacular colour changes. Their primitive relatives, the coelenterates, also adopt eye-catching garb during courtship. The Common American Squid, for example, woos his partner with a series of colour changes that dazzles and seduces her. Coloured dots first appear on his arms and then spread over his whole body in a process not unlike the blushing of a shy schoolboy on his first date. This bashful behaviour brings out tender feelings in the female and the two eventually copulate side by side with their arms entwined. Indeed, the underwater world can be an amazing journey into brightly coloured coral and luminescent and strangely patterned fish.

The beach, that undecided stretch of sand or pebble between land and sea, is a favourite meeting and even mating place for humans and crabs are no different. When ready to mate, one species of coastal crab known

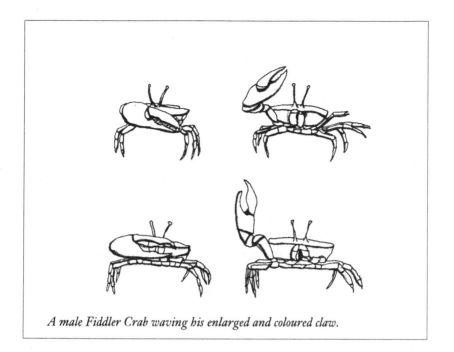

A male Fiddler Crab waving his enlarged and coloured claw.

as the Fiddler Crab, waits on the sand for a sweetheart to appear. So that she may spot him easily on the vast strip of white he waves a huge coloured claw in the air to attract her attention. During the mating season the colour in the claw may suffuse the entire body of the male crab, often changing from green to white to blue and even purple. The rest of the year he is as drab as the female. Indeed, even during courtship, the Fiddler Crab only dresses up in his finery when the sun is high in the sky and the tide is out. Sex hormones make his coloured shell even more spectacular and when the female responds he begins to dance wildly, driving the female into a state of feverish sexual excitement. When both crabs have reached a similar state of unbridled lust some public fondling takes place before the male leads the female to his hole in the sand. Once inside he plugs up the entrance with mud which is quickly read as the 'do not disturb' sign in crab language.

Some amphibians will also put on striking courtship displays. The tailed variety, newts, use a winning combination of visual, olfactory and even violence to entice the females to mate. Although they are close cousins to the toads and frogs their courtship practices are much more refined than the bump and grind that makes up the frogs' mad scramble for each other. Another major difference between the mating of frogs and newts is that the newts favour internal fertilisation. The male does not have a penis but instead produces a spermatophore which is picked up by the female. The object of the male's spectacular courtship is to attract the female to the spermatophore and persuade her to pick it up. Firstly he releases a sex scent from glands in the skin near his tail. He then fans his tail so that the perfume wafts over to the female. If she is unresponsive and starts to move away he may block her path and pose in front of her displaying his decorative tail of frills and spots. Next he brings the tail she has been admiring crashing down on her, often knocking her backwards. This series of wooing measures may continue for some time as the male does not give up easily. Finally when the female accepts that masochistic sex is her only chance of survival the male starts to play what is commonly called 'hard to get'. He gradually moves away in an effort to lead the female to the spermatophore. It is a delicate operation manoeuvring the female into position and he must be careful that her eyes are fastened on him during the whole procedure. Otherwise he must start all over again when the next female comes along.

Terrestrial life equals the beauty of the aquatic world. There are many splashes of colour in the wings of butterflies and the plumage of birds. Even the agile lizards are a colourful and active group during courtship. The chameleon, or green anole, is probably the most famous of the lizards because of its ability to change colour for camouflage purposes. During the breeding season the male inflates a pouch around his throat that is coloured yellow, green and blue. The pouch is so large that he has to hold his head right back to stop it from touching the ground. Like the tropical fish, the chameleon has also developed a system of signals to distinguish male from female. If one male comes across another, the resident male will stand on tiptoe next to his rival with his legs outstretched and his tail waving about. However, if the intruder is a female she comes towards him without the enlarged throat pouch. The male then grabs her neck in his jaws and twists his tail under hers so that their sex organs are together and they copulate. The chameleon also has African cousins, the agamas, who have a colourful courtship in more than one sense of the word. Sometimes this may resemble a slapstick farce. During the breeding season the male agama shows off a blue throat to attract females and nods his head to scare away rival males. As agamas are polygamous animals they often keep harems of up to six females at one time. Territorial struggles with rival males can become quite heated and sometimes this leads to violent confrontations in which tails have been

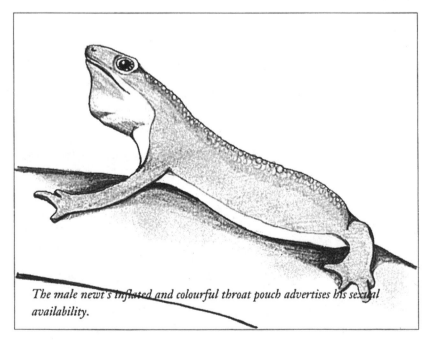

The male newt's inflated and colourful throat pouch advertises his sexual availability.

known to break off. At the end of the day however, a ceasefire is called, the courtship colours fade and the males retire peacefully to a communal tree for the night.

Avian Beauty

Although it is often denied, appearance does play an important role in the initial attraction between members of the opposite sex in the human world. Hair and eye colour, height and weight all count towards creating a favourable first impression that leads to that second glance. Some behaviour experts have suggested that during the initial meeting between man and woman, the man spends five seconds looking her up and down and 1.2 seconds of this time is spent gazing at her face. Yet humans are not the only species to place such faith in physical looks. Fish adopt bright colours and striking patterns to attract the eye of a mate during courtship while birds probably remain among the most visually arresting sights in the natural world. Indeed, the beautiful plumage of some species of birds often attracts as much human attention as does their exquisite song. This is because birds and humans both enjoy a keen sense of eyesight. Birds are also blessed with good hearing but for humans, sight has become the sense that we are most dependent on. The history of our keen eyesight harks back to the days of the apes and monkeys who developed forward facing eyes that allowed them to judge distances and the speed at which objects move. This was essential for successful arboreal life as it was necessary to be able to perceive things quickly and accurately as they swung from branch to branch. Thus the snout found in some of the earlier primates such as the lemurs and tree shrews gradually shrank and our reliance on smell was replaced by sight. The development of our vision was aided by the evolution of forward facing eyes which allow greater depth of vision and make the judgement of speed and distance a lot more accurate.

As mentioned earlier, most of the beautiful colours and patterns seen in the natural world are worn by the male. It is the female who is usually the dull or plain looking one. This often comes as a surprise to small children who are learning about nature, as they have become accustomed to images of beautiful women and handsome but considerably duller looking men. The reason for this difference between males and females, referred to in scientific circles as sexual dimorphism, is explained by Darwin's theory of sexual selection. Although sexual selection works in the same way as natural selection the end result is different. Natural selection results in a fitter species in terms of being adapted to an environment while sexual selection refers to the advantages certain individuals have over others of the same sex solely in respect to reproduction. Certain males acquire a particular feature that sets them above other males in the sexual stakes and this advantage is then passed on to their offspring.

Thus Darwin was assuming that sexual selection is always a matter of female choice; that is females make a definite choice of their sexual partners. He was proven to be correct in his thinking and almost everywhere you look in the animal world there are examples to back up his theory. Females prefer the most brightly coloured or patterned males and their sensibilities are stirred by the magnificent plumage of the male birds of paradise for example. Thus, they choose the most aesthetically appealing males, who are then able to pass on these advantageous characteristics to their offspring. In this manner a species is gradually modified. At the time of its release in the late 19th century, when women had not even begun to agitate for the vote, Darwin's theory of sexual selection and the basic premise that it was always a matter of female choice, stirred up considerable controversy. Today, the idea is more or less accepted by the scientific community although there is still no substantial proof apart from evidence derived from behavioural research. However, it is wrong to think that all sexual dimorphism is a result of sexual selection, a lot is clearly natural selection at work.

The lyrical beauty of birds, Class *Aves*, is possibly unsurpassed in the natural world. For centuries humans have been impressed by the magnificent colours of peacocks, birds of paradise, pheasants, hummingbirds, ducks and kingfishers. The function of these colourful birds is to show off. They strut, parade and flaunt their natural assets throughout the breeding season in order to attract a female. Indeed, just as birdsong is a delight to human ears, so the visual displays of birds are a pleasure to watch. Birds' finery is often accentuated by graceful movements or dances, the beautiful feathers catching the eye of the female while the dance steps hold her attention. Their plumage, which endures a lot of wear and tear, can begin to look a little tatty after some time. In most species it is replaced at least once a year in a process known as moulting and some varieties will moult twice or even three times a year. Moulting occurs gradually so that the bird is never left completely bare.

The peacock is perhaps one of the best known of all birds and is often held up as a symbol of pride and vanity because of the brilliance of its green and gold tail feathers and its habit of prancing around during the mating season. As a result the expression 'proud as a peacock' is often used to describe a ridiculously overdressed man strutting down the street. The tail feathers of peacocks, with the huge eyespot at the tip, have been favoured by milliners throughout the centuries and at various points in time were the height of fashion. The Blue Peacock, *Pavo cristatus*, is found in South-East Asia and India but has been bred in captivity for its beauty for some 2000 years. It is also much admired in its home countries as it kills young venomous snakes such as cobras. The peacock's tail with the eyespots often causes it to be confused with the giant pheasant, the Argus Pheasant, found in South-East Asia, whose wing feathers and those in the middle of the tail are also decorated with eye spots and are also brilliantly coloured. However, the peacock's glorious display involves a long train of tail feathers which can be spread out like a fan, making it easily distinguishable. It also has a longer neck, a head crest and long legs equipped

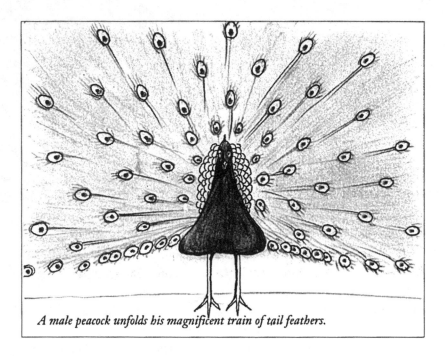

A male peacock unfolds his magnificent train of tail feathers.

with small spurs.

The magnificent iridescent colours in peacocks, pheasants and other brilliantly coloured birds are caused by pigment flowing through the thousands of tiny capillaries found within the thick tissue that makes up the tail. When pigment enters these capillaries the previously colourless plumage springs to life in brilliant colour. The most common pigments are yellows, browns and blacks which are produced by melanins found in nipple-like structures or papillae on the skin. These are incorporated into feather growth during the early years. The vivid red colour of some species like the flamingo is caused by aoerythrin, blue is produced by a combination of reflection and pigment while white is pure reflection. Most birds have keen eyesight and are able to see a range of colours similar to humans. The iridescence is caused by tiny colourless plates which are positioned to reflect the light. For a time it was thought that male hormones caused this colour change, but today a commonly held view is that sex hormones do not change the appearance of the male but rather it is the female who assumes a courtship dress under the influence of hormones during the breeding season. Unfortunately for her these hormones account for the dull, drab appearance of the female birds as they cannot afford to attract the attention of predators when hatching their eggs and caring for their young. This has been proven many times over by scientists in numerous experiments. Castrated male birds retain their beautiful feathers but if the ovaries of a female are removed she eventually assumes male plumage. Thus, it seems certain that it is the role of the female hormones to stunt the development of colourful or striking plumage during the breeding season.

When the male peacock wishes to attract a female, he unfolds his truly magnificent tail and spreads it out in front of her. At the same time he cries out to ward off other males from his territory. The sight of his beautiful tail feathers stimulates the female sexually and after a while she crouches down, ready and willing for his sexual advances. The courtship of the Argus Pheasant is particularly striking. Named after the multi-eyed giant from Greek mythology who guarded Io with the four hundred eye spots that adorned his wings, the male Argus is a huge bird about two metres long, of which the tail makes up over a full metre. The cock courts his hen by stretching out his wings so that he seems completely encircled by brilliant feathers. Just in case the female is a little world weary of beauty, he rocks back and forth in a courtship dance to make sure her eyes stay glued to him and him alone.

For most peacocks, pheasants, kingfishers and birds of paradise it is rarely enough for the male to sit back and rely on the brilliance of his feathers to attract a female. He must show off what nature has given him to its best advantage and he does this by striking poses and performing dances which involve the spreading of his gorgeous plumes. Birds of paradise, found only in New Guinea and nearby islands, are a case in point. Considered by many to be the most spectacular of all birds, they were for centuries only known outside New Guinea by their preserved skins from which the natives had trimmed the feet. This gave rise to the idea that these ornamental creatures lived ethereal lives and had descended directly from paradise and never touched the ground. Thus they became known as birds of paradise. Their beauty is unparalleled in the Animal Kingdom. The Greater Bird of Paradise, *Paradisaea apoda*, is a marvellous sight in full courtship dress. The male has a bright yellow head and neck, an emerald green throat, a velvety black chest and chestnut tail, wing and belly feathers. Long gold feathers hang down from the tip of the wings, becoming wine red at the ends. Today we know that birds with such heavy, ornamental feathers cannot fly well and spend most of the time with their feet firmly planted on the ground. Although it would seem that the brilliance of the male's plumage would be enough to sweep any female off her feet, it is not sufficient. The male also whistles, calls out to the female and dances with his plumage shimmering at every step until he wins over the female.

Unfortunately most birds pay a price for their beauty as they are unable to fly well with the additional weight of their colourful feathers. However, the tiny hummingbird, *Apodiformes*, is an exception. These enchanting birds match the peacocks and the birds of paradise eye for eye in terms of colour but far outshine them with their graceful aerobatics. Hummingbirds are able to drop down from the sky like stones falling from the heavens and then pull up in the nick of time in front of a female perched on a twig. When courting, the male hovers in mid-air with wings quivering until the female invites him to sit next to her on the branch. Their extraordinary flying ability is due to the speed at which they can move their wings, sometimes so rapidly that they become invisible. This agility is due to the fact that the wings are attached to the shoulder by a swivel joint which allows the leading edge of the wing to point forwards during the forward wingbeat and backward during the backward wingbeat. This enables the bird to fly in any direction or hover in the air. Small species of the hummingbird are able to make 60-80 wing strokes per second which can carry them through the air at a speed of up to 80 kilometres/hour. During courtship, males from other species can increase their wing strokes to an incredible 100-200 per second. In addition to flying ability and physical beauty, nature has also endowed hummingbirds with singing voices which are impressive for their size, although they are not strictly classified as songbirds.

Other birds which are both colourful and musical are parrots, lorikeets, lovebirds, canaries, budgerigars, cockatoos, macaws and lories, all of which belong to the Family *Pittacidae*. They are popular cage birds because of their gregarious nature, colourful feathers and powers of mimicry. The wild tropical forests, especially those of South America and Australia, resound with their incessant shrieking calls. They are also brightened by their vivid plumage, predominantly green, although red, yellow and purple are also quite common. Sometimes all four may appear on the one individual. One of the largest of the birds also has the distinction of belonging to a select and vibrant group. The Common Cassowary, *Casuarius casuarius*, is found in Australia, New Guinea and some parts of Polynesia and comes from the same family as the unique Australian bird, the emu. Like the emu and its relative the ostrich, the cassowary is unable to fly but is equipped with powerful legs that enable it to run very quickly. While most of its body is brown or black, these severe colours are relieved by the blue naked skin of the head and neck which contrasts with vivid red wattles and the horny casque on the top of the head. During courtship the throat panel of the male cassowary is brightly coloured and is used as a feature of attraction. Although these birds are normally placid, they have a razor-sharp nail in each foot and humans have been badly gashed. Be wary of the cassowary!

Seabirds too are not totally lacking in colour. The Frigatebird, *Fregata*

Male Frigatebirds inflate a spectacular red sac during courtship.

minor, gives one of the most spectacular courtship displays in the avian world. Found in the tropical waters of the South Atlantic, Pacific and Indian oceans, its body is a metallic black with the male being distinguished by a red pouch of naked skin under his throat. During courtship he inflates this so that he can only just peer over the top of what looks like a huge, inflated, red balloon stuck to his chest. In the Magnificent Frigatebirds, *Fregata magnificens*, this spectacular red sac can reach the size of a human head.

Casual sex

Although mammals are structurally more advanced than birds or fishes, they are not nearly as impressive in terms of colour. Humans still find many shapes, sizes and activities of mammals appealing such as the sight of a horse galloping through a paddock with its tail streaming out behind. However, the startling and eye catching brilliance evident in other species is missing in mammals. There are many reasons for this.

Firstly, most mammals spend their lives roaming in open areas and have dull, drab coats so that they do not draw unwanted attention from predators. Secondly, the sexual dimorphism responsible for the vivid plumage of birds is just as strong in mammals but is merely represented in different ways. Generally, the male mammal is larger than the female and in some cases may have one outstanding physical characteristic such as the mane of a lion or the antlers of a stag. Courtship colours are not necessary to attract a male as the use of scent is widespread in the mammalian mating game. This is because mammals have a highly developed sense of smell but lack the keen eyesight found in the birds. Reproductive advances in mammals have also played a major role in diminishing the importance of eyesight and hence visual displays. The female has her own in-built system of feeding the offspring through her mammary glands and so the male does not need to be involved in the feeding or consequent rearing of the young as with birds and other species. So much for women's liberation! It follows therefore that elaborate courtship is not necessary to ensure the correct choice of mate, although the passing down of top quality genes is still important. This choice, however, has usually been made for the females by the dominant male, who fights other males or scares them off, thus proving his worthiness as a suitor and father of her children. Once he has won supremacy the male mammal has only then to discover whether the female is in oestrous or not. He does this by sniffing at her genitalia or getting a whiff of her sexual scent. Thus, in some ways the female mammal takes a more passive role in the sexual process. Even solitary mammals such as the predators who come together for sex and then return to their lonely lifestyles rely on scent rather than sight when choosing a sexual partner. Early primates also depend on a good sense of smell and are equipped with a long snout which aids them in their search for food.

WHAM, BAM, THANK YOU MA'AM

When bulls are ready to copulate their penis turns bright red. Only one thrust is needed for the bull to have sex, so copulation lasts less than a second. The bull's penis is made of fibrous tissue which becomes springy when dried. In this form it is known as a pizzle and is often used to make whips and riding crops. Talk about breaking a fella's balls!

The development of eyesight and the consequent visual means of communicating sexual desire did not evolve until the primates began to colonise the trees. Keen vision is needed when monkeys swing from branch to branch. They must be able to judge distances accurately and so the long snout of the lower primates gradually shrank and was replaced by a flattened face with forward directed eyes. Visual signals became more effective than scent signals although olfactory messages have never been entirely abandoned by higher primates. Some use a combination of both while others produce loud calls that echo through the forest in their search for a mate. On the whole, however, courtship remains relatively uncomplicated between the primates.

Female monkeys and apes have a menstrual cycle like humans but sexual receptivity is still tied in closely with oestrous. As schoolchildren have often observed with horrified delight on trips to the zoo, this eagerness to have sex is indicated by greatly enlarged, pink-coloured external genitalia. The sight is usually repulsive to humans but is a source of great sexual arousal for the male chimpanzee. So much so that the female is often followed around by a number of eager suitors who will wait in line to mate with her. Some naturalists have observed the one female chimpanzee mating with eight different males in the space of 15 minutes! Human society would consider this behaviour promiscuous to say the least and in common parlance the term 'gang bang' would seem appropriate.

The mandrills, a species of monkey very similar to the baboons, are perhaps the one truly brilliant splash of colour in the primate world. Mandrills, *Mandrillus sphinx*, live in small troupes on the ground and eat

A female monkey indicates she is ready for sex by crouching, left. Actual mating is very brief, right.

a mixture of plants and other food. Found mainly in the rainforests of Africa, they are easy to recognise by their multi-coloured faces. Their long noses are covered with bright red skin and surrounded on both sides by a patch of pale blue with grooves running along them from the eyes to the nostrils. Mandrill buttocks are always bare and display brightly coloured areas of pigmented skin which act as a threat signal to other males. When courting a female the buttocks are an attraction and they become even more vivid as sexual excitement mounts.

The evolution of mammals and the higher order of primates brought with it communication by way of facial expressions. By twisting its face in a particular way or tightening and relaxing some face muscles mammals can visually express their different moods. However, just as birds only express themselves in song during the mating season, so all mammals

A male African Buffalo displaying the "flehman" grimace common to most hoofed animals.

except some primates and humans, only use facial expressions in the oestrous cycle. As already mentioned, oestrous is usually signalled by the release of pheromones from the female's genital region. Some male mammals then sniff the female to find out whether she is 'on heat' and hoofed animals will smell the female's urine for the same purpose. When these hoofed animals are trying this they will make a characteristic grimace known as flehmen, a word of German extraction. The male lifts up his head and rolls his lips, displaying his gums or wrinkling his nose. The significance of this is not really known but occurs in cattle, buffalo, antelopes and many other hoofed animals.

Some of the higher primates have developed facial expressions which are remarkably similar to humans. Chimpanzees, for example, have different expressions for different emotions. The four basic ones are excitement, happiness, fear and sadness but of course, there are many others. As anybody who has seen a Tarzan film will remember, his pet chimpanzee Cheetah would jump up and down with his lips jutting out ululating 'Oo Oo Oo Oo Oo Oo' to express excitement. Gorillas too use a mixture of visual and auditory means to communicate what they are feeling although they are not as sophisticated as the chimpanzee.

Things that go bump in the night

Just as humans have little knowledge of the colourful, underwater world of tropical fishes, so too do they miss out on the escapades of nocturnal animals. Those who do catch a glimpse of these creatures usually find them to be slow and sluggish as most sleep during the day and only come alive at night. As soon as the sun goes down nocturnal animals emerge from their daytime hiding places and the night is filled with the sounds of their movements and calls to their mates. Yet it is only keen natural scientists or nature lovers who head out into the night with torches in hand to spot these normally invisible animals. Of course, not all nocturnal species are land animals. Some are also aquatic creatures like the increasingly rare British Crayfish, known as the 'White Claw'. They are found only in freshwater containing lime which is essential for their shells. Mating takes place in the autumn dark. After the two sexes have met up the male spins the female around while placing his spermatophore onto her belly where it sticks to the hairs among her swimming legs. When she lays her eggs they also stick to these hairs and her 'pregnant' condition is known commonly as being 'in berry'.

Owls are probably the best known of all nocturnal animals and like many other birds they have been immortalised in literature. Probably the most famous tale is Edward Lear's *The Owl and the Pussy-cat* 'who went to sea in a beautiful pea-green boat'. The owl is also regarded as a symbol of wisdom, probably because it has a flat human-like face and is usually spotted sitting sedately on the branch of a tree. It also gives out a distinctive call which sounds like the English word 'who', giving rise to the term hooting. Owls are particularly well adapted to night life with their silent flight and acute sense of hearing. The asymmetrical position of their ears, whereby the right ear tilts upwards and picks up sounds from above while the left ear points downwards and locates quite small sounds from below, allows them to hear sounds at a distance. Whether it is the rustling of a mouse through the grass or the croak of a frog, an owl can pinpoint the source very accurately. Indeed, some scientists believe that the owl actually hunts by sound rather than sight.

The owl's breeding season is in spring along with most other birds. As a species they favour monogamy and choose their partners before sexual maturity. A long engagement takes place before then. As owls are nocturnal birds they have little use for brightly coloured plumage and rely on their excellent hearing to attract a mate. The male hoots first and the female responds with a higher pitched cry. Owls build rough nests for their young usually in the abandoned nests of other birds, holes in trees or the ruins of houses. The eggs are incubated for less than a month and the male and female rear the offspring together. Within several weeks of hatching the young owls are ready to fly from branch to branch.

Frogmouths are a relatively rare bird and a close relative of the owl. Only a dozen species exist and these are found in South-East Asia and Australia. One in particular, the Tawny Frogmouth, *Podargus strigoides*, lives in the forests of Australia and feeds on insects, small rodents and birds. It is a strange looking bird resembling an owl but with a wide bill that gives its face a half-pert, half-surprised expression. Frogmouths are not well equipped for flying and can only keep it up for short distances. As they are nocturnal and quite scarce little is known about their sex life although it is thought that they are monogamous.

Nightjars, like the frogmouths, are another relative of the owls although they are more widespread. Open woodland is the nightjar's preferred environment and it hunts at night for large insects like moths and beetles. The nightjar has large eyes and a wide beak with bristles around it to help it catch insects in mid-flight. It also has a deep, sticky throat that acts as a trap for insects. The European Nightjar is a mottled mixture of brown, red and black like the colour of dead leaves; an excellent camouflage. As soon as evening falls it starts hunting in the air or on the ground. It also begins to sing a monotonous tune from which the bird gets its name. Nightjars are solitary birds except during the mating season when they pair up and share the rearing of the young.

Another unique creature of the night is the bat. For centuries they have

ANYTHING GOES

Most frogs and toads have sex in the dark and are often so eager to copulate that the male will grab anything that passes by. They have been observed keeping a firm grip on strange objects and even small animals in the hope that they might turn out to be females. Croak!

been portrayed as evil creatures that swoop down on innocent victims and drink their blood. Indeed, there is one group, the vampire bats, which bite and then lap up the blood of animals. It was around this variety that the legend of the vampire grew from the superstition of country folk in Transylvania to multi-million dollar horror movies and best-selling horror fiction. One of the best researched species of real vampire bats lives in an area of South America. Blood is its only source of liquid and much of this will be gained from latching on to basking sea mammals such as seals. Contrary to popular belief, vampire bats are very small and less than half the size of tropical fruit bats.

Despite the fear, superstition and hype surrounding the vampire bats, there are many other interesting species of bat worthy of study. As animals, bats are unusual, in that the oldest bat fossils show the same structure and adaptations to flight as modern bats, proving them to be a very old species. Bats are instantly recognisable by their small furry bodies and large wings made up of membrane. They are the only mammals with the ability to fly although some others such as gliding possums are able to glide from tree to tree. Some bats, such as the fruit bats, are also migratory like birds. They are nocturnal, sleeping during the day upside down in roosts and then emerging at night to feed. The Greater Horseshoe Bat, *Rhinolophus ferrum-equinum*, roosts in caves throughout the year, hanging by its claws with its wings folded around its body. Bats usually sleep *en masse* as divided they may freeze but united they stay warm. Some species have very good eyesight in dim light, putting to rest the old adage 'blind as a bat'. Others see by sound, using echolocation in a similar way to dolphins. These are the small, insect-eating bats, *Microchiroptera*, that find their way around in the dark by emitting high frequency sounds that bounce of targets. In this way they can discern what objects are ahead, how far away they are and whether or not the are moving. To make these sounds and others that are able to be detected by the human ear, most bats have what is called a nose-leaf or complex folds of skin through which they produce sound. The nose leaf works in a similar fashion to a transmitting antenna, sending the out-going sound.

Bats mate in autumn before hibernation. When searching for a mate, the male produces a variety of acoustic signals to find a female. Fruit bats, or flying foxes as they are otherwise known, have an amazing repertoire of courtship calls. Males whine as they approach females and trill during copulation. The screeching commonly associated with bats is usually heard when the male is trying to bring his harem of females to order around him. Little Brown Bats also have a mating call. The male makes a 'weep weep' sound that rises in frequency and is used during sex to calm the female who often struggles with him. Sexual dimorphism is obvious and the male has a long, hanging penis with some species having a penile bone. The female's sex organ, on the other hand, is hidden from view. Sex is a topsy-turvy affair. While the female finds something to grip the male takes hold of her, hanging upside down with his stomach against her lower spine. For any other animal this sexual position would be impossible but the male bat has a penis specially designed for sex at this angle.

The reproductive cycle of a bat is unlike any other. After mating, fertilisation is delayed until the following spring and occurs upon the awakening of the female, at which time she produces her ova. During hibernation the sperm remain frozen in time as it were, they are nourished by a substance secreted from the vaginal walls. Gestation lasts roughly two months and the baby bats are born naked and blind but develop rapidly. Almost all the females roosting together give birth at the same time. This striking fact is not all that surprising when you consider that most bats wake each other from hibernation and thus ovulate at the same time. The mother then proceeds to educate the young bat in flying and hunting before they eventually fly away for an independent life.

A number of other primitive mammals are active at night and sleep during the day. Many are marsupials or mammals which have no placenta but retain the embryo until after hatching. However, the foetus is born at such an early stage of development that further incubation must take place in a pouch before the young are ready to face the outside world. For example the offspring of the opossum is so small that a dozen do not even fill a teaspoon. Sometimes the pouch may be little more than a couple of folds of skin with mammary teats to feed the helpless young. So weak is the foetus at this stage that it cannot even suck on the teat. Instead muscular action of the mammae squirts milk into its mouth every now and then. Modern marsupials are only found in Australasia, South America, with one species existing in North America. In fact they are the most common mammals in Australia and inhabit every part of the continent. Australian marsupials such as the koalas, kangaroos and the Tasmanian Devil, found only in Tasmania, are tourist attractions. Nocturnal varieties include the Australian possums, bandicoots, phalangers, cuscus and wombats.

The Australian possum looks similar to a squirrel as almost all varieties

---

FURRY FECUNDITY

The American Opossum has the shortest gestation period of all mammals. The only marsupial to exist in North America, its gestation period is between 8-13 days. The young weigh in at barely 2 grams when born. At one time it was a widely held belief that the female opossum gave birth through her nose. This myth probably arose from the fact that the female sometimes licks a path for her young across her fur and may pick one up in her mouth and place it in her pouch.

---

have a prehensile tail and forepaws and hind paws roughly the same size. The possum is distinguished by its short, woolly fur which is sometimes attractively patterned with spots or stripes. Roughly the same size as a cat, it leads a strictly arboreal life and enjoys a mixed diet of insects, leaves, eggs and birds. Considered pests by many householders as they often nest in roofs, they were also hunted by moonlight for their fur especially the Ring-Tailed Possums. Flying Possums were also much sought after for their beautiful and thick fur. They are found in eastern Australia and Tasmania and are set apart from the rest of the possums by a long bushy tail instead of the prehensile tail of the other species. Another beautiful species that lives in south-eastern and eastern Australia as well as New Guinea is the Sugar Glider. It is a charming sight with its grey back and white front and is able to glide from tree to tree due to the membrane which joins the limbs on either side of its body. The Brush-Tailed Possum, *Trichosurus vulpecula*, is found in Australia and New Guinea and often lives in back gardens on the outskirts of cities. Its trademark bushy tail is used to balance it as it moves around high up in the trees. It only breeds once a year, giving birth to a single offspring. Despite extensive hunting of most varieties of flying possums throughout the last decade they are still numerous owing to their fecundity. There are two mating seasons a year, in summer and winter, and after a 13 day gestation period the new born possum climbs into the mother's pouch where it stays for the next three months.

Just as possums often become the bane of a householder's existence, so too do bandicoots because of the damage they wreak on gardens as they search for food. Despite this, both animals are often kept as pets and become one of the family. Bandicoots sleep all day but become extremely active at night and their movements are very fast and lively; they jump and leap around in a similar fashion to the kangaroo as they have elongated hind legs. Wombats, which have some similarities with badgers, are thick-set, short-legged, lumbering animals with no tail that sometimes burrow for over 30 metres. They often live for a long time and some tame ones have been known to survive for 30 years. Like the Brush-Tailed Possum, wombats only breed once a year and the female rears the single offspring.

The Echidna is another lumbering mammal indigenous to the Australasian region. Also known as the Spiny Anteater, it is a monotreme or egg-laying mammal, like the Platypus which lives in creeks. Echidnas resemble hedgehogs in that they are covered in spines. When in danger or alarmed, it rolls itself up into a tiny spiky ball to protect its soft underbelly. The Echidna is nocturnal and also lives in hollow logs or cracks in rocks. In emergencies it burrows into the ground, performing something of a disappearing act. Burrowing is not done headfirst but rather they sink down as they dig into the earth with all four feet. It has a sensitive and elongated nose for probing ants and termites, which form the bulk of its diet, and a long sticky tongue. Echidnas lay eggs, although these eggs are not a rich source of food in the same way that birds' eggs are. They contain very little food but instead the growing embryo is nourished through the thin shell by substances secreted from the mother's womb. Despite their clearly mammalian characteristics, such as suckling their young and having body hair, they also have a number of features in common with birds. Firstly, only the left ovary operates and secondly they incubate their eggs in a similar fashion to birds. On the other hand their method of reproduction and their skeleton are reptilian in character. One unusual characteristic of the Echidna, found also in the Platypus, is a poisonous spur on the heel of the hind feet in every male. This makes the Platypus and Echnida the only existing poisonous mammals, apart from a few shrews. There is enough poison in their spurs to kill rabbits and small rodents as well as giving violent pain and symptoms of poisoning in humans. It is not known why the Echidna has developed this potentially deadly spur shaped like a dagger. The spur is actually hollow and leads to a gland on the thigh containing the venom. However, Echidnas and Platypuses rarely use the spur in defence. Some scientists think that it may be used during the breeding season as males only release the poison at mating time. It is thought that perhaps the male drugs his mate to get her 'in the mood' so to speak by ramming the spur into the female during courtship to stimulate her sexually. This could well be the case as the female Echidna has no instrument of sexual pleasure, that is she has no clitoris and so the injection may be a type of sex aid for her. On the other hand, no male has ever been observed giving the female a dose of his love potion. The exact function of the spur remains a monotreme mystery!

Dirty dancing

Some animals attract a mate with colours that beg to be noticed or by singing irresistible tunes that melt the heart of nearby females. Others make an effort to impress a female by dancing in a performance for her eyes only, although frequently this becomes a *pas de deux* before copulation takes place. Dancing together is just as pleasurable for animals as it is for humans but it also serves a number of important functions. Firstly, in many aggressive species the dancing of the male persuades the female to drop her hostile act and prepare herself for mating. By bringing the female into a state of psychological readiness for reproduction it synchronises the sex rhythm so that the female will be at the height of sexual receptivity when the male is ready to ejaculate. As George Bernard Shaw is reputed to have said: 'Dancing is the vertical expression of a horizontal desire'.

Courtship dances are also a foolproof way of establishing whether the individuals are from the same species as well as determining their gender. Only a member of the same species knows the steps to the dance while males and females have very different ways of responding to the lightfooted attentions of the male. These courtship dances have developed through an evolutionary process so that the various movements have become modified into stereotyped displays. From these movements other members of the species realise that it is breeding time. The dance steps may have originally developed from a chance movement by one animal that gave it an advantage over others when seeking a partner. Natural selection then came into play and gradually transformed this behavioural characteristic into a more reliable and conspicuous form of communication. In birds, for example, the head, tail and wing movements so common in courtship displays are reminiscent of postures adopted just before flight;

in some species the take-off and landing movements have become ritual-ised into elaborate courtship signals.

The dancing of birds is usually not nearly as graceful as their seemingly effortless aerial acrobatics. Most love dances consist of jerky and abrupt movements often accompanied by harsh shrieks and cries which are in-tended to capture the female's full attention. Those birds with the best dancing ability are usually the flightless species or those that are unable to fly well for long periods. Many varieties of waterbirds are also good dancers. Flightless birds, who on the whole boast the most spectacular plumage of all, often draw attention to their brilliant feathers by dancing. When the male bird of paradise dances, his magnificent plumage shim-mers and shakes with every step, thus showing it off to its best advantage. Peacocks, pheasants, lyrebirds and bowerbirds are also known to perform

The dance ritual of Crowned Cranes sexually excites both male and female.

little jigs which allow them to flaunt their feathers. In the case of the bowerbird, described earlier in this book, the male constructs an elaborate love nest and performs out the front with the intention of luring a female to the site.

The Crane family of birds is a particularly talented group of dancers. The spectacular Crowned Crane, *Balaericqa pavonina*, is found in the African tropics although at one time it lived as far north as the Balearic Islands in the Mediterranean, hence its name. It is a striking bird with a black velvet cap from which spring tufts of bristly feathers. During the breeding season the male and female perform a highly ritualised dance which reduces mutual hostility and brings them to a point of sexual stimulation. The Crowned Crane's close relative the Sarus Crane, *Grus antigone*, is also an accomplished dancer. So it should be as dancing forms an integral part of its life outside of the breeding season. During courtship both sexes take part in the dance. They strut about with outstretched wings, perform balletic leaps into the air and bow to each other. The two also add a juggling act to the courtship dance by throwing sticks into the air and catching them with their beaks as they fall. One particular species found only in Australia, *Grus rubicundus*, even became the subject of a film about its dancing and nesting behaviour. Known as 'Dancing Brolgas', these large cranes are found mainly in the tropical region extending from Northern Queensland to the Kimberley Ranges in Western Australia. Their sex life is closely tied to regional weather as the Dancing Brolgas reproductive schedule is linked to the monsoon season when food is abundant. At the onset of this wet period, male and female come together and perform their well-known courtship dance. The couple then wander off and nest apart from the rest of the group.

Many varieties of waterbirds also have dance acts and are as nimble on their feet on land as they are when propelling themselves through the water. The Crested Grebes, *Podiceps cristatus*, are one such species that are not only light on their feet but are also talented choreographers. Both sexes join in a complicated courtship dance resembling a water ballet with a definite prelude and climax. Firstly, the two dive in the water and rise facing each other with wings partially outstretched. As they usually some up with some distance between them, they rush straight towards each other until they meet. Then the two rise neck to neck and breast to breast in a sensual and languid dance movement most modern choreographers in the human world would give their eye teeth to write and have performed so gracefully. Often when the Grebes face each other they have beaks filled with weed. This phase of the dance has sometimes been described as the 'penguin dance', no doubt because of their upright stance and the sleek lines of their body.

It may seem that the birds have the best of many worlds. Not only can they be breathtakingly beautiful but some are frequently exquisite sing-

Crested Grebes face each other with laden beaks during their courtship dance.

ers, fliers and dancers too. However, birds and other creatures are judged very much within the parameters of what humans define as beautiful. During the 19th century it was common among naturalists and the general public to attribute human characteristics to animals. Thus storks became a symbol of fidelity, doves were admired for their gentle and loving natures and reptiles such as snakes and crocodiles were considered the epitome of all that is evil and ugly in the world. Thankfully it is no longer accepted scientific practice to place these sorts of value judgments on animals although the general public can still not quite resist.

Spiders are a case in point. To some human beings these eight-legged creatures are pure anathema and many people are mild to extreme sufferers of arachniphobia, an obsessive fear of spiders. However, many species of spiders build webs that are of infinite beauty. Their silken threads are frequently stretched between trees and create intricate patterns that shine when caught in the sunlight. Most spiders are accomplished dancers and this, in the case of males, is usually for their own safety. Firstly, male spiders are usually considerably smaller than the females they are wooing and so they must be most gentle and cautious suitors. As a consequence rape is practically unheard of in the arachnid world. Secondly, the copulation of spiders is an extremely complex process which requires certain essential initiatives on the part of the male. But before he can even think of beginning to win the hand of the female the male first has to attract her attention. It must be remembered at this point that the male spider has no penis but instead uses his maxillary palps at the front of his body to transfer sperm to the female. Thus, the urge to have sex is only aroused in the male spider once the maxillary palps have been filled. After this brief prelude the show begins.

Male Wolf Spiders wistfully wave their sperm-filled palps at the female and at the same time perform a number of intricate dance steps. Male Jumping Spiders too, can often give extremely funny performances. As the name suggests they are very agile creatures and their lithe bodies and quick movements are those of born dancers. When the time comes to approach the female in her web, these small and normally stealthy spiders spring to life. The male, with an enormous burst of energy, raises himself high in the air and then with his first pair of legs waves at the female from his new vantage point. He then begins to play the clown and brings a smile to the face of the deadly female by running in zigzags back and forth in front of her. Finally he stops when face to face with her. If she remains still and peaceful the male seizes his golden opportunity and leaps on top of her, inserting his sperm-filled palp into her genital cavity. Some spiders even hold hands before they mate like human lovers on a walk along a moonlit beach or strolling through the park. However, for spiders this endearing gesture is often a matter of life and death. The male grabs the female's forelegs in defence as these claws contain poison which she might readily drive into him if she has not been coaxed out of her predatory mood by his dancing performance.

Scorpions are another deadly variety that engage in courtship dancing. They are among the largest and most feared arachnids and they are also among the most primitive, terrestrial arthropods living today. The severity of their sting depends upon the species. Tropical varieties are the most deadly to humans as their nerve poison paralyses the heart and chest muscles. This poison is located in the tip of their tail which curves over when they are ready to inject their prey with a lethal dose. The tail is placed in the same position during the scorpion's love dance. This complicated rhythm begins with the male and female facing each other with pincers outstretched and often touching; this is cheek-to-cheek dancing, scorpion style. Next, the male grabs the female's palps with his own and takes the lead in the dance, stepping from side to side in a slow waltz-like movement that can last for hours. Others species eventually intertwine their deadly tails until the male releases a spermatophore which is picked up by the female. Young scorpions, like humans, are later born alive and spend the first part of their lives on their mother's back.

However, it is not only the arachnids that have been blessed with eight nimble limbs capable of beating out an infectious dance rhythm. Many insects have also been blessed with a natural sense of rhythm. The Dancing Flies, as their name suggests, are the undisputed dance champions of the insect world. There are some 3000 species of these flies that live near water and it is just above the surface of the water that the male flies dance, turning tiny pirouettes from time to time. These flies are also quite an avant garde group of dancers and often use props, which the male makes himself, to enhance their routine. These all-round entertainers then spin delicate veils which trail behind them as they dance and spin around. Good use too, is made of natural lighting as the sun shines

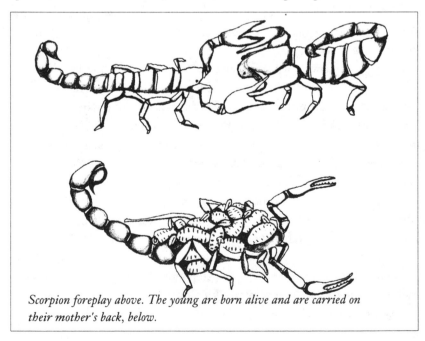

Scorpion foreplay above. The young are born alive and are carried on their mother's back, below.

on the threads of the veil so that it shines like silk and attracts the eye of the female. However, these males have rivals who are only too eager to cut in on a dance and steal the first male's girl from under his nose. No fights break out as a rule since most insects have more generous natures than humans.

The erotic dancing of butterflies is another fascinating sight. With their brightly patterned wings tracing arcs and circles in the air, their courtship dances become truly wonderful spectacles. However, by the time the sex play of butterflies catches the human eye, a significant amount of courting has already occurred through the scent released by the female. For this reason the male is in a very excited state as he searches for the willing female who has so tantalisingly indicated her availability. Every butterfly that flutters past is assumed to be a potential mate even if they are only vaguely the same colour and size as the females of his species. He flies up hopefully to almost every passer-by, only swerving away when they are from the wrong species. If the butterfly hovers and buzzes its wings, however, he knows that she is a female from his species and the two then begin a wild erotic dance in the air. The male flies in circles around the female, looping-the-loop and generally going all out to impress her. Sometimes the female settles down on a twig or flower to watch the male's show and spreads out her beautiful wings. The male then gradually winds down his performance, flying in increasingly narrow circles until he finally alights beside her and fans her with his outstretched wings. He then caresses her with his antennae on the G-spot of butterflies, i.e. a spot on her head which is reputedly an erogenous zone for butterflies and then nature takes its course.

It is not hard to visualise the effortless dancing of lightweight insects and spiders. However, the imagination has to be stretched in order to think of the rather cumbersome crustaceans as being light on their feet. One particular coastal crab, the male Fiddler Crab, *Uca zamboangana*, not only dances like Fred Astaire but uses colour to create an even more arresting visual spectacle for the female. This crab has borrowed from many different dance styles to put together a non-stop show full of energy, sensuality and colour and these dances are easily distinguished from each other. Sometimes he dances *sur pointe* with his huge claw held high above. At other times he sways sensuously in a style reminiscent of the Latin American salsa or he may even draw inspiration from modern dances and begin a wild jitterbug. Generally, the males all perform at the same time of the day, making the beach a spectacle of colour and movement as thousands of crabs writhe to an inaudible beat. In the dance of one species the female joins in too, instead of just watching from the sidelines like a wallflower. She is quickly infected by the rhythm of love and is whirled around and passed from male to male.

Even the more primitive underwater creatures like the squid perform a water ballet of sorts to impress the female. Some of their dances so entranced the ancient Greeks that they featured prominently in the literature and art of the time. When the male and female join together and embrace they remind us of old-time ballroom dancing as they rock back and forth cheek-to-cheek, so to speak. At the same time their delicate nervous systems produce dazzling changes of colour in the male, sweeping the female off her feet. Seahorses are another marine species that often remind humans of the romantic partner dancing of yesteryear. When the male and female mate their graceful movements are one of the most tender spectacles in the animal world; they are in fact the Fred and Ginger of the underwater kingdom.

Erotic smells

For most humans the notion that animal smells can be erotic must seem like a contradiction in terms. Anyone who has been backstage at a circus or works in a zoo, knows that the everyday scent of animals is not usually pleasant. Indeed, one of the most infamous animal smells is that of the Striped Skunk, *Mephitis mephitis*. The offensive odour emitted when the animal is frightened has inspired much literature and animation. In the famous cartoon strip *Pepe Le Pue*, about a lovesick French skunk, the whole thing is treated very lightheartedly but for those who have been caught in the olfactory cloud of a skunk, it is no laughing matter.

Unlike the skunk which releases its scent when in fear, most other animals in the wild use smells to either mark territory or attract a sex partner. The practice of secreting sexual scents when ready to mate is one of the most simple yet efficient ways of attracting a partner in the animal world. Musk, for example, is used by such animals as alligators, some deer, turtles, beetles and oxen as a natural aphrodisiac. Musk and other fragrances that occur naturally, such as castor and civet, are widely used as a perfume base in the human world. Before humans learnt to manufacture perfume many of these animals were massacred for their scents. Civets, which resemble cats, except they have longer jaws and non-retractable claws, are well known for the perfume of the same name which they release from their anal glands. Civets have often been kept in captivity for their scent which is collected twice a week with a small spatula. Whether men and women wear perfume to arouse sexual desire in a member of the opposite sex is unclear but in nature there is no uncertainty. The release of sex smells as a means of courting is an age old tactic used by both males and females to bring the sexes together and increase sexual excitement.

The Musk Duck, for example, is so called because it produces a very strong, heady, musky scent during the breeding season from an oil gland at the base of the tail. The male also has a rather ugly sac of skin under its bill which becomes filled with blood when he wishes to attract a mate. To show it off he throws back his head, lifts his tail up over his back, then kicks his legs sending a fountain of spray two metres high behind him. The Hoatzin, *Opisthocomus hoatzin*, also produces a very strong smell of musk which has earned it the nickname of the 'Stinking Bird'. Found in South America it was once thought to be the missing evolutionary link between reptiles and birds. Its strange combination of primitive and highly specialised features still confound scientists who to this day consider it to be something of an enigma.

MARATHON LOVERS

Stick insects are not the first animals to spring to mind when thinking about high libidos. Yet these skinny, awkward-looking insects can actually enjoy up to 79 days of continuous copulation!

Most of the sexual scents used by wild animals cannot be detected by the human nose. Some of the most primitive of these sex odours are pheromones, a word derived from the Greek meaning 'to transfer excitement'. Pheromones were originally used by unicellular animals to find food and thus smell was probably the first of the five senses to develop. As life became more complex and sex more sophisticated with the advent of sexual reproduction, chemicals were used to increase the chances of the two sexes finding each other and copulating. By releasing pheromones animals may attract a mate, inform a prospective partner of their sex and receptivity to their advances, and identify which species they belong to.

Pheromones act very much like hormones; they are both chemical messengers but pheromones carry information between individuals instead of within individuals.

Insects have provided scientists with much of their knowledge about pheromones as they tend to favour the use of odour more than any other group of animals. For these tiny creatures who usually lead fairly solitary lives before and after mating, scent is a very effective way of attracting a mate. Scent can penetrate almost anything to stimulate the male wherever he may be. Pheromones are also used by many mammals to identify which species they are from, as well as determining age or social status. A female arboreal snake, known as the African Boomslang, secretes a special scent to bring the male to her. The two then entwine and copulate. The Black-Tailed Deer *Odocoileus hemionus columbianus*, for example, secretes scent from the tarsal gland for individual recognition. Female dogs, including domestic varieties, release pheromones when 'on heat' or sexually receptive and their special sex smell attracts appropriate males who are ready for mating. This is why pet owners often witness the sniffing of female genitals by the male. In fact a major part of courtship in mammals involves the male discovering whether the female is sexually receptive and ready to copulate.

Like mammals, male insects must also search for the female. The female secretes the pheromones which must be able to travel over long distances and survive dilution in the air. In turn the male has remarkably sensitive receptor organs and only needs a tiny trace of scent on his antennae to race off in the direction of the female. An example of this is when drone honeybees are attracted to the queen by scent secreted from glands near her mouth. This scent is so powerful that it may attract a swarm of drones from several hundred metres away. The scent produced by moths is also particularly effective as most species are nocturnal animals and cannot rely on visual displays to attract the opposite sex as do butterflies. Only a virgin female moth is able to tempt a male with her scent and after she has mated the males will have nothing to do with her. When ready to mate the female flutters her wings so that air rushes past the scent glands on her abdomen and her scent is dispersed downwind. The male only needs one tiny whiff to become sexually excited as the scent has told him that there is a female from the same species who is ready, willing and waiting for him. The female's scent has become such an irresistible lure in some species of moth that she has given up flying and instead concentrates on producing the maximum number of eggs. In rare cases like the moth *Orygia splendida* of Southern Europe the male also has a sexual scent. He is still attracted to the flightless female by her scent, which she releases as she lies on top of her cocoon, but when he arrives he too wipes his own scent over it. As soon as the female smells his scent, she rips open the cocoon and they both lie down to mate. Sadly, after the eggs are laid the female dies alongside them. Many male moths also boast feather-like antennae which are covered with chemoreceptors which allow them to smell a female moth up to three kilometres away.

One of the most famous scent moths is the Indian Moon Moth, *Actias selene*. This species has the most acute sense of smell in the natural world being able to detect a female's scent five kilometres away. He does this with the aid of two specially modified antennae which are similar in appearance to feathers but with long hairs sticking out horizontally from the main stem. This increases the surface area for picking up chemical odours as the hairs are covered in tiny, ultra-sensitive scent-detectors. To follow the smell to its source the male simply follows the trail by calculating the scent's strength and moving off in that direction. He is able to ignore all other scents and can follow the trail around obstacles despite its dispersal in the air.

Of all the insects, the butterfly is the most admired and popular and is considered the great beauty of the insect class. Its metamorphosis from caterpillar to graceful flyer has long inspired human admiration. Like its more homely relative the moth, butterflies also release erotic smells as part of their sexual process although scent is mainly used as a stimulant during the physical act. The coloured or brightly patterned wings of the butterfly are more than enough to attract the opposite sexes to each other. Once together the female's antennae press against the patches of perfumed scales on the male's wings. This scent contains a pheromone that acts as the final stimulus for the female to receive the male and they couple.

Although the majority of insects release their scent into the air, there are some species that mark the ground with their odour. This is usually to give directions to other members of the species so they can find their

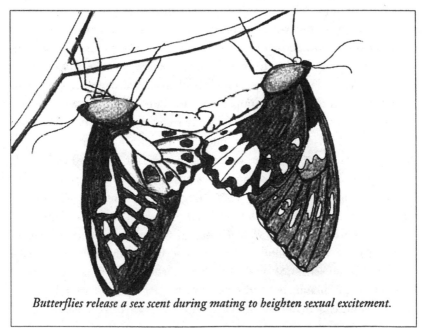

Butterflies release a sex scent during mating to heighten sexual excitement.

way to a food source or back to the nest. Secreting scent onto the ground or vegetation instead of into the air is a much more permanent way of leaving a mark as the smell will linger for many hours after the animal has left. This method is much favoured by mammals, most of whom possess scent glands. Some species have scent glands near their genital areas and use urine and faeces as scent carriers. A classic example of the use of urine in scent marking is the dog, which walks around lifting its leg at regular intervals on trees, posts, car tyres and other objects. Some monkeys spread their scent onto branches as they move along by urinating on their feet, while deer and some other animals actually have scent glands on their feet and thus leave a trail as they move about. Then there are those species which carefully prepare a site before marking, such as the African Oribi, *Ourebia ourebia*. This species chews tall stems of grass down to size before depositing its scent from a gland located in front of its eye. The most important use of scent in mammals is to mark territory or ownership by urination, defecation or by secretion from special glands. This keeps out members from the same sex but attracts those of the opposite sex. Some mammals even mark their sexual partners with scent as well. Scent is of particular importance to some mammals because they are social animals and by rubbing together constantly the members of a group tend to develop a common odour. The main function of this type of scent marking is, like the insects, primarily for sexual purposes. It usually only occurs when an animal is sexually motivated and is more frequently performed by the male, although female squirrels, like female dogs, leave scent trails when they are 'on heat' which the males follow.

Mammals are particularly well adapted to attracting each other by leaving scent on various landmarks or releasing it into the air as they have developed acute senses of smell. Elephants have the most acute sense of smell of all the mammals, and probably the largest nose as well. Their famous trunk is actually an elongated nose which is prehensile and ex-

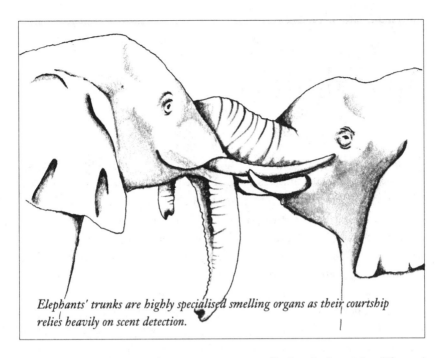

Elephants' trunks are highly specialised smelling organs as their courtship relies heavily on scent detection.

tremely sensitive. Apart from using it to smell, the elephant also lifts and carries objects with it; gives itself a shower and uses it to carry food and water up to its mouth. Ivory tusks are located at either side of the trunk, otherwise known as upper incisors, and these grow to a great length in the males. The rhinceros comes second to the elephant in the smelling stakes; hearing and smell being its most developed senses, although its eyesight is generally poor.

Aphrodisiacs

The giving of small gifts during courtship is a very old tradition observed by many animals and humans alike. Some presents, such as chocolates, are aphrodisiac in nature i.e. they are thought to arouse sexual desire and are given by suitors eager to put the lady of their choice into a sexually receptive mood. The Banded Coral Shrimp, for example, courts his lady with a gift of love in the form of a tasty morsel although it may well be rejected if she is already feeding.

The ritual of giving presents in the natural world is perhaps more correctly called courtship feeding. It generally involves the male presenting food or similar objects to the female in an effort to impress. These offerings are actually a ritualised form of everyday life as indeed are all other courtship displays which echo normal activities such as drinking, eating, preening and flying. Thus, in many animals a common form of display during the breeding season is the passing of food from one to the other. In some species this helps to maintain the bond between the pair while in others it actually saves the male as the female eats the gift instead of the giver. The amount of food the female receives is usually much smaller than her normal daily intake. In some cases, however, courtship feeding extends well past copulation and the gestation period. This usually occurs in animals where the male and female stay together for extended periods and develop a long-term bond. When the male feeds the female it lifts some of the burden of motherhood from her shoulders as she may have more than enough on her mind with the developing offspring. In this way courtship feeding has a certain ritual value in maintaining a bond between the male and the female but it also has a practical purpose.

The giving of aphrodisiacs is very common among spiders and with good reason. As any person who has studied first-aid knows, the female spider is usually larger than the male and also deadlier in that she has the more poisonous bite. For this reason, male spiders are some of the smoothest and most eager to please suitors in the animal world. The offering of the present may be a shy and hesitant gesture or there may be a sneaky and rather desperate tactic behind it, as is the case among certain tropical spiders. These males court the females with a heady mixture of bravado and foolishness. The more fearless male spiders wait patiently for an insect to fly into the female's web. They then dash in, wrap the insect up and hold it out to the female in such a way that it serves half as an ahprodisiac and half as a protective shield. The less courageous resort to sneakier tactics and wait until the female has snared her prey. Just as she is devouring her meal, the male rushes in and quickly transfers his sperm before beating a hasty retreat. This has to be the riskiest sex of all.

NEW, IMPROVED ORAL SEX

The mouthbrooder fish is so called because fertilisation actually takes place in the female's mouth. First she releases her ova into the water, then she turns around and swallows them. When the male swims by she mistakes the distinctive spots on his anal fin for more of her eggs. She opens her mouth to swallow them and catches his sperm instead. In this way fertilisation occurs.

Conversely, there are some species to whom the aphrodisiac is more than just a trick but rather a gift of love. The Hunting Spider, *Pisaura listeri*, is a more genuine suitor than the tropical variety. The male catches a fly and then wraps it up into an attractive bundle using silk from his spinneret. This he gives to the female with his heart brimming over with love. It may take some time for the female to accept the present as she is quite rightly suspicious of his motives. While he waits for her to accept his offering the male spider becomes increasingly nervous and his whole body quivers. He then stretches out his arms as though pleading with her to take the gift and return his love. Often his hopes are dashed. The heartless female ignores the gift and the male creeps away with his pride and heart in millions of tiny pieces. The more aggressive female believing the whole business to be nothing but a sham, threatens the male and curtly chases him off the web. Others draw back in fright as though they are protecting their virtue and saving themselves for Mr Right. However, occasionally the gift-wrapped fly will be accepted graciously by the female although the male must still be on his guard. After all it is a woman's prerogative to change her mind and she may still suddenly turn round and gobble him up. Thus, the male moves slowly towards her, feeding her as he goes along, and then quickly sticks his palps laced with sperm into her vagina. Wise spiders do not attempt to push their luck for some after-sex caresses but turn on their multiple legs and run for safety.

Insects too go courting with gifts to please the female. However, unlike the spiders these presents do not signal a truce offering but simply satisfy the female's belly during sex. The male Dancing Fly, for example, prepares a complete wedding feast to be consumed during the act of sex. They catch small dayflies or gnats and wrap them up in their own homespun silk. Sometimes he dispenses with the laborious task of wrapping the gift and carries the insect between his legs to the female like a sacrificial offering. The tasty morsel is then consumed by the female or perhaps the pair, as they are having sex. Another species, the Emphid Fly, *Hilara sartor*, has the same spinning talents and makes silk balloons to present to the female. However, unlike the delicious gift of the male Dancing Fly, the emphid's silk balloon is empty. One male Emphid Fly may be joined by many other males all carrying silk balloons which they display as a group

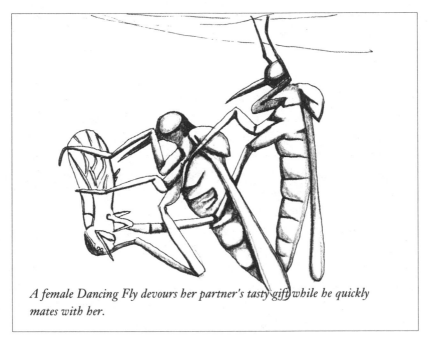

A female Dancing Fly devours her partner's tasty gift while he quickly mates with her.

when females come to visit. The females then make their selection by judging the best balloons and the happy couples disappear towards the proverbial sunset.

Some birds have also taken up the practice of offering aphrodisiacs to a female they are courting. Unlike the insects and spiders who, gift in hand and swooning with love will then turn around after a rejection and try the same thing with another female, birds usually have more genuine motives. The first gift is by no means the last and birds and will often continue to give gifts over a period of time. The Black-Headed Gull, *Larus ridibundus*, is a perfect example of courtship feeding. Once the male and female have found each other, the female begins begging for food like a baby chick and the male regurgitates it for her. This ritual foreshadows the feeding of chicks later on, who plead for food in a similar manner to the female during courtship. They will be fed by the male or female in the same way that the male fed the adult female. Bird behaviour is strangely similar to the baby talk and gestures of human lovers when they are courting. Terns, moreover, illustrate the long term practice of feeding the female long after courtship has achieved its purpose. In some species the male tern carries a small fish in his bill and shows it off to potential partners. Later when he has paired up with one of them the female relies more and more on food brought to her by her mate as she is busy laying eggs. The quantity of food that he brings is critical at this stage as the more she eats the larger her eggs and consequently the bigger the offspring. Larger chicks have a better chance of survival and so the female must choose a male who will be a good provider. Thus, the initial aphrodisiac offered by the male at the beginning of the courtship ritual is very significant. In some species of tern courtship feeding has reached a very advanced stage. These birds go through the motions of feeding but no food is actually passed between them. Instead courtship ritual consists of sudden and jerky movements of the bill. Who says birds have no imagination!

Most aphrodisiacs used by birds have a higher purpose than simply coaxing the female into a sexually receptive mood. The gift serves to develop a long-term bond between the male and female which can only be advantageous to the survival of their offspring. Two parents are always better than one. The male feeds the female who needs the energy to lay her eggs. Often he also helps incubate the eggs, feed the chicks and protect the nest from danger. This is particularly common in monogamous varieties as the male is investing just as much time and energy as the female in producing the young. For example, in the African Dabchicks the male feeds the female which helps to build a bond between them even if it only lasts for the breeding season. By receiving plenty of food the female can also produce more eggs. One rather curious aspect of their courtship is that the male and female eat their own feathers. Why they do this has never be explained.

Timing is everything

Apart from man and a few other species who can enjoy sex all year round, the rest of the animal world must pick a time to reproduce that will ensure the survival of their offspring. Most have seasonal cycles during which they are sexually active; spring is a particularly popular time for the birth of new creatures as the weather is warm and plants produce new foliage which provides food for both parents and offspring. Most animals have an internal clock that triggers the first stirrings of sexual activity. It happens annually, just as horses for instance grow a winter coat as the days grow shorter and the first signs of cold weather appear. This internal clock tells animals when the optimum time for reproduction is approaching and is usually closely related to the climate regularly experienced in the normal habitat. For example the Great Tits of the British Isles lay their eggs in April. If there is a warm spring the eggs may appear a little earlier but if the weather is slightly cooler than usual, egg laying may be delayed for up to four weeks. Longer days and rising temperatures arouse sexual activity in the birds. At the same time warmer weather also means that food is likely to be more abundant for the strenuous business of laying eggs and the feeding of young chicks when they hatch. For other species variations in rainfall may signal an open season for sex.

There are some animals that are so reliant on the perfect set of environmental conditions that they will actually switch to a completely different way of having sex if their habitat deteriorates. The *Hydra* from the Phylum *Coelenterata*, for example, reproduces asexually at a terrific rate when there is ample food but at the first signs of change it will conserve its energy and reproduce more slowly using a primitive sexual method.

That the moon wields a strange power over some members of the Animal Kingdom is well-known. Many dogs will throw back their heads and howl at a full moon and even humans can be affected by lunar peaks. Throughout human history, lovers have found balmy moonlit nights to be romantic and conducive to love. The moon's control over the rise and fall of the tides also indirectly affects the lives of all water creatures who must arrange their eating, sleeping and fornicating timetables according to the tide.

The sex life of the famous Palolo Worm, *Eunice viridis*, relies heavily on the phases of the moon. For four days every year in October and November the South Pacific seas around Samoa and Fiji fill with these worms which come up to the surface of the water to mate. Their spawning crisis is so accurate that South Pacific Islanders, who consider the worms to be a great delicacy, go out on their boats and scoop up huge quantities of them. The Palolo Worms first appear at dawn on the day preceding the last quarter of the October moon and continue spawning throughout the next day until the water is alive with worms and discoloured with their sperm and ova. Then in November they repeat the procedure before disappearing until the following year. The spawning times of these worms are so predictable that Fijians have named two periods in their calendar *Mbalolo lailai* (palolo little) and *Mbalolo levu* (palolo large).

Some strange biological clock regulated by a combination of tidal rhythms and changes in daylight hours controls the spawning of the Palolo Worms. During the rest of the year they live at the bottom the sea hidden in coral. As spawning time grows nearer the rear end of the worm changes; internal organs break down and two rows of paddles appear while the worm prepares itself for sex. When ready, the reproductive end snaps off and heads for the surface to join countless others like it. Then, just before releasing the ova and sperm into the water, their bodies disintegrate. By concentrating their sexual activities to a specific time and place, the worms increase the odds of successful fertilisation and reduce sperm and ova wastage.

Choosing the right time for sex seems to be something of a family trait among the annelid worms. Some relatives of the Palolo Worm also tie in their sexual activities with the phases of the moon. *Leodice fucata* is found along the coast of West India and will spawn only during the third quarter of the June-July moon. Another variety to be controlled by cosmic events is a worm found around the coastal waters of eastern Asia and in the Caribbean seas south of Florida. They choose the periods immediately after the full moons in March and April to spawn furiously, but are quiet for the rest of the year.

Some species of fish find moonlight quite intoxicating. The Grunion, *Leuresthes tenuis*, is an unremarkable looking fish but has the most remarkable love life. Their breeding season is restricted to three or four nights after a full or new moon and again for only a few hours after high tide. This timetable of sexual activity extends from late February to early September. When ready to spawn these fish swim into shallow water and allow themselves to be swept ashore, beaching themselves so they can fornicate. Once on the beach the females partly bury themselves in the sand where they lay the eggs. The males then fertilise them and the adults let the next wave carry them back to sea. For about two weeks the eggs lie hidden in the sand until the next high tide when they too are taken out to sea.

THE ONLY WAY TO GO

The Swamp Antechinus , a mouse-like marsupial, is the only mammal that dies after mating so its breeding season is very brief and intense. The males give themselves up to continuous copulation until they literally drop dead. Most die of starvation because they have no time to feed although some are eaten by predators as they search for their next mate.

Two species of Cricket Frogs found in North America only mate on one night of the year. They come out of hibernation as the weather becomes warmer and on the night of nights the evening air is filled with the mating calls of males.

Porcupines also regulate sex to a definite time and place; in their case the female porcupine is only 'on heat' for four hours of the year. Presumably sex between porcupines is already a somewhat prickly affair but to add insult to injury the males must deal with constant, frigid rebuffs from the girls for 364 days of the year. Yet for the female porcupine her all too brief sexual awakening is frustrating for her too for as she actually begins experiencing sexual stirrings some months earlier. Some females have been observed toying with sticks or branches in an effort to satiate their sexual longings. As the time draws near, erratic behaviour increases and the female wanders around biting trees or climbing up and down trunks without any purpose. Occasionally she can be heard emitting a low moan or whine. To satiate her sexual longing she often rubs her vulva against any object in her path or drags her bottom along the ground. Sometimes she straddles objects like sticks and branches, holding one end in her paw while dragging the other end along the ground with its tip pressing against her vulva. Nearby males notice her behaviour and if she drops the branch they promptly pick it up, sniff it and then imitate her 'riding' actions. Sometimes they even hop around on three paws while the fourth holds their penis in order to try and relieve the lust which is welling up. These months of sexual tension for the male and female accomplish a purpose, however. When the night of love finally arrives the female has reached such a state of anticipation and excitement that her eggs are ready for fertilisation. The frigid lady's icy manner then melts and she is anybody's for the next four hours. Lady porcupines become crazy nymphomaniacs, offering their bodies to any male that passes by. Indeed, the sexual activity in these four hours is phenomenal and the forest floor comes alive with the sounds of writhing and moaning porcupines. The question that begs to be asked, however, is how the male manages to mate with the female without being impaled on her spines. The answer is that the ever considerate female flattens her spines and even raises her tail up over her back to provide a cushion for the soft underbelly of her mate. Porcupines remain locked together in sexual bliss for about five minutes before each moves on to a new partner.

Some animals have refined their sexual habits so that they do not suffer the same sort of time restrictions on their copulatory activities as the porcupines. Instead, breeding occurs in much the same way as other animals but they have the ability to delay the implantation and development of the egg in the uterus or even its fertilisation. Top Minnow fish found in South America and Africa, for instance, mate during the rainy season and bury their eggs in the mud. When these areas dry up, all the adults die but the eggs survive because they are encased in a tough coating. They remain dormant until the following rainy season when they hatch and begin the cycle all over again. In Australia, some animals, like the kangaroo can actually delay growth of the embryo as a safety measure when environmental conditions such as drought make reproduction unfavourable. Most animals, however, have incorporated these delay tactics into their normal breeding cycle. In the northern hemisphere, for instance, where bats hibernate in winter, delayed fertilisation is the accepted norm.

Delayed implantation is somewhat different. When the female's egg is initially fertilised by the sperm, a clump of cells known as the *corpora lutea* is formed. This formation is responsible for releasing the hormones which control the development of the embryo. When delayed implantation occurs the *corpora lutea* remains in an immature state and only continues to develop after a suitable length of time. As it grows larger the hormones responsible for triggering the preparation of the uterus wall for the implantation of the embryo are released. The pregnancy then continues as normal. Seals tend to favour delayed implantation instead of fertilisation as the adult seals have not yet adapted sufficiently to their marine life to mate in the water. They are tied to land for the breeding season and so combine their mating and birthing into one terrestrial outing instead of two. At the onset of the breeding season the pregnant females haul themselves onto rocks to give birth to their offspring. They then have sex with the males almost straight afterwards. After being fertilised on land the seals return to the sea but as soon as their fertilised egg becomes embedded in the womb all development stops for several months. After some time the egg starts to grow again, reaching full development by the time the next breeding season comes around.

For land animals that must survive harsh winters with scarce food, delayed implantation is something of a godsend. The Roe Deer, for example, mate in the northern hemisphere's autumn but the fawns are not born for five months. If born any earlier the young animals would not survive the cold so the fertilised egg remains dormant in the mother until the end of winter. Then it becomes firmly implanted in the uterus wall and development continues until parturition. This is why Roe Deer, unlike most other mammals, mate in the autumn for if they bred in spring the young deer would still be too weak to survive the oncoming winter. Many rodents, such as stoats, weasels and badgers also suspend the growth of their foetuses for several months. Like the Roe Deer, mating is in autumn but the fertilised egg does not become implanted until close to the end of winter. The reproductive cycle of the stoat is particularly interesting as it carries the process of delayed implantation to the extreme with embryos remaining dormant for up to seven and even ten months. These northern hemisphere rodents are born between March and May and their mothers mate immediately after giving birth. By June or July the original offspring are also sexually mature and ready to mate.

Both generations of females then delay development of the embryos until the following March. Despite carrying a fertilised egg for such a long period, actual gestation is only four weeks.

Sex machines

There are many animals in the natural world that tend to treat sex like an assembly line and produce a constant stream of offspring. Marine creatures in particular will spawn an incredible quantity of eggs in the hope that just a few of them will escape the predators and maintain the species. The cod, for example, is an extremely efficient producer of eggs and a single female has been known to shed as many as eight million at one time. Like many other fish, they produce copious quantities of eggs in the sure knowledge that many of them will be swept away by the currents or eaten by passing predators. External fertilisation, or the dispersal of ova and sperm in the same area, is just one example of how successfully fish have adapted themselves. The more primitive marine species such as mussels also have an incredible rate of reproduction. Female mussels are capable of producing up to 25 million eggs, yet only a handful of these will survive to sexual maturity. At all stages of their development mussels are the favourite diet of many different animals so their only chance of ensuring future generations is to produce large quantities of eggs.

Some land animals, in particular insects, can rival the underwater species in the extraordinary numbers of offspring they produce. Insects are fascinating although in general humans fail to appreciate them.

The fly is a perfect example. It is regarded with the utmost contempt by humans as it revels in dirt and disease which it often passes to humans. Indeed, flies have caused numerous plagues down through history by carrying disease causing bacteria. Another possible reason why humans regard flies as the scourge of the earth is that they are so many of them. In fact there are over 60,000 recorded species (including mosquitoes) and probably many more waiting to be discovered. Although insects are responsible for the spread of malaria, yellow fever and typhoid, there is much to admire about them from a scientific point of view. To begin with flies have the distinction of being the fastest insects alive in the air. Their speed is due to the incredible flight muscles in their wings which allow them to beat their wings at amazing speeds. The common housefly, for example, can beat its wings 200 times a second for one and a half hours before becoming tired. Its relative, the mosquito, tops the fly's efforts with ease; mosquitoes can beat their wings 600 times per second while some of the tiniest species manage over 1,000. Aside from speed, flies are also extremely agile and able to perform amazing aerodynamic feats. This combination of speed and agility allows the male fly to pursue sex to his heart's content as it will take hours of exercise to exhaust him.

Compared to many animals the male fly has been granted enormous sexual freedom by nature and is ready, willing and able to copulate at any time and in any place. The female fly too is always keen on sex although she must take a breather occasionally to lay her fertilised eggs. Most varieties do not waste much time, if any, on courtship and copulation is usually a 'wham, bam, thank-you ma'am' affair. However, the more advanced species do take time out to woo the female before copulation. Some males go courting bearing a little gift or aphrodisiac that allows them to prolong their sexual experience while the female is unwrapping the present. The courtship of the Fruit Fly is particularly fascinating. The male approaches the female and determines that she is from the same species by tasting her legs. He then circles her and vibrates his closest wing in order to arouse her sexually. After some time he uses his foot (in which his taste organs are located) to lick her vagina and this simple gesture proves to be the female's undoing. She then abandons herself to unbridled lust. In contrast, the male housefly has absolutely no consideration for the female's pleasure. He approaches a female, discerns whether she is from the same species and without further ado jumps on top of her, stroking her head to allay any doubts she may have about the sudden union. The pair may then copulate several times in succession, although the female must stop after each mating to lay her eggs. When she returns she extrudes her vagina and the male happily mounts her again. This alternation of egg laying and sex can last for some time before the two become sick of each other and move on to find other partners. In this way, the flies are able to produce vast numbers of off-spring. Not only is copulation incredibly brief but the laying and hatching of eggs is very fast. Most fertilised eggs quickly hatch out into maggots and are then transformed into sexually mature flies in no more than two weeks. If they all survived it would be possible for a single fertilised fly to have trillions of descendants within a five month breeding season but luckily pesticides, predators and unfavourable environmental conditions manage to keep the population under control.

The amazing ability of the female fly to breed so quickly and prolifically is surpassed by only a few other species in the insect world. Take the queen bee and ants for instance. They add new meaning to the term sex machine but not because of their fantastic sexual tallies. In fact they only have sex once in a lifetime, but this one sexual experience is enough to keep them producing offspring for between six and twelve years.

Everyone knows that bees make honey and can inflict a nasty sting. That they are social insects is also well-known and their rigid society has long been a source of admiration and fascination for naturalists. However, little more about the lives of bees is common knowledge which is a pity as they are some of the most advanced insects existing on this planet. Not all species are social insects by which we mean insects that function better as a whole than as individuals, but the two best known varieties can claim this title. They are the Honey Bee, *Apis mellifera*, and the Bumble Bee, *Bombus*. Bumble Bees nest in the ground, often forming their colonies in deserted mouse nests, while Honey Bees congregate in caves or hollow trees in the wild and in artificial colonies in captivity. These bees are incredibly specialised. The prime example of this is the complex and fascinating collecting of nectar with which bees make honey. Nectar is sucked up through an extendible tube in the mouth and then stored while the pollen sticks to the bee's hairy body as it delves into a flower. It is then scraped off by a second pair of legs and placed in pollen baskets on the hind legs. Equally impressive is the bee's sense of direction which allows it to fly to a pollen-laden flower and then return to its original starting point. More amazing still, it is able to tell its fellow workers the

---

UNDERWATER BREEDING FACTORIES

Considering their size, usually about one metre at maturity, it is most unusual that almost three quarters of the total body length of the Ocean Sunfish is made up of its head. They are also one of the most fertile of all fishes. One female can produce up to 300 million eggs and some larger individuals may exceed this number several times over.

---

exact location of the flower by performing a little dance. The angle of its body and the routine of the dance tell the direction and distance of the flower. As it dances it releases a pheromone, geraniol, which supplements the information given by the dance itself. So precise are the directions that a swarm of bees is able to fly directly to the flower. The bee is also endowed with keen eyesight and a superior sense of smell; so what it does not see, it smells.

A colony of Honey Bees may have a population of about 50,000 workers with one queen and a changing number of drones whose only role is to be on hand when a new queen has to be fertilised. The drones' chance to copulate comes around only once on the nuptial flight of the virgin queen bee, when she decides to found a new nest. She will then buzz off into the distance with about 200 eager drones hot on her tail. Although these drones are the pick of the bunch and have been bred specifically for the wedding night, the queen bee can easily outfly them until she is ready to bed down. At this point one lucky male swoops down and copulates with her in mid-flight. For these two it is love on the wing and they fly united although the whole affair only lasts for a couple of seconds. When they pull apart, the male's penis snaps off and plugs the queen's vagina to prevent the millions of sperm he has deposited in a pouch from being wasted. Having performed his sexual duty, he falls to the ground and bleeds to death. Although it could be said that he died happy, the other drones meet a quite horrible death by slow starvation when they return to the hive. It is from this single impregnation that the queen will produce, over the next five years, more than two million eggs. She alone makes the decision as to whether the eggs she lays will be fertilised or unfertilised. If she fertilises the eggs they develop into sterile female workers or queens, while unfertilised eggs develop into fertile drones. Workers also have the ability to create a new queen in case the old one dies or stops producing eggs. They secrete a substance with a high hormone level known as royal jelly on to fertilised eggs which would normally become sterile workers. These are transformed into fertile females and one of them, after an in-hive sting-to-death session, becomes the new queen. This royal jelly was once prized by humans who believed it contained the elixir of youth. Aging ladies bought it, often at great expense, in the hope that it would reverse the aging process and it is widely available today.

Unlike the honey producing bees, ants are not revered by humans but regarded as pests as they are extremely hard to get rid of once they invade a house where sugar or some other food source has been spilled. They can also inflict a painful sting on humans with the American Fire

Ants and Australian Bull Ants being the most notorious. There are over 6,000 known species of ants in the world, half of which are the social variety in that they form colonies and function more effectively as a group. Ants generally live in underground nests, although some species found in Latin America and Africa are nomadic and form a nest-like structure by swarming together. Others like the European Wood Ant, *Formica rufa*, build huge mounds out of twigs and pine needles over their underground nest which are often over a metre high. There are normally two castes within the ant society; one concerned with reproduction and the other with the collection of food and defence of the nest. These colonies may number anything from just ten ants to groups of several million over which the queen ant presides. Fertilisation of the queen ant takes place in much the same way as the bees. At certain times of the year the virgin queen flies from the nest followed by many hopeful suitors and mates in mid-air with one lucky male. This is the only time that she copulates as once she has been fertilised she can keep on reproducing for many years. After this aerial fertilisation and nourished by food materials stored in her body fat the queen ant lands and starts to dig out a small chamber in which she lays the first eggs. The first eggs develop into workers who build an underground palace for the queen and supply her with food. These workers form the first of two castes. They are always wingless, sterile females and are often very numerous. In some species they include forms with larger heads and mandibles known as soldier ants that defend the colony. The second caste are the sexual ants which develop from unfertilised eggs and these are always fully winged flying adults that are sexually mature.

Wasps too belong to the same group as bees and ants, the *Apocrita*. On the whole these insects are beneficial to farmers as wasps kill many insect pests while bees assist in the pollination of flowers. Many wasps are solitary animals, perhaps due to their predatory nature. However, there are some species of wasps that are social insects such as the European Hornet, *Vespa crabro*, the Paper Wasp, *Polistes* and the Common Wasp, *Vespula vulgaris*. Hornets build their nests above ground in trees or buildings but most wasps generally prefer to go underground. The Paper Wasp builds a small nest above ground. It is a very elaborate affair with several tiers enclosed in an outer envelope and it may be built on the ground or suspended from trees. These nests may hold anything up to 5,000 workers. Yet not all wasps' nests are so impressive. In *Polistes*, for example, the nest only consists of one tier and the workers are barely distinguishable from the queen. Perhaps more bizarre still are the solitary wasps, known as the Potter Wasps, which build a nest in which they live in solitary splendour. Found mostly in temperate regions, they build nests resembling miniature vases which are composed of tiny particles of clay glued together with the insect's saliva. A steady supply of caterpillars is provided to feed the larvae which emerge from the single egg. Amongst these larvae will be one adult who then breaks out of the walls of the cell.

With over a million known species of insects it is no wonder that some of the most bizarre and fascinating sexual practices can be found in the world of these tiny creatures. From cannibalism to rape and bondage, the sex lives of insects are as varied as the number of different insects species themselves. There are even rare cases of monogamy among insects despite the fact that lifelong fidelity is not a quality usually associated with the insect world. The royal couple in a termite nest, for example, lead a regular married life in which the male and female remain together for life. Yet there is a twist to this fairytale union. The monarchs rely on the enslavement of an entire society of termites each of which has a special role in maintaining order in their kingdom. This leaves the two bluebloods free to indulge in sex around the clock; the termite queen actually becomes a huge sex machine with a grossly enlarged abdomen and in some species she is capable of laying an egg every two seconds.

Termites are often referred to as White Ants, a misnomer as these insects are not members of the ant family and on close inspection resemble cockroaches. They are deplored by humans as they are extremely destructive, especially in the tropics where most species are found. Termites destabilise the foundations of houses by eating away at the wooden beams until they collapse. They can also destroy furniture in the same way; even books and papers are not safe from their ravenous appetites. The mounds that they build in the open to house the termite society are known as termitaries. These can be several metres high and are a nuisance for farmers since they actually have to be removed by exploding dynamite. For this reason termites are often viewed as a scourge to the extent that they have sometimes featured in science fiction horror films as the inheritors of the earth. Yet despite their evil image, the social organisation of the termites is on the same level as the much admired bees, probably even superior to them. Termites live in large colonies and are either found inhabiting a network of tunnels in soil or wood or in their own large and elaborate nests. The nests of the African Termites, *Macrotermes bellicosus* and their Australian cousins, are the skyscrapers of the insect world. Made of hard, watertight balls of earth and plant material cemented together with saliva and excreta, they can sometimes reach a height of up to six metres. Life in these mounds is very regimented but successful in terms of reproductive capabilities. Social insects such as termites, bees and ants clearly benefit from living together in a community, although they prosper as a whole at the expense of any individuality. Not only have they engineered a social way of living but the organisation of their society relies heavily on a complex communication system so that members of the society can react promptly to any problems that may arise.

Termite society is made up of four castes; each caste has a different function just like the division of labour found in other social insects like bees and ants. The first caste can be identified at the beginning of a new colony of termites; they are the fully winged termites that swarm out from established colonies and mate, each king and queen founding a new society. The aim of swarming is to spread the species as far as possible and it is a spectacular sight. Thousands of sexually mature termites form a cloud which drifts on the air for days and in the country can cast a shadow over a sunny field. The second caste, which are smaller and have non-functional wings, act as extra reproductive bodies. These termites develop in societies that have lost one of their founders and take over the sexual role in perpetuating the colony. Then there are the worker termites. They are small, flightless and sterile and are responsible for building and maintaining the nest as well as feeding the sexual termites and their young. Finally there are the soldiers, also wingless and sterile, who defend the colony. These soldier termites have a large head and a nose-like projection from the face from which they secrete a sticky substance that paralyses enemies.

Reproduction is a casual affair although once a pair have mated they remain together for life. Sexually mature males and females find each other during the swarming which occurs at certain times of the year when winged males and females fly away from a nest to mate. They do not, however, have sex in mid-flight but instead upon landing. As soon as they hit the ground the male and female shake off their wings and form pairs. They then set out on a walk to determine the best site for their dream home. Once they have found the perfect spot they begin to build and it is during this stage that they reach sexual maturity. Finally they move into their new dwelling and copulate. It is thought that the bond between the two is due to secretions from the tail end of the female which attract the male and keep him following her until they lie down in a blissful sexual union. Thus, the period between landing on the ground and moving in to their own home could be viewed as a type of 'engagement period', one of the few in the animal world. After copulation there is a honeymoon period where the male and female share equal responsibility. They both build the first tunnels for the new nest and they both care for the eggs and feed the larvae with a liquid secreted from their bodies. The larvae grow into worker and soldier termites, taking anything from three months to almost a year in some species, to develop. Once there are sufficient numbers of workers and soldiers, the king and queen stop working on the nest and devote themselves to a life of sexual pleasure, never again stooping to menial tasks. The worker termites gather around the couple and clean and feed them, licking up their excretions and carrying away eggs. Workers may also raise additional kings and queens from existing larvae and these sex maniacs are fed special hormones so they become sexually active. However, the workers must make sure that they do not raise too many additional kings and queens as the stability of the termite society is very much a numbers game. A whole termite nest may perish if there is not enough labour to support the monarchy or if the royal couple dies without any substitutes ready to take over the kingdom. Thus, a complex system of communication has evolved which influences the whole balance of the colony and pheromones play a key role in transmitting the information. For example, termite larvae are reared on pheromones. The royal couple release pheromones which retard the sexual development of the larvae so that during this period only workers are born. When there are enough workers they in turn secrete pheromones which encourage the development of soldiers and sexually mature, winged adults. The soldiers too secrete pheromones which stop the development of more soldiers and in this way a harmonious balance is achieved and the colony hums along at maximum efficiency.

The tiny Naked Mole-Rat lives in an ordered society similar in some ways to the honeybee. Also known as the Sand Puppy, *Heterocephalus glaber*, this rodent spends its whole life underground in a network of tunnels often covering an area up to 15 hectares. Their burrows are well insulated which explains their bizarre appearance as they are the only mammals without any kind of fur or hair. Instead their naked and wrinkled bodies resemble a mammal foetus. They live in colonies of between 50 and 100 members dominated by a single queen. She is the only female capable of breeding and her offspring form different strata of workers, each with specific tasks to ensure the smooth running of the colony. The smallest and youngest dig tunnels and bring back food to the central nest. Bigger Mole-Rats guard the tunnel system and repair collapsed sections and the largest have the enviable responsibility of mating with the queen and a few other fertile females who leave to form new colonies.

Prairie Dogs also build underground colonies thought to be the largest in the natural world. A typical tunnel system consists of a single wide shaft plunging down into the ground with a number of horizontal tunnels branching off it. A cone of soil at the top of the main shaft stops rainwater from coming in. Guards can also poke their heads above it to watch for approaching predators. Colonies usually consist of about a thousand members and division of labour is very rigid. Amongst the different levels of society the Prairie Dog is the breeding group or coterie. In order to make the society function effectively as a whole, Prairie Dogs have developed many different ways of communicating. For instance whenever individuals meet another colony member they engage in a long 'kiss'. It is a very human-like embrace that serves as a way of telling each other their station in the life of the colony.

However, one of the most prolific breeders in grass land countries is the rabbit. These mammals need not rely on the enslavement of thousands of workers to go forth and multiply since they have other ways of reproducing quickly. Indeed, their fecundity is notorious throughout the world giving rise to the well-known expression 'breeding like rabbits'. It has been calculated that one breeding couple can produce over 13 million

For Prairie Dogs kissing is a way of communicating social status.

descendants in three years if environmental conditions are favourable. Such large numbers often swell to plague proportions as frequently happens in countries like Australia where the rabbit is an introduced species. The devastation caused by rabbits can be seen in many parts of the country where formerly lush green fields are now dusty, arid plains littered with craters, the remains of rabbit burrows. Although rabbits feed mainly on grass, they also eat other vegetation and can ravage whole fields of crops, gnaw the bark off trees and even attack their roots. Although it has many enemies such as foxes, badgers, wild cats, wild boars, dogs and humans, the rabbit always has been able to withstand the onslaught; a tribute to their amazing breeding capabilities.

Unlike many other mammals, breeding in rabbits can take place at any time of the year although it is most common in spring and summer. Courtship is conducted with characteristic mammalian casualness, the male sprays the female with pheromone drenched urine, displays its little white, tufty tail and then mates with her. The female, or doe, generally has three to four litters a year with a gestation of one month. Litters consist of between four to ten young each time. Within four to six months the newborn rabbit is sexually mature and it too reproduces with young females being able to breed before they are fully grown. The doe usually mates again immediately after she has given birth as the physical act of sex causes her ova to be released and guarantees fertilisation. Some rabbits are able to produce a litter every month although over sixty per cent of these will not survive. When environmental conditions are unfavourable or there is a shortage of food, the embryo simply does not develop but instead is reabsorbed into the womb lining. Some rodents too use this as a natural form of population control.

Possibly the only other animal to rival the procreative power of the rabbit is the rat, another animal repulsive to humans. Much to people's horror, rats and mice have found it advantageous to live in close contact with humans as they tend to consume anything that humans eat and thus try to live close to their food source. They have an enormous appetite due to their constant desire to gnaw on something and grind down their teeth; the word rodent actually means 'a gnawer'. Not only do they eat and destroy large quantities of stored food by contamination with their droppings, they also cause structural damage to buildings. As well, they are carriers of many human diseases such as typhus, bubonic plague and Lassa fever. Indeed, one species, the Black Rat, was responsible for the worst plague ever to hit Europe. Introduced by crusaders returning from Asia, the rats quickly spread and in the fourteenth century were instrumental in causing the notorious Black Plague which decimated the population of Europe.

When environmental conditions are favourable rats and mice can breed all year round. Gestation varies between three and four weeks depending on the species with the female usually producing about six litters a year. A litter will average six offspring and the young are ready to breed when they are only four months old with litters per year varying from two to seven, and each yielding three to 14 young. Thus, the yearly offspring of a pair usually number six or over and may even come to 98, all capable of the same rate of reproduction when they mature. In this way rats and mice can assume plague proportions like rabbits. The Brown Rat, *Rattus norvegicus* is a particularly successful species and is thought to be the greatest biological competitor to the human race. The cousin of the dreaded Black Rat, the Brown Rat is the larger of the two and in recent times has colonised every continent except Antarctica by sneaking aboard ships. A burrowing animal, it is also a capable swimmer and is found in rubbish tips, sewers and around farms. It lives in family groups and will fiercely defend its territory against rats from other species. Sometimes it will even duel to the death although it usually just pushes the other rat away by kicking it.

BACK-BREAKING PREGNANCY

The sex life of the Surinam toad is the most bizarre of all the amphibians. The female uses her back as an incubator for her eggs. With a flat body, tiny eyes and no tongue or teeth it is a strange looking animal but highly specialised. The female's flat back actually has tiny depressions on it where each egg sits, protected by a thin layer of tissue. Here the young remain throughout their tadpole stage for as long as two to four months. They only emerge after changing into the immature toad form.

Other rodents like hamsters, gerbils and lemmings are also noted for their incredible breeding capabilities. In all there are about three thousand different species throughout the world and they can be found living successfully in almost every kind of habitat. Most have a strong instinct to build, either underground or by damming rivers like beavers, and often use their shelters as storage spaces for food during the winter months. Some such as mice, hamsters and gerbils are often kept as pets and white rats even became the preferred pet of the punk movement in the 1970s. However, one of the most interesting rodents is the lemming, a species subject to great cyclic changes every couple of years. Mating of lemmings usually takes place in spring when litters of between four to six are produced. Then, every three to four years they will suddenly produce litters of more than ten. This leads to a population explosion which in turn causes the total destruction of all vegetation in the area and results in the famous mass migrations. Normally shy nocturnal animals, lemmings suddenly venture out into daylight in search of food. Once they start out on a path they are not diverted and continue in a singleminded manner, pushing past any obstacles in their way. If they come to a river they will look for a crossing point but if none can be found they dive in and attempt to swim. Thus, many drown during migration while others become victims of predators such as foxes and wolves. Often entire migratory parties are destroyed. It is not known what drives the lemmings to embark on these trips. Perhaps survival of the fittest is their way of natural selection. Those that do stay behind continue breeding until the following cyclic population explosion forces them to embark on the next doomed migratory trip.

Another group of animals that undertakes aimless migration is the locusts. They belong to the same family as the grasshoppers and are renowned for periodic devastation of crops and natural vegetation in warmer regions. Travelling locusts in plague proportions can appear suddenly and without warning anywhere from Africa to Australia. They appear like a low, dark cloud on the horizon and attack and devour every living plant in the area in a massive feeding frenzy. A medium sized swarm of locusts may number a billion insects that consume up to 3,000 tonnes of vegetation in single day. As their brief but highly destructive visit draws to a close, mating takes place *en masse* and the fertilised eggs are deposited by the female in pods in the soil. Each pod contains up to 120 eggs and after hatching into embryonic, grub-like forms, they spend their time living underground. When they finally grow into mature locusts they live a peaceful life above ground until the next overcrowding suddenly sends them on their way again.

There even exists a bird that is insect-like in the size of its population, breeding and feeding habits. Known as the Locust Bird, the Red-Billed Quelea, *Quelea quelea*, often descends on crops in the same manner as locusts. A flock of tens of thousands, sometimes millions, of birds will swoop down on fields of corn, rice and wheat to feed. These feeding frenzies can often result in half or even all of the crop being destroyed within a couple of days and do as much damage as a plague of locusts. The damage such a flock can cause is sufficient to destabilise the economy of many small African countries that rely on a good harvest.

Another insect detested by humans is the cockroach of which there are over 3,500 species. Most live in the wild although the best known varieties are domestic species such as the dark brown *Blatta orientalis* with its reduced wings or the smaller *Blattella germanica*, a light brown species with dark stripes. Despite the human revulsion for cockroaches, they are one of the oldest and most resilient of all animal species and have been around for some 300 million years. There are a number of reasons why they are such survivors. Firstly, cockroaches will eat just about anything from garbage scraps to electrical wiring. Also, they tend to come out and eat at night, thereby avoiding the daylight hours when they can be spotted more easily. Another of their strengths, as many a despairing house-holder knows, is their seeming immunity to so many pesticides. But undoubtedly the main reason cockroaches survive is because they are continually active sexually and breed in great numbers.

Cockroaches have a highly developed libido and are always interested in having sex. When the female is ready she releases her sex scent in the form of pheromones as does the male when he feels like copulating. Unlike most other prolific breeders, however, cockroaches actually do engage in a courtship ritual and may often remain lovelocked for up to two hours. Indeed, there are no quickies on the sofa for this sexually active species. In some varieties courtship begins when the male and female face each other and rub antennae. This arouses the male who then presents his rear to the female and raises his wings. If she is in the mood she climbs on top of his back and eats a special substance the male has secreted. This gentle and erotic nibbling on his back gives the male cockroach multiple erections as he is blessed with several hook-shaped penises. He begins to back further under her until one of his male members connects with her tail. He then quickly turns around so that they are now tail-to-tail and hooks in the remaining penises. The loving couple can remain locked together in this loving position for many hours. Virile male cockroaches from other species impress their lady lovers with their physique practising push-ups in front of them until, overwhelmed by the size of their biceps, the females give in to sexual pleasure. Others dispense with preliminaries and busy themselves with the task at hand, copulation. After she has conceived, the female cockroach carries her fertilised eggs around with her in a packet, eventually leaving them on a floor or shelf to fend for themselves. More advanced species actually give birth to their young and although the female drops the egg container, she will later retrieve it and put it back inside her body where the young will hatch later.

Love on the wing

Both children and adults sometimes dream of being able to fly like a bird, soaring high above the earth without a care in the world. Humans who are fascinated with the aerodynamics of flight in the wild have often attempted a take off themselves. No-one has ever been successful. The most famous failure was that of the legendary Icarus, a young man who took off with wings fixed to his body with wax. The flight was going quite well until Icarus, who had been warned not to fly too close to the sun, got carried away. As he approached the fiery orb, the wax on his wings began to melt until he finally plunged to his death.

No doubt aerodynamics enthusiasts would be surprised and probably delighted to learn that some animals with the ability to fly are also able to have sex in mid-air. There is frequent talk of those united in the air and on the wing experiencing new heights of sexual ecstasy. However, while humans may yearn for sex in the sky, dragonflies derive routine enjoyment by flying united. They are among the oldest of the million or so known insects and when they first appeared about 300 million years ago they were enormous. Fossil evidence has shown that some dragonflies had wing spans of up to two feet, making them the largest insects that ever lived. However, they eventually died out with the dinosaurs and gave rise to smaller versions until the successful modern form evolved. Unlike its more cumbersome ancestors, today's dragonfly is one of the quickest and most agile insects . It also has 360° vision so that no prey can escape its line of sight. They are even able to dive underwater for their food as they can trap air between the hairs on their bodies and carry it down with them. However, this manoeuvre makes them prey to fish living close to the surface and fly-fishermen often use plastic imitations of dragonflies when angling.

Adult dragonflies are, as their name suggests, fierce winged creatures. Slender and stick-like in appearance, they prey on small animal life and have even been known to catch worms, tadpoles and little fish. In small species, dragonflies spend a year developing their adult bodies, during this stage they are known as nymphs. Larger species often take up to two or three years to develop. Once they reach adulthood, however, their days are numbered. Mature dragonflies only live for about four weeks, but this is all the time they need to mate and lay eggs, after which their usefulness is over and they die. But oh what a sex life they lead in this short time! Indeed, their mating habits are quite unlike those of any other insect. Before the male even approaches the female he must first transfer his sperm from his reproductive organ, located in the second last

101 WAYS TO HAVE SEX

There is an incredible variety of copulatory positions in the Animal Kingdom yet only a handful of animals actually have sex face-to-face like humans. They include whales, hamsters, beavers and the Two-toed Sloth. On the other hand, humans can enjoy almost every sex position seen in the wild!

body segment, to special organs on the abdomen. He then grabs the female by the head with his tail. The female must then bend forward until her reproductive organs in the tail touch the male's sperm. With each body bent into a rough semi-circle the aerial lovers form an irregular wheel shape. At this point fertilisation occurs but for some species it does not stop there. The male and female fly off in their tandem copulatory position to the nearest aquatic plant, partly submerged in water. The female then deposits her eggs into the plant, sometimes drilling holes in the stem into which she drops her precious load.

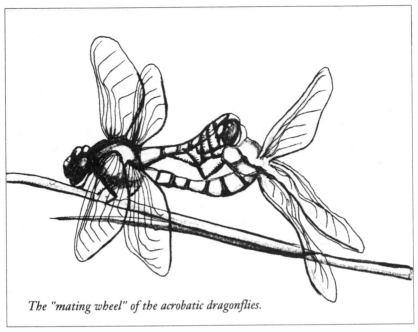

The "mating wheel" of the acrobatic dragonflies.

The mayfly is very similar to the dragonfly and the two are often mistaken for each other. The confusion arises because they are similar in appearance; adult mayflies are slender with three long tail filaments and huge forewings. However, the *Ephemeroptera* as they are scientifically known, are not a predatory species but rather they are vegetarians. Adults do not even stop to eat, for their sole aim in life is sex, sex, sex and then some. Their lusty behaviour is more than understandable: with only one day to live they might as well make the most of it. Hence their name *Ephemeroptera* or 'winged insects which live for a day'. Mayflies live the nymphal part of their life in the water and once they have matured, they rarely wander far from home - they don't really have the time anyway. As well as being stay-at-homes they are weak at flying. Flight for mayflies is characterised by a kind of vertical dance where they flutter up about half a metre with quick but feeble wing beats and then fall back to their starting points with wings motionless. Males usually congregate in a vibrating swarm which from a distance it looks as if it is just hovering above the water surface. However, within this cloud everyone is performing a vertical dance which plays an important part in mating. When a female approaches, several males break away from the pack and fly hot on her heels until they catch up with her. The first to reach the female copulates with her immediately and egg laying follows shortly afterwards. Usually the poor girl is so exhausted from her mid-air sexual work-out that she just drops the eggs on the surface of the water, often into the waiting mouths of fish. However, enough are generally produced to survive these hazards and the whole cycle begins again. Other insects, like the fly, bee and ant that are dealt with elsewhere also have sex in midflight.

Section 3

MATING STYLES

Group sex

At the beginning of this book it was established that sex is one of the great instincts that dominates all living things. It is the instinct in all creatures that ensures that male and female come together and multiply. Group life developed because it ruled out the search for a mate by ensuring that a potential partner was close at hand. At the onset of the breeding season it only takes one member of the group to become sexually aroused before this feeling spreads through the entire colony, signalling to male and female alike to pair off and copulate. This is social behaviour at its most primitive. Each member of the group renounces his or her individuality and instead the animals act as a whole. Even some relatively advanced creatures like birds congregate at special breeding grounds where preparations for mating take place. These large colonies are extremely effective in transferring sexual excitement as the gregarious birds indulge in mass courtship rituals before pairing off and coupling. Group life also offers the individual greater protection than if each member lived in isolation. In fact the only animals that lead a solo existence are usually predators who are more than able to take care of themselves. Most other animals such as schools of fish are more able to locate food sources as a group than by themselves. Finally, group living also gives individuals a greater guarantee of security and protection from predators.

However, to humans, who are the most individualistic species on earth, group life in nature seems to exist at the expense of any expressions of individuality. Some of the most primitive forms of society, for example, are the bee and termite colonies, where members are all part of a greater scheme to make the group function as a whole rather than the other way around. For these insects living, loving and working together in unison is much more beneficial than living alone or in a partnership. Yet, despite the unchallenged position of humans at the top of the animal kingdom, early human sexual practices such as group sex can still be observed in tribes relatively untainted by the spread of modern civilisation. Primitive tribes in Africa, for example, often hold religious festivals which develop into sexual orgies, a practice frowned on in western cultures. Indeed, it seems they are a lot less coy about the expression of sexuality than inhabitants of more modern countries although many of their erotic customs seem barbaric to us.

Most animals who indulge in sexual orgies as a group do so because this method has proved to be the most effective in perpetuating their kind. It only takes one couple in a group to begin courting and before too long the entire colony is engaged in the same activity. In short, each member of the group has paired up with a member of the opposite sex and is busy copulating. Love or affection simply has nothing to do with it. Even among some of the most primitive forms of life known to scientists today group sex flourishes. Take the unicellular *Paramecium* as a case in point. Although they tend to favour solo reproduction, by simply dividing into two, they have by no means limited their sexual options. When environmental conditions become unfavourable and pose a threat to their survival they suddenly change course and decide that divided they perish but united survive. They do not copulate in the strict sense of the word, but instead multiply by a similar process known as conjugation. Two individuals come together and join at the mouth; this results in some sexual changes and a male and female nucleus are produced and then exchanged. Certainly, it adds a new dimension to oral sex! Once this couple have taken the first step the rest soon follow; indeed, the first act of conjugation triggers a chain reaction through millions of protozoans living in close proximity to each other and for a while the entire population indulges in conjugation. The purpose behind this social form of sex is to introduce some variation into the species so that it is better equipped to face environmental change.

Some species of snails, on the other hand, have sexual habits which could offer a blueprint for sex orgies. For example, when Mud Snails have sex they form the original love train. About half a dozen snails line up in a row and copulate simultaneously. At the beginning of the breeding season, the first snail in the chain acts as a female. The next snail in line acts as a male to the first female but when joined by the third snail it also acts as a female. Thus all snails from second to fifth position in the chain have a dual sexual role; the best of both worlds, so to speak. The last and sixth snail acts only as a male. Once the six have sorted out their respective roles they fall into formation and lock together, acting as a single entity. Although this seems almost too close to an assembly line for comfort, the snails must get something out of it otherwise they would copulate in the more conventional manner of some of their relatives.

There is nothing ordinary about the way their close cousins, the Slipper Snails, have sex, however. In fact their scientific name, *Crepidula fornicata*, gives some indication of their unique sexual habits. Not only do they

---

NECKING IN THE WILD

It comes as no surpise to learn that the long neck of the giraffe plays an integral role in its sex life. First the male tastes the female's urine to ascertain whether she will be receptive to his advances. If she is ready and willing the two giraffes then indulge in a little foreplay by entwining and rubbing their necks together.

---

form love chains like the Mud Snails but they also change sex as they enter a change of life. When young the snail is male and slithers around with complete freedom of movement. However, once he gains sexual maturity, the male is stripped of his ability to move around and becomes sedentary, attaching himself permanently to a base. At this point in time he also loses his manhood, undergoes a sex change and emerges as a female. Although still reeling from this swift series of changes, the new female snail must then accept the amorous advances of a male from which there is no escape; they are locked together forever in sexual unison. This 'Johnny- come-lately' is then mounted by a third snail and he too begins to change into a female!

And so the process continues until there are up to fourteen snails in the permanent love train. The largest snails make up the front of the train, those in the middle are medium sized and change from male to female, while the ones at the end are the smallest but retain their masculinity. It is an ingenious way of reproducing. The sperm of fourteen young males is used before they are transformed into fertilised females capable of producing millions of eggs in the love train. Indeed, these snails are a bizarre example of monogamy and group sex combined, proving that the two need not be mutually exclusive.

Snails are not the only species, however, to favour this contradiction in terms when the time comes to breed. There are other animals which also share the same curious double standards as the Slipper Snails; these are the Callicebus Monkeys of Colombia. They are unusual in that they mate for life and settle down with their lifelong partner on a small piece of territory that is ferociously guarded. The line between territories is clearly marked and if another monkey steps over the line he is immediately chased off what is private property. In this way, the life of these monkeys becomes a series of feuds with their neighbours and these have formed the basis of their social relationships. Partners are guarded just as closely as territory and opportunities for extramarital affairs are few and far between. However, at a certain time every year the female Callicebus Monkeys come into oestrous and it is then 'on' for young and old. Old boundary disputes and quarrels between neighbours are forgotten as the

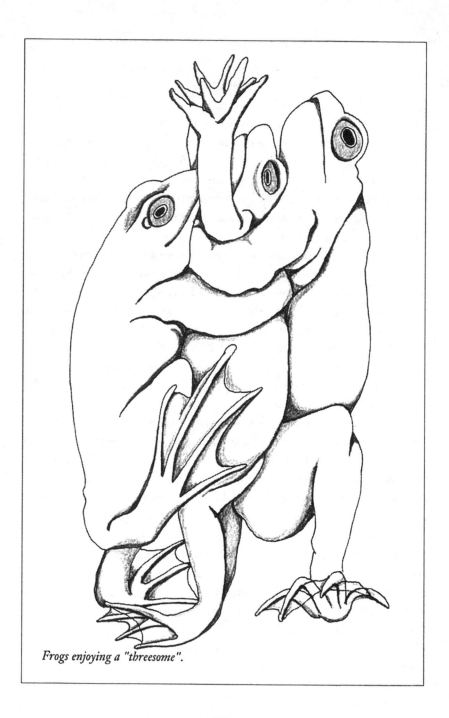

Frogs enjoying a "threesome".

entire population throws itself headfirst into a period of unrivalled sexual activity. Fidelity becomes a thing of the past and for the duration of oestrous the whole community revels in the throes of a wild and frenzied sexual orgy. Sworn enemies suddenly make love instead of war and the old biblical commandment 'love thy neighbour' is observed night and day with great passion. But then after a few days, these couples lose that loving feeling and abruptly revert to their old ways. Territories are re-formed and the walls go up again until the same time the following year when they can all let their hair down again.

Frogs too indulge in group sex from time to time as described else-where. They are often clumsy and fumble around in the dark and there is much bumping and grinding. Many other species of frog also indulge in group sex although most would consider the common toad or frog's approach a bit close for comfort. The Pacific Tree Frogs for example gather together for sex *en masse* but leave a polite 15-20 inches between every copulating pair.

Indeed, the idea that orgies or group sex must always involve the sweaty writhing of more than two intertwined bodies is somewhat misleading. Many birds that reproduce in breeding colonies technically engage in group sex. Gregarious species such as gannets, gulls and even flamingoes flock to communal nesting sites during the breeding season, breeding colonies being particularly common among sea and migratory birds. Take for instance the Artic Tern, *Sterna paradisaea*. This variety makes one of the longest migratory trips of all. Every year they migrate from north to south in a round journey which can cover up to 35,000 kilometres. Considering the average life expectancy of these birds, up to 30 years, a single member can become an extremely well travelled individual. In their life-time they may end up travelling over one million kilometres, an amazing feat for an average-sized bird. By travelling from their mass mating grounds in the Arctic Circle right down to the Antarctic they are able to enjoy a second summer with an abundance of food. Breeding colonies often consist of hundreds or sometimes thousands of pairs. Understandably they are very noisy places but if an intruder suddenly appears a deathly silence falls over the colony. Then they all fly up together and swoop down at the stranger, pulling out only at the last minute to frighten it away. This is one of the advantages of breeding in a colony; group life affords more protection for the individual. It is also thought that mass courtship increases the sexual excitement of these birds, thus ensuring that there will be a fertile union.

The spectacular flamingoes breed in huge colonies; sometimes one colony consists of up to a million pairs. When they congregate in such large numbers they often appear like a red cloud or pink haze from a

The mating of flamingoes involves a flurry of long legs and pink feathers.

distance. Flamingoes have a number of conspicuous habits. They emit a raucous squawk and are able to stand on one leg, with the other folded under the belly and their head resting on their back, for hours on end. Most migrate to warmer climates at the onset of winter and the lesser flamingoes conduct their migratory trips under the cover of darkness so as to avoid predators. Their ability to fly is also used as a retreat tactic when they are frightened. Indeed, the flight of a flock of flamingoes when disturbed by an intruder is an unforgettable sight. It only takes one to sound the alarm and the rest start marching in single file squawking loudly. Gradually they increase their pace into a trot and then a gallop. At the same time their wings begin beating and they eventually lift off the ground in a swirling cloud of pink.

Promiscuity

Humans are the only animals with the ability to enjoy sex at any time of the year. For the rest of the animal world nature has preordained strict seasons for sex. As a result of these strictures, those creatures who desire more pleasure from sex must try and satiate their desire before the mating season finishes. For this reason sexual activities are often very intense, especially when the mating season is short.

It only seems just that the King of the Beasts, the lion, should enjoy a full and busy sex life. Indeed, *Panthera leo* is one of the best known sexual enthusiasts in the natural world and both male and female just can't get enough of it! Although debate rages over whether the male lion is simply a miserable male chauvinist, a super sexual athlete, or more probably both, there is little argument over his lusty performances. In fact both the lioness and the lion share an insatiable desire for sex and have been caught in the act repeatedly (indeed, they have repeated the act many times) by numerous scientific observers. Perhaps it has something to do with the sociable way of life that the royal beasts lead since, unlike the rest of the big cats from the genus *Panthera*, lions live together in small groups called prides. This more social way of living is thought a natural adaptation to life on the plains where a pride of lions is easily able to surround a herd of prey. Prides are generally made up of related lionesses who form the core of the group. The males are replaced every two or three years by stronger males, which is not surprising when you think of the hard work they have put in. The new male ousts the presiding male and usurps his position as the head of the pride, thus ensuring the influx of new blood. Hunting is usually undertaken by the lionesses who kill zebras, antelopes and wildebeests. Lionesses are beautiful animals and there are few more beautiful sights in the wild than a big lioness stretched out in a lithe, indolent manner with the natural feline grace showing in every line of her body. The male lion with his face framed by the famous mane has a magnificent and regal appearance. The lion's undisputed position as King of the Beasts and his distinguished looks have made him a popular symbol of nobility on many coats of arms. The lion is also renowned for its tremendous courage although this is rarely challenged in the wild as lions are stronger and more dangerous than any other animal they are likely to meet. Size and strength are usually enough to scare off lesser animals.

However, the strength of the lion may be called into question during the mating season by the lionesses' insatiable appetite for sex. Sometimes a male may falter with exhaustion but he always get his second wind and begins another wild burst of sexual activity. For this reason they are able to copulate an amazing number of times, often with the same lioness, because the duration of sexual intercourse is so brief. Far from being the loving couple and indulging in the gradual build-up of sexual excitement, lions belong to the school of what is commonly referred to as 'Wham, bam, thank-you, ma'am'! Copulation usually takes no longer than one minute and at its briefest lasts for only six seconds. During the physical act the lion often grabs the neck of the lioness in his jaw, sometimes even drawing blood. He can also be heard miaowing during copulation while the lioness gives out a continous low growl. The male lion's sexual prowess was watched and recorded with amazement by one observer who noted that a male lion he watched for two days copulated 84 times in the first 24 hours. In the following 24 hours he had sex a further 62 times, eventually ending with a sexual tally of 157 times in 55 hours. After such an amazing bout of coitus another male usually takes over and copulates with the lioness, who possesses a prodigious sexual appetite when on heat.

When she falls pregnant, she will confine herself for three months after

Lovebites enhance sexual excitement during mating in the big cats.

which two or three cubs are born, with their eyes open. Lion cubs are as big as domestic cats when born and at six months they are ready to be weaned. By the end of one year they are about the size of big dogs but the distinguishing mane of the male usually only becomes noticeable in the third year. However impressive the number of notches on the lion's bedstead may be though, its sexual performance has been far outshone by a common little Desert Rat named Shaw's Jird, *Meriones shawi*. This animal was observed copulating an astonishing 224 times in two hours. However, despite their eagerness to mate with several different partners in succession, male and female jirds will form lifelong partnerships to raise their young.

The female chimpanzee too has an appetite for sex to rival the lioness and a sexual stamina to match. Their lax morality would be abhorred by human society and the sexual submissiveness to males would no doubt have women liberationists up in arms. However, for this species, quantity over quality has proved the most successful way of reproducing. The female chimpanzee has even gone one step further than the lioness in ensuring that she is sexually satisified all year round. Her ability to have sex is not limited to a mating season but rather she is sexually active throughout the year. Like female humans, ovulation takes place every month in the chimpanzee. Special tissues supplied with blood for the placenta are formed in the womb to prepare for a fertilised egg. If conception does not occur the bloody tissue is discharged. With such unique sexual freedom it is no wonder that promiscuity is the byword of the chimpanzee's sexual life. Whenever a female feels ready she flaunts her willingness to copulate and the males line up. As the old saying goes it pays to advertise and the genital area of the female becomes pink and swollen when sexually receptive. Then, in order to leave the male with absolutely no room for doubt, she also releases sex pheromones from her genitals. The combination of sight and smell arouses the males who line up to mate with her in turn. One female chimpanzee was observed by scientists mating with eight different males all within the space of 15 minutes. When ready to have sex the male usually adopts one of several signals to let the female know he is in the mood. These include squatting with shoulders hunched and arms extended or shaking a branch at the female and are the only forms of courtship visible in this species. The female in return crouches before the male and offers him her posterior. He then squats in an upright position and enters her quite nonchalantly. Foreplay simply does not exist and copulation itself is very brief. Perhaps this is why the performance is repeated over and over again to gain some sort of sexual gratification. The female usually receives a succession of sexual partners who have been patiently waiting their turn. This sex orgy or 'gang bang' usually lasts for about ten days in a month after which the female recuperates, a bit bruised and battered. Pregnancy usually lasts about seven or eight months and at birth the young chimpanzee weighs close to two kilograms. For the first two years of its life it is completely dependent on its mother but as it grows older it will be supported by the rest of the troop.

It is possible that the chimpanzee's casual approach to sex has something to do with its social lifestyle. Like the lions, chimpanzees live in small groups and individuals are free to come and go as they please. They are essentially forest dwellers although they are not particularly well suited to arboreal life and tend to spend most of their time with their feet firmly planted on the ground. The fluid nature of their groups also means that they live a relatively peaceful life with little aggression between group members. There is a rank order whereby large males are treated with deference and have a high status but this is not rigid and any conflict that arises is usually solved when one of the individuals leaves to join another troop. Subordinate animals do defer to their superiors, but this does not really affect their mating behaviour. Relations between different troops are usually calm as well and when neighbouring groups meet they are

---

NO TIME FOR POSTNATAL DEPRESSION

The female Egyptian Spiny Mouse acts as a midwife to other females once she has given birth. She bites through the umbilical cord and licks clean the newborn infant while the mother gives birth to the rest of the litter. Two of the unusual defences of the Spiny mouse against predators are a strip of spiky hair along its back and a tail that can snap off if caught in the attacker's mouth. The mouse can thus literally escape the jaws of death

---

able to mix without hostility.

The sex lives of lions and chimpanzees reveal an important fact about most promiscuous species. This is that generally it is the male who chooses the female and then has his way with her, often many times over. Even in those species where the females line up for sex, the male still has the upper hand and she considers herself lucky to receive his sexual favours. Such is the case with the well-known Sage Grouse. For three months the males strut around flaunting their brilliant plumage and securing the tiny pieces of ground upon which they will copulate. Then, on only one night, flocks of hens descend and begin to look for a sex partner. They are immediately attracted to the most colourful male with the finest piece of real estate and converge on him. There are usually only about five of these superb specimens available and since time is of the essence they begin copulating straight away without any foreplay. The males continue this down the waiting line, taking a breather every now and then to recover their strength. When they are exhausted and can perform no more the lesser males sneak in and service the unsated females still waiting patiently for their turn. This seems like one of the more unjust laws of nature and the rest of the male population must be genuinely peeved as they stand and watch the few privileged ones having all the fun.

Promiscuity is rife in the world of birds. Just as some of the most tender examples of monogamy can be found among the feathered species so too can just as many callous heartbreakers. The polygamous species, or those that make a habit of having more than one mate, usually boast the best territories while monogamous species defend comparitively poor land. Polygamous males use short and simple songs to defend their territory and attract a mate and may often be brilliantly coloured as well. Yet the female is often more interested in his land than his looks as she is familiar with the male's 'love 'em and leave 'em' ways and is aware that more often than not she will be left holding the babies. For this reason she looks for territory with an abundance of food and water close at hand. Indeed, every aspect of the male's behaviour shows a marked lack of interest in nest- building, incubation and general care of the young.

On the other hand he goes out of his way to make sure the female has everything she wants, calling her when he has found food and always letting her eat first.

The largest living birds, the ostriches, are a particularly promiscuous species although the male Casanova actually has a heart of gold and helps rear the children. Averaging two or more metres in height, ostriches are the largest birds on earth. They are unable to fly but have powerful legs which enable them to run very fast, and speeds of more than 50kph have been recorded. Their huge wings are usually tucked in at the side while they run but can be used as brakes or when turning at speed. Sexual dimorphism is very marked. The males boast black body feathers with white wings and tails and it was these white plumes that once adorned the hats of society ladies. During courtship the male also inflates his throat which is coloured pink, to add to his dazzling display. Although he mates with several females, the cock does have some paternal leanings and builds the nest in which the hens will lay their eggs. The nest of the ostrich is a mere depression in the ground, which is usually sand or mud. The cock scrapes a hole about 30cm deep and the hens then lay their eggs in what becomes a communal nest with all the other wives. The eggs are huge, about 15cm long and 10cm in diameter with a tough ivory coloured shell and each weighs well over a kilogram. Once the chicks hatch, the male does not abandon the young as is the case with so many other polygamous birds but rather takes charge and protects them.

Most polygamous male birds leave the female holding the baby while the male finds a new wife with no burdens, but the ostrich is one of the exceptions to this rule. It is reasonable to assume that brilliantly coloured male birds have a somewhat flighty nature and are never satisfied with just one female. Of course their magnificent plumage and lusty nature serve a purpose in making them desirable to the females so they can fertilise as many of them as possible and thus perpetuate the species.

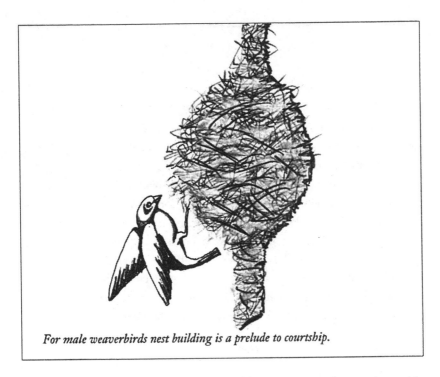

For male weaverbirds nest building is a prelude to courtship.

A male pheasant is a typical dandy and he is a spectacular specimen; his long tapering tail, which reaches a length of over six feet in some species, being his most outstanding feature. His head is also ornamented with a colourful ruff. During the breeding season he calls the female with a harsh cry and attracts her with a display of fine feathers but once they have mated he shows no sign of parental tenderness towards the chicks and leaves the rearing of the offspring to the female. Even the nest is built by the female without any help from the male, who, by that stage, is out looking for another partner. She makes do, however, building a nest which is usually just a small depresssion in the ground sheltered by a nearby shrub or bush and similar to that of the ostrich. The small olive green eggs are laid and the young usually hatch about 25 days later, staying with their mother until the onset of autumn when they forge an independent life.

Apart from the ostrich, there are some other birds which despite their promiscuity, show some responsibility for their actions and look after their children. One such creature is Brewster's Blackbird found in North America. The male blackbird courts a female and has a child with her, then runs off and mates with another female in a process which may be repeated more than three times in a season. However, he does not abandon any of the females but instead searches for food and protects all his offspring and lovers. The Common Starling has a similar approach to fatherhood. He usually takes a couple of lovers as well and once his girlfriends are pregnant he becomes a loving father to all his offspring. To begin with he builds a shelter for all the eggs, then takes turns incubating them until they hatch. He then helps the female by collecting enough food to feed the hungry mouths he has fathered.

Two male Sea Elephants challenging each other's breeding territory.

The male weaverbird is unique as he actually builds a communal nest for his harem among the treetops. Of course his lovers are completely under his control or else they might peck each others' eyes out in an effort to win his attention. One particular species found in Africa, the Black-Headed Weaverbird, builds his nest as a prelude to courtship. The nest is something of an engineering masterpiece as the male collects vegetable fibres and then shapes them into elongated pouches. The main opening is at the top but a smaller hole is located near the bottom which allows secondary access. When it is finished the male hangs upside-down from the nest to attract the attention of passing females to his handiwork. Often there are several of these amazing nests in the one tree making them very conspicuous. Another species is the Quelea, *Quelea Quelea*, which suddenly descend upon the African plains in their thousands at the onset of the breeding season and begin frantic nest building. Sometimes a male becomes a little carried away and his nest takes up the whole tree. Observers have often underestimated the promiscuity of this bird and when a few males decide to share lodgings their nests can house hundreds of females busy rearing their young. The weight of the nest with all these birds in it occasionally becomes so great that the tree actually collapses.

Some more advanced animals, with no claim to beauty like the birds, also indulge in the habit of having more than one mate. One rather unlikely example, not only because of its poor looks but also because of its slow, cumbersome motion and blubbery body, is the Sea Elephant, *Mirounga leonina*. So called because of its resemblance to the large land mammal of the same name, this huge creature often grows to weigh up to three tonnes. Most of this weight comes from the extraordinary amount of blubber and fat insulating its body and one large Sea Elephant can in fact yield a tonne of oil. It is hard to imagine the male of this species being much of a suitor but he does enjoy an active sex life. The Sea Elephant belongs to one of only three groups of mammals which are fully adapted to life at sea. However, they must perform their most important functions, including mating and giving birth, on land. When the breeding season comes around the male inflates his pendulous nose to form a proboscis twenty inches long, certainly one of the few features to recommend him physically. Older bulls also have a bony crest rising from the top of their skull which adds to their strength and dominance in the group. These fine specimens are also the biggest, reaching up to six metres in length at the height of their maturity. The females come ashore in September after a gestation period of up to eleven months. They gather in small groups on the beach and after some time give birth to a single calf. At this point the males arrive on the beach and begin to fight amongst each other for possession of the cows. The most pugnacious bulls win a harem of cows and calves as their reward and will mate with them throughout November. Sexual intercourse is long by mammalian standards, usually lasting up to 15 minutes and may be repeated many times. Meanwhile the mothers suckle their young with milk until, after two months, they all leave. During this time both males and females shed a lot of weight as they have been living off their reserves of fat. In these eight weeks, before they return to sea, the sea elephants must go out on foraging expeditions usually in the season of squid. However, they return to sleep on shore.

Harems, those situations when a few dominant males mate with most of the females, are a common feature in the sex life of mammals and are linked closely with territorial species and their behaviour. Harems are particularly popular with hoofed animals, whose herd leader will change before and after the breeding season. The rutting season, as it is otherwise known, is a time of intense sexual activity but only for a select minority. Marriages of this sort are particularly common among mammals and like marriages of convenience they are also marriages for protection. In exchange for turning a blind eye to her husband's many sexual dalliances the female receives his protection, as do her offspring. Indeed, protection is the keyword in the development of herd life. The dominant males' role is to protect his females and their young as well as servicing them. For this reason the youngest and weakest generally travel on the inside of the herd for protection while the stronger males are found on the outside. This arrangement also allows most of the herd members to graze continuously without constantly lifting their heads and looking around to make sure danger is not near. If a predator reaches it must first get past the strongest of the herd before it attacks the more vulnerable and easy prey. Thus, the question of fidelity is superfluous in herd life and what really counts is that the social structure remains intact. Indeed a definite and quite rigid social structure does exist complete with hierarchy. The herd acts as a group and there is little room for individuality with all members having to obey the laws and customs of the species. Those at the top of the herd hierarchy are called *alpha* animals by scientists; the next rank is *beta* while the lowest in the herd are the *omega* animals. Like most orders this hierarchy is complicated and often challenged by sex. When males of a high rank mate with females of a lower rank the status of the female is instantly upgraded. However, the reverse rarely occurs. A low ranking male does not often get the chance to mate with a high ranking female unless he can steal some moments of sexual pleasure behind the dominant males' back. Incidentally, the dominant rank in a herd is not always occupied by a male. Among deer or cattle it may well be a female who has fought other females to reach her place at the top.

Baboons are considered the most extreme example of group behaviour. Scientifically speaking they cannot strictly be called herds which is a term that sits more comfortably with hoofed animals. Rather it is more appropriate to call their social lifestyle a loose grouping of individuals into a large family, or a small community consisting of several small families. Each family has a sire, wives and offspring and some unmated males as

The pink, swollen genitalia of a female baboon indicate she is ready for sex.

well. The dominant males attract the most females while the lesser males are lucky to collect two or three. Furthermore, it is unwise for them to protest if the dominant male suddenly indicates a sexual interest in one of their wives. Yet if the lower male casts a longing eye at one of the wives of the dominant male there are often serious consequences. This may seem unfair but nature has spent many years developing the best way in which baboons can live and prosper as a species and as a result a strict hierarchy has evolved.

Yet one can understand and empathise with the lower males feelings of resentment and sexual frustration. Dominant baboon males are selfish creatures. They steal all the best food for themselves and severely punish all challengers to their authority. This can be justified to a certain extent as the sires of the herd must keep their strength up so that they can service the females. They also have a duty to protect the herd from predators, their most dangerous natural enemy being the leopard. For this reason, lower males will bow to superiors when they approach food and the dominant male always gets the first pickings. Sexual order is governed in much the same way which is unfortunate for the lower baboons but an essential mechanism to keep up the population of the species. In the baboon herds, females gain or lose status depending on which male they engage in sex. This is a familiar echo of the human world where social mobility may be attained by a poor person marrying someone rich and well-known. Perhaps it is no wonder that the lower males are always hoping for a revolution. They watch their leaders closely for some sign of aging or sickness and will usurp him on the first sign of weakness. This is essential too as the day will come when the dominant male is too old and worn for his job and new, fresh blood is needed to maintain the strain and protect the herd.

The most famous examples of herd behaviour, especially during the mating season are male deer, or stags. The Saiga Antelopes from Russia live in unisex herds until the onset of the mating season when the dominant males suddenly choose a harem of females from the main herd and form a breakaway group. Often a single male may head a harem of up to fifty females which he defends against the other males he used to run with on the plains. Many males die as a result of pre-mating battles where they suffer wounds or become exhausted, making them vulnerable to the freezing cold of winter. Another antelope, the Uganda Kob, is renowned for its promiscuity. At the onset of the breeding season, the males select small territories and defend them in a similar fashion to the Sage Grouse. The females then descend upon the males, choosing those with the best real estate towards the centre of the communal mating ground. When a male sees a female approaching he prances forward to meet her with his head held high, displaying his fine, white throat. The female then wets herself in the heat of the moment and the male comes forward to sniff her urine and caresses her body with his forelegs. Mating takes place not long after but actual copulation is brief and usually performed several times for greater satisfaction. However, although the males appear to be having the time of their lives, most can only stand the pace for a very short time before letting others have a taste of the high life. Holding onto the central piece of territory preferred by the females is a difficult task for a male as there is usually a shortage of food, so he will be unable to keep up his strength for a long period. Nevertheless, he still has to fight off fierce competition from other males.

Fur Seals experience similar problems. These mammals come ashore during the breeding season and the selection of territories takes place on beaches with each small patch of sand being ferociously guarded by the resident male. For the male seals this is an exhausting business as their mating seasons are longer than is usual because they coincide with the females giving birth. For this reason, bull seals are huge when they haul themselves up on the sand as they will be unable to leave their yet to be won territories for fear of some other male taking over. Therefore, they eat and eat before coming on to land and live off their thick layer of blubber during the mating season. It is a hard life at the top though and they are constantly fighting to keep their positions. Eventually, the continuous assertion of their authority, combined with frequent sexual activity, wears them down and they relinquish their territories to other eager young males. But we need not pity them as they will have enjoyed many sexual liaisons with different cows. The arrival of the females occurs very soon after most of the initial squabbling over territory has subsided. However, as they are usually about to give birth they do not bother searching for the best male or land but plonk themselves down on the nearest stretch of sand. Thus the bull who has won a flat territory stands a good chance of snaring quite a few cows while those behind the beach or on the rocks must try and herd some pregnant females up to their lovenests. Because of this they will generally be unsuccessful. Once the cow has found a home, a protector and a lover, she gives birth to the baby she has been carrying for most of the year. Within a week these cows will start getting interested in sex once more, although they must still take care of their calves and suckle them for another six months. The Fur Seals are a good example of sexual selection at work as the most dominant males who win territories on the beach pass on their characteristics to the offspring. The same qualities which attract the females to them also allow them to defend their territories and stay on shore living off their fat reserves for extended periods of time. Thus, size and strength are of the essence and it is not by chance that male seals are four times the size of the females.

The ability to stay on land is just as crucial in the Grey Seals, a species whose numbers have been seriously diminished due to hunting and the encroachment of human civilisation. The bull Grey Seals are extremely cumbersome on land, having stored away months of food supplies in their bodies. If another male enters his territory he generally does not even bother to fight it but instead co-exists peacefully with him, conserving energy so that he can stay longer on the beach. The biggest bulls remain ashore for up to eight weeks, most of which is spent sleeping but their waking hours are devoted totally to the pursuit of sex. However, as Grey Seals do not defend their territories they do not have exclusive rights to a cow and thus mate with a female whether she is 'on heat' or not.

Just as the soft and fluffy seal pups with their huge black eyes inspire feelings of tenderness in human observers so too do horses, both young and old. Wild horses live and breed in much the same manner as the seals despite being strictly land animals. The aesthetic appeal of the horse lies in its perfectly proportioned body with small, neat feet, powerful hind quarters, a sloping triangular head and a soft muzzle. In the wild, and indeed in captivity as well, horses live in herds with a dominant stallion who leads the group to good grazing land and protects it from predators. It is a stable society of one stallion for each harem until the onset of the mating season. Then his authority will be challenged by younger blood and fighting usually ensues using teeth and hooves. Frequently the loser suffers fatal wounds and bleeds to death. Humans admire the sex drive of the stallion and indeed, its promiscuity has worked its way into the vernacular.

Other hoofed animals that have been harnessed for use by humans are those beasts classed as cattle. Cattle rearing is widespread throughout the world, and meat from cattle forms a substantial part of many people's total food intake. Dairy farms are also plentiful as cows yield milk which is considered to be a dietary necessity for humans. Like horses, cattle live in herds, although these usually include more than one dominant male and are much larger. The ancestors of all modern cattle were the Aurochs, *Bos primigenius*, from India. Selective breeding has since improved both the size and quality of cattle to produce higher yields of meat for the beef market. Such breeds include Herefords, Murray Greys, Aberdeen Anguses, Shorthorns and the Polled Herefords. Breeds used for dairy products

---

BABY BOOMERS

The fastest breeding mammal in existence is a tiny rodent known as the Multimammate Rat. One female is capable of producing up to 120 offspring a year if conditions are favourable. This is because she has 24 teats, the most out of any female mammal. It is rare that all of them are used but when they are a Multimammate population explosion can occur.

---

include Friesians, Ayrshire, Jerseys and Guernseys. Cattle do not have a clearly defined breeding season although spring still seems to be the most favourable month. The same rule applies for cattle as for most other hoofed animals when mating. In cattle it is always the dominant bulls which service the herd's females. Buffalo and bison are very similar to cattle but can be distinguished by their greater size and horns. They live in much smaller herds than cattle; a herd usually consisting of one bull and his harem. During the mating season the possession of the harem is challenged and fighting can become particularly violent and bitter. Rival bulls charge at each other with horns lowered and crash their heads together with considerable force and it is surprising that these contests do not result in serious injuries. Bison differ from buffalo in that they have a large mane and beard as well as small curved horns. Today their numbers are greatly diminished, having plummeted from roughly 60 million in North America in 1700 to a low of just 840 animals in 1860 before they become protected. Other hoofed animals of great importance to humans are sheep and goats. Both are widespread throughout the world, having been part of human culture for more than 10,000 years. They are easily domesticated as they can survive on almost any pasture and require very little supervision. They are bred for their wool and to a lesser degree, for meat. Both sheep and goats live in a herd-like manner known as flocks, with the females grouping together to the exclusion of the males.

To the human world the habit of keeping a harem appears chauvinistic, if not downright sexist. But males from the hoofed variety of animals are very progressive creatures when compared to ducks. Male ducks, or drakes as they are more properly called, are the last word in sexism and are among the most lecherous of all creatures great and small. Ducks add new meaning to the term promiscuous.

Mature and immature ducks usually form pairs in autumn and then spend the winter together. By the time spring comes around many have already discovered whether or not they are sexually compatible. In contrast to the chaste engagements of many of their near relatives and cousins like the jackdaws or the swans, ducks often live together in sin before finally tying the knot. Such matings do not produce offspring as the birds are usually still sexually immature but they are not play acting either. Both male and female ducks possess fully developed sex organs and they are merely lacking in sex cells at this stage of their development. Come spring, when the winter relationships either result in marriage or fizzle out, the whole situation changes. The drake becomes a two-timer extraordinaire. Every female that goes past is a potential conquest and the drake goes after all of them with great enthusiasm, leaving his partner to turn a blind eye to his extramarital affairs while she waits for him. The marriage becomes sexually barren although the pair still feed together on the same pond as the female prefers to stay with her husband for protection if nothing else. He too prefers to stay with her as he can keep an eye out for the wives of other drakes on the pond and make advances while their husbands' backs are turned. No matter how much his wife protests, once a drake has caught sight of another female he is off and there is nothing the duck can do but wait until he returns to beg her forgiveness. Often her husband does not live up to his end of the bargain and allows his wife to be molested by other drakes while he paddles by. Indeed, it is not an uncommon sight to see three ducks flying together, the first one being a female while the other two are her husband and a strange drake. The stranger is pursuing her with decidedly dishonourable intentions while the husband joins in the chase so that he knows where to find his wife later. It is obvious that the female is not a particularly sexual being. She cries in alarm when pursued, flies faster, hides in bushes or even strikes out at the stranger until exhausted. It is at this point that the insatiable male has his way with her using his long corkscrew shaped penis. However, there have been cases where the female has died in the course of the chase rather than submit herself to the lust of a stranger.

The lifestyle of some animals makes it difficult to decide whether they are monogamous or polygamous. Take, for example, the mighty whales; they have fascinated naturalists for centuries and their beautiful song has been extensively recorded. However, despite this scientific scrutiny, comparatively little is known of their sex lives. It has been established that some whales mate in the water and others out and it is also known that the female's gestation period is extraordinarily long. Although whales are thought to be polygamous no-one really knows for certain as their watery environment has proved a great barrier to detailed study.

Whales, or cetaceans as they are scientifically called, are huge creatures with the rare Blue Whale being the largest animal on earth. Fully grown Blue Whales have been known to reach lengths of 20-30 metres and weigh over 100 tonnes. However, because of extensive whaling, this variety is no longer seen and even a 20 metre long representative is a rarity these days. Their proportions are huge: 50 tonnes of muscle, 60 tonnes of skin and bones, eight tonnes of blood, one tonne of lungs and a heart that weighs about 700 kg and measures one metre each way. If stranded on a beach it soon dies because the weight of its body is so great that its lungs collapse under it. These amazing creatures are also the most fully adapted of all mammals to a marine environment. To begin with they are able to survive in sometimes freezing waters because of a layer of blubber around their whole body which helps stop body heat escaping and provides an alternative source of energy. Whales move swiftly through the water due to a streamlined shape and use their huge tails, with horizontal fins sticking out on either side, as a rudder. Their enormous lungs allow them to store enough air to dive down to depths of between 80 and 200 metres and stay there for up to an hour before surfacing again. When they do finally surface, the top of the head where the famous blowhole is found comes up first. From the blowhole a huge spray blows up high into the air. It was once thought that this spray was water, however, now it is known to be the condensation of warm moist breath hitting the cold air. These blowholes are the only exhalatory outlet and watching whales "blowing" has become a tourist attraction.

Mating takes place towards the end of winter. Smaller species mate on the ocean's surface lying side by side. Larger varieties also mate belly to belly as their shapes allow very few variations in copulatory positions. Whales are thus one of the select number of animals which mate face to face. When the male is ready to mate the pair shoot high out of the water together with their bellies touching. The male must then insert his huge penis and fertilise the female in these few moments, usually no longer than about eight seconds. For this reason, the whale's penis is very elastic as it is made up of thin but hard fibrous tissue. It can reach lengths of up to three metres and a width of about 30 centimetres. Once the male has used his member it is stored away in a special body pouch until it is needed again; otherwise it would act as a drag and slow down his movement through the water.

Whales are notoriously slow breeders. Each male has a harem of several females which he services. They only mate once a year and since the female's gestation period lasts for about 10-11 months they may only give birth once every two or three years. A female will suckle her young calf for up to six months on her nutrient rich milk and it is this slow breeding cycle together with large numbers killed by hunting that has contributed to the alarming drop in numbers. Some species are now extinct while others remain endangered as it takes a long, long time for them to build up a sizeable population. Most species live in herds and are easy targets for whalers with radar equipment and harpoons.

Monogamy

The practice in many countries of making it law to have only one wife at a time is reflected in nature with the monogamous pairings of many different species of mammals and birds. Of course, this is not to say that some cultures with accepted customs of each man having a number of wives, are wrong or unnatural. In fact, polygamy is far more widespread in the natural world than the one-on-one style partnerships. Yet it is these monogamous pairings which evoke feelings of tenderness in human observers as the courtship and sexual behaviour often resemble the loving antics of humans. There are many examples of monogamy in the world of birds as discussed in the next chapter, in mammals it is not nearly so popular.

Some creatures take monogamy to the extreme and the parasitic blood flukes are prime examples. Not only do these worms remain partners for life but they literally become joined at the hip, as the saying goes. Once a pair of flukes have met and copulated they lock themselves in a permanent sexual embrace. They become Siamese lovers, never to be separated again until death does them part.

Mammalian monogamy

The gradual development of mammals involved a leap from the sky to the ground. While the birds soared high above and sang from the trees, mammals kept their feet planted firmly on the ground. However, birds have paid a price for their high-flying lifestyles as most of their brain is occupied with controlling their flight and as a result they have adopted rigid patterns of behaviour. It is only in courtship that they truly come into their own, with melodic songs and displays of vivid plumage. Mammals, on the other hand, are able to devote much of their large brains to intelligent thinking and considerable learning. They have also evolved a keen sense of smell which plays a major role in courtship and other sexually related activities. Most mammals release pheromones to attract a mate and use other scents to deter rivals from their territory. Thus, courtship can often appear all too brief to the human observer whose nose cannot detect the release of these significant pheromones. The emergence of mammary glands in the female mammal with which she feeds her young, have also contributed to briefer courtship periods and casual mating. Because the female suckles her offspring she releases the male from most of the responsibilities of rearing the family and so a lasting partnership is not necessary. This also leaves the male free to explore other sexual possibilities and the number of the species is increased. Thus, it is quite rare to come across examples of monogamous mammals in the same way that loving, avian couples can be found. Among those mammals thought to be monogamous are the gibbons, gorillas, Orang-Utans, beavers, the Hooded Seal, badgers, foxes and mongooses. The Roe Deer, hyraxes and rhinoceroses lead a quasi-monogamous lifestyle in that they live in small family units but it does not usually follow that they are content with the one mate.

The Roe Deer, *Capreolus capreolus*, are spread widely from northern Scandinavia to southern China. They do not live in herds like many other species of deer but instead are found in pairs or by themselves. They differ to larger varieties of deer in that the males bark instead of bellowing and their short, velvety antlers grow up almost vertically between their ears. As for loyalty to their partners, this is a still a debatable point. Some scientists have argued that the Roe Deer is temporarily faithful to his mate as a family is usually often formed after the breeding period and generally stays together until the following rutting season. Other evidence suggests that there is no monogamy, temporary or otherwise, among Roe Deer. These observations point to a polygamous lifestyle with the male serving any female that attracts him by her bleating during the rut.

The fox is an animal equal in beauty with the Roe Deer although much maligned. Foxes are often represented in cartoons as sly and tricky animals or as the enemy of the chicken coop. In England they are considered the bane of the farmer's existence and a grand, upper class tradition sprang up whereby the landed gentry organised hunts to eradicate the fox. The aim of the hunt is to provide an exhilarating horse ride, accompanied by hounds that will corner the fox and then kill it. Thus, the hunter has become the hunted in a manner of speaking but the foxes do have some redeeming qualities. Their appearance is one. Foxes are characterised by their pointy snouts and ears and their long bushy tails, otherwise known as brushes. Some also have distinctive colouring such as the Old World Red Fox, *Vulpes vulpes*, which sports a beautiful red-brown coat on top and soft, white fur on its underside. Humans have not been slow to appreciate the beauty and warmth of the fox's fur and their pelts have been worn as coats or stoles.

Their courtship is a particularly charming sight. The pair play together by rolling around on the ground and chasing and tripping each other up as their cubs will do some months later. Sometimes they lunge at each other with mouths open as if trying to bite but this is just a sign of enjoyment. Towards the end of this spirited courtship the female releases the characteristic 'foxy' smell that lets the male known she has had enough play and is ready for copulation. This well-known scent is released from an anal gland near the base of the tail. Like the Roe Deer, the fox's fidelity is also in some doubt. According to some it is monogamous while others insist it leads a busy extramarital sex life. There are cases for both. The charming courtship play of the fox and the role of both parents in rearing the young seem to suggest the creature is monogamous. However, during the physical act of sex the male dog's penis swells and locks inside the female for ten to thirty minutes. This is a common occurrence in polygamous dogs and is known as a guard against any other dogs gaining access to the female before it is certain that the dog's sperm has fertilised the ova.

The passion of the primates

Those primates that resemble humans are known as the anthropoid apes and they include the gibbons, Orang-Utans, gorillas and chimpanzees. Anatomical features that they have in common with homo sapiens are the lack of a tail, an upright posture and a highly developed brain. They have an upright stance although they often walk on all fours. In addition, not only are they like people in form and brain capacity but their mating styles also uphold the values of monogamy that humans supposedly cherish, but do not always practise. In most species the mother and father pair up for life and form a family that stays together until the offspring grow up and leave.

Gibbons are probably the most primitive of the anthropoids as they have a large brain in proportion to their size but are not nearly as intelligent as the other apes. They also have longer arms which drag along the ground when they walk in an upright manner. For this reason they are sometimes excluded from the anthropoid classification and placed with the family *Hylobatidae*, or 'tree walkers'. They move around their habitats in South-east Asia by swinging from branch to branch, with their hands acting as hooks. At first the gibbon's behaviour seems more like that of birds than mammals, perhaps not surprising given that they live in dense forests like birds. Adult gibbons live in monogamous pairs and each defends its own territory by loud shrieks and calls that echo through the jungle. The male and female look after their young until they reach the age of about six when they are driven from the group to start an independent life away from the family unit. The bond between the pair is usually reinforced by hours of grooming each other and feeding together.

The Orang-Utans are among those mammals most similar to humans as they are the only apes to have twelve ribs like humans and a high arched forehead. They also display many human-like characteristics such as building shelters which are usually platforms of small branches flattened in the tree fork. When it rains or becomes cold they pull some leaves over their bodies like a blanket. Covered in orange hair, which is thicker and longer in the male, they tend to move about on all fours but occasionally walk upright. Orang-Utans are very rare and only one species, *Pongo pygamaeus*, survives in Borneo and Sumatra. The words Orang-Utan mean 'man of the woods' in Malaysian. Their ability to learn puts them almost on a par with the chimpanzees and in one famous experiment an Orang-Utan learned to say 'papa' after six months and a little later 'cup' when it wanted water. The other main characteristic they share with humans is their monogamy.

Gorillas are definitely the most frightening looking of all the anthro-

ONCE IS ENOUGH

After sex the male garter snake cements up the female's sexual opening with a plug made from kidney secretions. This natural kind of chastity belt prevents any further sexual activity, guaranteeing that a female is fertilised by the first male to mate with her.

poid apes and are the biggest and strongest of all the primates. They have a ridge across the top of their head which gives extra height to the skull and small eyes sunken under huge, jutting brows. Powerful jaw muscles and massive shoulders also contribute to their ferocious appearance. Adult gorillas rarely climb trees as they have become too heavy for arboreal life and thus build their nests for sleeping on the ground. Stories abound about gorillas destroying villages and kidnapping women and children, no doubt fuelled by the cult horror film *King Kong*. Another popular image has the gorilla jumping up and down beating his chest while he grunts ferociously. However, movies and stories such as these have a lot to answer for as humans need not fear gorillas at all unless they attack them first. They are actually shy vegetarians using threatening drumming of the chest and accompanying sounds and movements to scare off other males. Although gorillas are thought to be monogamous, little is really known of their sex life as they seldom breed in captivity. They are also difficult to observe in the wild because of their renowned shyness and the thick impenetrable forest terrain which they inhabit. Gorillas live in small troops led by a dominant male and wander through a home range in search of food. Gorillas do not defend territory as such and if two troops meet by chance they generally ignore each other. It is only when the male is walking with a female that he can become dangerous and attack. The female gestation is about the same as humans and like humans, baby gorillas are helpless at birth. At three months they are able to climb onto their mother's back and by the age of seven months can walk and climb on their own. However, the bond with their mothers remains very strong until she gives birth again about three or four years later.

Feathered fidelity

Of all creatures in the Animal Kingdom, the habit of having only one mate is probably most common among birds . This does not mean that our feathered friends should be revered for the moral manner in which they conduct their sex lives, although monogamous avian species are often used as examples for human marriages. Indeed, when the study of animal behaviour was developing it was accepted practice to interpret animals in human terms by holding up their sexual lives in comparison to humans. The tender parental care, courtship and chivalry of some species epitomised the ideal human relationship while the promiscuity, violence and lack of parental care observed in others represented the reverse. Today it is generally recognised that it is irrelevant to pass moral judgements on animals as each creature is merely obeying laws preordained by nature. In the case of monogamous birds it is their system of sharing parental responsibilities that makes monogamy the most sensible and successful way to mate. Both male and female take turns in feeding and caring for their chicks and this teamwork requires a strong bond between the pair. For this reason their home territory tends to be quite small and long flights are often necessary to obtain food. When choosing a mate the female therefore chooses the male with the loudest and longest song as an indication of his individual strength. Polygamous species, as we have already seen, are less concerned with the quality of their mate and more interested in a large territory with an abundant food source as the female will have to bring up the chicks on her own.

One monogamous species which has suffered countless parallels with human sexuality through the ages is the stork. This large bird has often been misrepresented and a number of misconceptions still persist. One strong image is of the stork perched on a chimney-top nest or flying through the air delivering babies. Another is the cartoon version which portrays the stork as a loveable old eccentric with a fondness for the bottle who creates dilemmas in a drunken muddle, in the tradition of *The Prince and the Pauper*; delivering babies to the wrong houses. Perhaps the odd and slightly worse-for-wear appearance of the stork has something to do with this humorous image. All 17 species have rotund bodies, a short neck that is hunched forward and long slender legs, making them well adapted to their preferred marshland habitat as well as to strong, easy flight. A more sober and lasting image of the stork, however, is of it being the ultimate symbol of fidelity. It has also won fame as a migratory bird with some storks having recorded distances of up to 10,000 kilometres on one trip.

It is not really known how the fable of the loyal stork came about but it persisted throughout the Renaissance and still enjoys popular support today. Every time a dead stork is found or has died after being attacked by the rest of the group, it is assumed that the dead bird is a female who has paid the ultimate price for her adultery. Legend has it that the male stork is able to smell the female's indiscretion and at once calls a tribunal of other storks to decide her fate. It is more likely, however, that the male stork simply drives the unfaithful partner away or abandons her.

In recent times the image of the stork has become somewhat tarnished by a controversial debate surrounding its previously unquestioned life-long fidelity. Some believe that storks do not lead exemplary monogamous lives as once thought. Storks do not always occupy the same nest each year and neither does it belong to the same couple. At the beginning of the breeding season, the male stork arrives before the female, often flying into the same nest as the previous year. Sometimes a younger owner arrives before him in which case the previous male must find another nest if he cannot persuade the intruder to move on. The female arrives a little later and searches for a nest occupied by a male. She is accepted by the male whether she was his wife the last season or not because the male is more interested in securing shelter than a lifelong mate since it is he who must incubate the eggs and raise the young. Nor is the female looking for a lifelong companion but rather a male who can offer her a nest and is willing to look after her eggs. The quarrels and subsequent killings witnessed by so many people and assumed to be punishment for adultery often occur when a third stork appears at the nest, usually a female who has not yet found an occupied nest. Fights break out between the resident female and the intruder and a fierce battle may ensue as the first female fights for her man. Thus, while it can be argued that storks observe a temporary fidelity during the mating season, or even several seasons, they are not the best representatives of sexual purity or monogamy.

However, there is one bird that does lead an exemplary marital life which has not been tainted by the slightest rumour. Neither male nor female have a roving eye and they stick together until death. These totally faithful birds are the Grey Geese who begin their search for a lifelong partner after they turn two years of age. Although sexually immature the gander is eager to tie himself down without experiencing premarital sex. He is a charming suitor, demonstrating great tenderness and affection remarkably similar to humans in love. Once he sets his sights on a female he hangs around her family and stares at her for long periods with a wide-eyed, lovesick expression. Sometimes the young gander snaps out of this trance long enough to impress the object of his affections with his courage and masculine strength. If a rival male walks by he is immediately attacked and the loud shrieks of the resident lover are calculated to attract the attentions of the female to his gallant deeds. If the young goose returns his love she may throw caution to the wind and run off with him, at which point the family, realising that the couple are serious about each other, finally accept the romance. When a goose or gander happens to fall in love with an already mated individual the

Wandering Albatrosses spread their wings and point their bills towards the sky during courtship.

result is disastrous. There is no way that a successful union can be broken up and the hapless lover must languish in misery until their ardour fades.

When the eager young male suitor finally wins the heart he so earnestly desires, his happiness knows no bounds. He swaggers about with his chest puffed out and his wings outstretched and cackles loudly to other males. If the young lovers are ever separated their rapturous reunion reaffirms the old adage that absence makes the heart grow fonder. These reunions may occur even if the pair have only been separated for a couple of hours and unlike most human partnerships this loving behaviour only appears to grow stronger after the first flushes of passion die. If the mate of a gander or goose suddenly dies or disappears the survivor is overcome by grief and cannot be consoled. It is one of the saddest sights to see the surviving individual searching frantically for their spouse. Usually they fall into a deep depression and look sad and dejected. As geese are on the whole strictly a couple orientated community the widow or widower falls right to the bottom of the pecking order and it is only after a long period of mourning that they eventually find another mate. The subsequent relationships are never as intense or true as the first and it is in these second marriages that a drake often has discreet love affairs on the side. Sometimes the goose or gander never gets over his or her grief and will remain celibate until death.

The approval of the moral majority must be sorely tried by the fact that geese also maintain monogamous homosexual marriages that are just as loving and faithful as the heterosexual variety. The only difference is that the homosexual pairings do not produce any offspring but they flourish in every other way. Sometimes a female goose will be accepted into the life of the homosexual pair. At first she is ignored by the loving couple but if she persists one of the pair eventually copulates with her and a successful and fertile mating occurs. She is eventually accepted by the other half of the pair although the two always put each first. When the female bears the fruit of this union the two drakes adopt her and help maintain the offspring. This new maternal role frequently arouses the second drake's interest in the female and he too will have sex with her. In this way a successful *ménage à trois* is established. The three are now more productive than the normal families and they rise to the top of the flock's pecking order as they are now producing twice the offspring of everyone else.

Pairing for life is common among birds, so geese are no exception. Monogamous relationships save them a lot of time that would otherwise be spent searching for a mate each year. Other birds prefer monogamy as the additional parental care helps ensure the survival of their offspring. Often this lasts for a whole year so that the couple find themselves still together when the next mating season comes around.

Like many other species of monogamous birds, the rearing of a young albatross is prolonged for a year so that by the time the immature bird is ready to fly away for an independent life, the breeding season has come round again. For this reason a long term relationship between the parent birds is necessary as both male and female invest a lot of time and energy in raising the young. There are fourteen existing species of this beautiful bird although some such as the Short-Tailed Albatross are endangered. Others like the Wandering Albatross, the largest species, are much more common.

Albatrosses have enchanted people for centuries with their serene beauty, gentle nature and feathers like shining white satin. The enormous wing spans, which may stretch to two metres, makes them the greatest of any living bird. They are also greatly admired for their effortless ability to glide along the currents of the sea air. Known as the nomads of the ocean, albatrosses are able to fly for five years without once returning to land. Their amazing flying prowess is due to their extremely aerodynamic shape; they also use their wings like sails, deflating and inflating them to make the best possible use of the prevailing winds. Although they are often thought to bring bad luck, thanks mainly to Coleridge's poem *Rhyme of the Ancient Mariner*, in most parts of the world they enjoy a much more positive reputation. New Zealand Maoris carve albatrosses on the bows of their boats to ensure a peaceful voyage while the writer Beaudelaire expressed his admiration for their regal appearance, describing one albatross as the 'monarch of the clouds'.

These birds have a complex and protracted courtship, once they touch down on land. It is much more drawn out than in other bird species as the right choice in partner is a lifelong commitment and there is no divorce. All the dancing and squawking help to create a strong and lasting bond between the two so that they stay together and produce fit offspring. In the Wandering Albatross, the breeding cycle of a female begins when she returns from the sea after four or more years although she will not actually lay an egg until she is at least twice this age. Meanwhile each young male finds a suitable nesting space on the rocky outcrop and builds the foundations of a nest. At this point he announces his sexual availability by assuming a spectacular stance with his huge wings out-stretched. He then points his bill to the sky and lets out a loud and clear whistle. The female, who is circling above, now swoops down and takes a closer look at him before finally landing and walking up to join in the courtship ritual. Sometimes it goes no further than this as they discover that they are not really suited. When this happens the female albatross will often walk around for days until she has found another with whom she really wants to have a long term relationship. Even then she cannot drop her guard as the male has an aggressive streak which must be tamed before any serious courting can occur. He may lunge viciously at the female as she draws close but she will try to coax him out of this by nibbling him on the neck. Indeed, from a human point of view, the courtship of the albatross is the height of romance. Not only do they indulge in kissing and caressing but they also dance together. These rituals have been known to last for weeks but the extravagant build-up is everything as sexual intercourse itself lasts for less than a minute. Once the female has copulated and laid an egg, she and her partner remain totally faithful to each other until one dies. This lifelong commitment saves time on future courtship ritual and the couple can spend more time raising their chicks.

The albatross has also developed its own hierarchy in the nesting ground. The older birds with the whiter plumage, tend to nest in the centre of the colony while the younger and darker birds sit on the outside. If an egg is pushed outside the nest it means that the chick inside is dead. As hatching grows nearer the couple grow noticeably agitated and engage in heavy preening and nuzzling. After the egg has hatched, one parent guards over the chick for the first couple of weeks while the other forages for food. As the chick's demands grow, however, it is necessary for both parents to go out searching for food as the young bird can now be safely left in the nest. Albatrosses may spend up to two weeks away from the nest during breeding and some birds, who were probably swept away in the strong winds, have been recorded more than 14,000 kilometres away from their nesting site.

Like albatrosses, penguins too are a monogamous breed. Many parallels are drawn between penguins and humans; some humorous, others more serious. Firstly, most monogamous birds are held up as models for human marriages and their courtship is often likened to young human lovers. Secondly, the huge colonies in which penguins congregate to breed are often compared to cities as the constant journey to the sea for food and then back to land again carves out roads and highways which from the air look like the rough outline of a major city. On a lighter note, it is easy to understand why men's formal wear is often referred to as a penguin suit. Plump men wearing the obligatory black tail suit and white shirt resemble the penguin both in appearance and the manner in which they walk. But this is perhaps a bit unfair to the penguin as these birds are very striking with their clean black and white coats and rotund bellies. In some species such as the King Penguin, *Aptenodytes patagonica*, the head is decorated with an orangey-yellow colour, which adds a bit of cheer to their otherwise stark and icy environment.

These unusual flightless creatures are remarkably mobile and can swim as fast underwater as seals, due to their webbed toes and wings which form strong flippers to propel them along. Conversely, they are awkward on land and waddle around with a clumsy gait that severely hampers their mobility. However, there is no need for them to move quickly as they have no natural predators except humans. Once penguins have heaved themselves out of the icy ocean which they inhabit they set about finding a suitable place to build a nest. Penguins are very sociable creatures and during the mating season they set up large breeding colonies often consisting of thousands of birds. However, with so many packed so closely

Kissing and cuddling is a tender sight in penguin courtship.

together it is inevitable that squabbles break out and bickering and fights are a daily event.

Apart from the rivalry between neighbouring colonies and the competition between males within the one colony, the penguins are some of the most delightful birds to observe during courtship. There are many similarities to human customs in that certain behavioural codes must be observed in the serious business of winning over a female. Bowing and scraping to the female object of their affections is common and necessary to awaken young love in both sexes. When two males fix their sights on the same girl they often duel until one falls to the ground exhausted and defeated. However, once a couple is established, penguins are extremely affectionate towards each other. They actually kiss by stretching out their necks and rubbing their beaks together and sometimes hug one another using their flippers. Penguins are also as devoted in parenting as they are in courting. When incubating the egg both parents share equally in brooding as they will in feeding the chicks once the eggs have hatched.

Collecting food for the young is a laborious process involving long trips to the ocean to catch food not only for the chicks but also for themselves. Once the offspring are able to stand they leave the nest and join others from the same age group in a type of animal kindergarten. At this point they are no longer their parents' responsibility but are cared for by the group as a whole. As they shed their down, which is water absorbent and could cause them to sink in the sea, the young penguins form large groups in the water, fishing together and warning each other of danger. Then in three to four years they too reach sexual maturity and head towards land to take part in the breeding cycle.

The habit of having only one mate, or sexual partner, is quite common among seabirds. Research has shown that the longer a pair stay together the more successful breeding is. Those birds that have already formed a bond arrive before the others and lay their eggs earlier in the centre of the colony where they can breed more efficiently. It is the younger newlyweds who inhabit the fringes where a lot of bickering and squabbling goes on which interrupts their breeding. Do they sound just like humans?

The swan is another bird that spends most of its life in water but breeds on dry land. Like storks, swans too have attracted their share of attention from writers, particularly the story teller Hans Christian Anderson. The story of how the ugly duckling became a swan is a well known fairy tale. Indeed, swan chicks are quite unattractive creatures but the transformation in adulthood is well worth the wait. Swans are among of the most graceful of all the water birds. Their sleek forms seem to glide effortlessly across the water and their beautiful slender necks are a byword for beauty. In some species, however, this graceful appearance hides an aggressive nature. The Mute Swan of Great Britain becomes particularly fractious during the breeding season and will drive off all other water birds and sometimes even drown their chicks. These swans are an exception though as most are gentle lovers during courtship. Male swans caress the head and neck of lady swans uttering soft cries and moans. The only aggression shown is when the male is driving off a rival, after which he swims back to his partner with his chin lifted in what is called a triumph ceremony. This is a particularly beautiful sight given the long, flexible neck of the swan and is enhanced in some species such as the Black-Necked Swan by the striking contrast in colour between the neck and the rest of the body. After sex, some swans, such as the Whooper Swans, go for a sensual dip in the water as bathing is a tradition after copulation. Once swans have mated they remain faithful to their partners for life.

The fidelity of one species, the jackdaw, has been immortalised by Konrad Lorenz in his book *King Solomon's Ring*. Unlike geese who meet their future partner while they are still young and immature, the jackdaws usually wait a little longer before falling in love. Their engagement

A male Black-Necked Swan lifts his chin in a "triumph ceremony".

lasts for about a year before the couple finally consummate their marriage and start to breed. There is some degree of upward mobility in the pecking order if the female makes a good match but the reverse is not true and male jackdaws never mate with superior females. The male and female jackdaw, once they have mated, seem like the definitive couple. They cannot bear to be separated, are extremely loyal and quick to spring to each other's defence at the slightest provocation. Affection between jackdaws grows with the years instead of diminishing and their bond is constantly refreshed by their sexual intimacy. Even after several years together the male still feeds his wife in the same considerate manner that he used when they first met.

Many colourful birds found in the tropical regions of the South Pacific and South America are popular cage birds because of their beauty and pleasant disposition. Most of them are strictly monogamous, such as the parrots and parakeets and many are capable of living for 70 years, even in captivity. Their monogamous nature means that they can become very attached to their partners. If they are a pet they often accept their human owner as a substitute mate and let themselves be scratched and handled without any pecking and often pine if their owners are away for protracted periods. Parrots, budgerigars and parakeets are also well known for their skills of mimicry and are always fun and pleasing pets to have around the house. They are easily domesticated and trained, especially parrots and cockatoos, who can be taught simple tricks very quickly. Parakeets, or *Agapornides* (lovebirds) as they are also known, are the favourites of many bird keepers. They are noted for their deep attachment to their mates and many owners find this tenderness towards each other endearing. Indeed, there is complete harmony between the male and the female. When one bird takes a bath the other joins in; if the male begins singing the female also raises her voice in song; when one is sick the other tends to its needs and feeds it. Often if one of the pair dies and is replaced the new bird is ignored for a long time until the period of mourning is over. Sometimes parakeets never come to terms with their grief and refuse to attract a substitute. The courtship behaviour of these chirpy and colourful birds differs from those of other monogamous birds. There is not such a concerted and frantic effort on the part of the male to win the heart of the female. He never comes on too strong but instead continues courting her until she is ready to go all the way and mate with him. Even then, it is a remarkably gentle and tender union. When ready to have sex the female nods her head. The male then grabs her and literally takes her under his wing by enfolding her body in his large wing, cuddling her in this way. He is also extremely attentive to the female during brooding and is tireless in ensuring that she has enough food and is comfortable.

Parrots and parakeets are not strictly classed as songbirds but they do possess a strong, shrill voice which is evident when they mimic sounds from their environment. One thing they have in common with many songbirds is their monogamy. However, it is a quasi form of fidelity since most songbirds do not take an oath to stay with their mates forever but just as long as the breeding season lasts. During this time the male and female have eyes only for each other and will not tolerate any other bird from their own species to come near their nest. This is the general rule among avian species that divides those that practice monogamy from those that are polygamous. When both parents are needed for incubating and rearing the young, the couple generally remain together for the season. Conversely, mating is more casual and having several partners is common practice when only one of the parents takes care of the offspring.

Pigeons and doves, like the above mentioned parrots and parakeets, also make ideal pets as their regular habits allow them to adapt easily to captivity. They move about in flocks during the day when they feed and drink then roost together at night. The domestication of these birds is so easy that at many points in history they have become integral to the progress of human civilisation. Carrier or Homing Pigeons were at one time the most efficient way of sending messages over a long distance due to this breed's speed and sense of direction. A rolled up message written on paper was slotted into a capsule tied to the bird's leg before it was released on its homeward journey. Today pigeons are generally bred as a hobby. A fully trained pigeon is able to fly home from a point several hundred kilometres away by the shortest and most direct route. Bad weather may slow it down but in general, the Carrier Pigeon will fly between 50-100kph. It is not really known how the homing flight of the pigeon works. Some scientists have suggested that the bird has some sort of magnetic sense and is guided by the magnetic pull of the earth. Others believe that it navigates by correlating the height of the sun or moon with its own movements. Pigeons also play a surprising role in tourism in some countries where flocks of pigeons have become tourist attractions in major European cities.

Pigeons and doves are monogamous and tend to mate for life. With their soft cooing and light colouring pigeons and doves are a pretty sight as they groom each others feathers. The courtship of the Domestic Pigeon, for instance, is on the whole gentle, although does have a few unexpected and quite unique twists. As the male bird reaches sexual maturity its cooing takes on a deep resonance in contrast with the more nasal and weak calls it makes during adolescence. When it begins courting the male makes elaborate bowing gestures to the female and coos almost constantly. The female responds by bowing in a similar fashion to the male, who then begins nuzzling her with his beak. Sometimes the pair may be silent for hours before one of the two begins running its beak through its partner's head feathers. They may then 'kiss' by intertwining their beaks. During the kiss the male regurgitates a milk-like substance which the female swallows and this is thought to contain some hormones.

These in turn probably stimulate the sex glands of the female to make her sexually receptive to the male's next move. She indicates her readiness to mate by crouching by the side of the male who then mounts her. After sex, he chooses a nesting site and begins building a crude but strong structure. Incubation of the eggs is a shared responsibility although neither show the same devotion to their eggs as the penguin. When the pigeon chicks hatch they stay with their parents for about a month, by which time they have started to grow feathers and are able to fend for themselves.

Another species that has played an active role in the lives of humans is

---

ALL WORK AND NO PLAY...

Never disturb a pair of copulating donkeys. An Iranian farmer once dragged his male donkey away from its mate and was savagely bitten to death by the furious animal. According to Iran's Islamic Republic New Agency the donkey grabbed its inconsiderate master by the throat, choking him to death.

---

the partridge, although unfortunately at the wrong end of the gun. The partridge comes from that brilliantly coloured group of birds which includes the incomparable birds of paradise and peacocks. Like its gregarious cousins the parrots, the partridge is thought to favour monogamy. Although they tend to live together in groups for protection, they are poor fliers and cannot escape predators swiftly. Partridges mate in pairs and like most other birds, courting and mating occurs in spring. The group breaks up into pairs during courtship and the female then lays up to 16 eggs in a primitive nest in the ground. By late summer the eggs have hatched and the family unit soon breaks down, with the young birds joining groups of their own age and the adults returning to the parent group. These birds were once some of the most abundant game birds in Europe but today their numbers are depleting and often require restocking before the hunting season.

In the majority of cultures where monogamy is supposed to be the rule, there are constant exceptions and variations. This is the same in the world of the birds. Just as in a monogamous human society there is bigamy, occasional polygamy, desertion, divorce and broken marriage, so too are there deviations in the world of birds. Pigeons, swans and birds of prey are thought to mate for life but it is difficult to be sure without banding them and monitoring them year in and year out. Although some presumed monogamous species have often revealed themselves to be less than 100% faithful, others have demonstrated quite remarkable fidelity. In the case of the Montague Harrier, monogamy even manages to survive the long migration from breeding grounds to winter palaces and back again. The male arrives at the breeding ground where the couple reared their young the previous year and prepares everything, from building the nest to claiming the territory in anticipation of his mate's arrival. The female usually appears about ten days later by which time the male bird has fought off most of his rivals and is ready for a loving reunion. The female has made a special effort with her appearance and arrives in sultry black plumage instead of her normally drab brown feathers.

Most birds of prey are either solitary animals that only come together for mating or else they live in pairs except when migrating. Whatever the case, whether together forever or for only part of the time, these birds are universally monogamous. It seems like a wild contradiction to imagine the vulture, with its horrifying eating habits, carrying on a loving relationship but it does. Certainly there is a no more macabre image than that of vultures circling in the sky or waiting in tall trees for an animal to die so that they can eat the remains. Small carrion are usually held in their sharp and powerful talons where they are plucked of fur or feathers and then pulled apart to make bite size pieces. Larger animals are ripped apart, starting from the limbs. Vultures do not cut a graceful figure like the majestic swan although some are truly magnificent creatures. The Andean Condor, *Vultur gryphus*, is a huge, predominantly black bird reputedly able to soar to heights of between 5,000 and 6,000 metres. Once high and out of sight they are able to glide effortlessly for hours on end, using their remarkably keen eyesight to spot food on the ground. Others such as the Griffon Vultures, *Gyps fulvus*, fulfil the gruesome image vultures have earned both in appearance and eating habits. The feathers on its huge wings often look tatty and it has a long skinny neck and small bald head. This long and skinny neck is in fact extremely handy as it allows the vulture to dip its whole head into the corpse which it is tearing apart. At the base of its neck is a kind of ruff that looks like a moth-eaten fur from a second hand shop. Indeed, some species look not unlike the carcasses from which they pick their daily meals. In order to digest what is usually a rough and bulky diet, the vulture has strong digestive juices which are able to break down even small bones. In some parts of India and Africa, where they occur in large numbers, these birds are accepted by villagers as they remove not only carrion but animal faeces too. In the human world vultures are often depicted as symbols of greed and evil just as doves and lovebirds are held up as the living epitome of peace and love. During courtship, male vultures may sometimes fight in front of the female who watches with keen interest. Once the couple have had sex they become partners for life. At brooding time the task of incubating the egg is shared equally between the male and female as is the feeding of the chick once it is hatched. From birth Griffon Vultures have ravenous appetites which increase as they grow older.

Other monogamous birds of prey like the hawks, falcons and eagles hold a more revered place in the human world and feature widely in art, literature and mythology. The bald or American Eagle is the national emblem of the United States and is used frequently as an image of the country's greatness. The Golden Eagle is the largest and most majestic species found very occasionally in the forests of Northern Europe, Asia and North America. Its strength allows it to swoop down from a great height and pick up quite large prey with its talons. All eagles lead a monogamous lifestyle although they are not prolific breeders which accounts in part for their rarity. Pesticides, hunting and the destruction of their natural habitats by humans have all contributed to the decline of these magnificent birds.

Rape

While most animal mating styles are mirrored in the human world, rape would have to be the exception. It is a common occurrence among humans, sadly, but remains almost completely foreign to members of the Animal Kingdom. Sometimes sex in the wild appears rape-like to human eyes but the female is usually in a sexually receptive condition when the male forces himself on her. Nevertheless she may try to escape her suitor's amorous advances and sometimes she may become embroiled in a violent scuffle when asserting her right to say no. In most cases this behaviour, horrific to humans, is justified, as only the strongest male is able to overcome her resistance and thus the female receives the best possible genes for her offspring. Yet, it seems unfair that nature has preordained that female submission in many animals is necessary to carry on the species while the male gets away with often brutal sexual behaviour. The male Wolf Spider that rapes the female in passing is a perfect example of the often unjust laws of nature. Some frogs too are mad rapists but cover up their crimes by indulging in midnight sex orgies, as covered earlier in this book. The male's tendency to resort to rape usually occurs after he has sung himself hoarse for half the night serenading a female with no apparent response. He becomes increasingly frustrated as his song not only arouses the female but also makes him more and more excited as the night wears on. When a female frog finally hops up to him he will jump on her back without further ado and latch on to her with his front legs. Yet although he has literally forced himself on her he cannot go 'all the way' in the conventional sense because the poor fellow does not possess a penis. Instead he must wait for the female to release her eggs for fertilisation, often squeezing her sides extremely hard to induce their release prematurely. Meanwhile the delay causes havoc among other unmated males searching for females and they croak their loud disapproval behind the pair. Occasionally tensions reach a flashpoint and the frog on top is attacked by desperate males who try to dislodge him from his privileged position. Sometimes the battle over the female becomes so heated and violent that she is actually injured or even inadvertently killed by her ardent admirers.

Among the birds too, the taint of rape creeps into the lives of happily married couples. Finches, for instance, usually pair up into very satisfactory marriages of convenience but if a new female appears on the scene these partnerships can disintegrate very quickly. Normally the male tries to rape the newcomer although his efforts are often futile. The male finch then switches to the more conventional way of achieving copulation through courtship. This love affair enrages the abandoned hen so much that she may launch ferocious attacks on the other bird. Frequently this is to no avail and the husband runs off with the new girl anyway. Then to add insult to injury, the newly formed couple attack and drive the old wife away from their area. However, on those occasions when the wife's fight to bring her husband back to the nest is successful, the other bird must flutter away with her tail between her legs.

In the case of another bird, the duck, it is well-known that the males indulge in extramarital affairs with the full knowledge of their wives. At the same time they happily give their consent to any passing drakes who may want to have sex with their own wives. This free and easy approach to married life only occurs once a year and for the rest of the time the swinging pair are a model of monogamy. Interestingly, ducks are one of the few birds to possess a penis as the rest simply rub their respective clocae together to have sex. At times, however, they misuse this natural asset and particularly during the mating season their sexual hunger can be almost insatiable. As a result faithful husbands suddenly become uncontrollable lechers while the females, whose sex drive is considerably lower, spend a great deal of time fleeing the unwanted advances of other drooling drakes. As she is a lot quicker, the duck can usually get away but unfortunately for her the drake often thinks she is playing hard-to-get and gives himself up to the thrill of the chase. Sadly, this sometimes results in the death of the female as he pounces on her when she dives into a pond to escape, and this can result in death by accidental drowning. On those occasions when she does want to mate with her pursuer, she crouches down in the mating position waiting for his corkscrew-shaped penis.

Indeed, violence and rape go hand-in-hand as they must when one individual forces their will on another. The sex life of the mink is certainly something to ponder when spotting a mink fur coat. This inoffensive little creature that graces the backs of so many humans is actually an accomplished swimmer in the wild and lives off fish, frogs, snakes and rats. There are many species of mink, the most valuable being the North American Mink, *Mustela vison*. Its coat is thicker and softer than other breeds and it was once hunted for its fur although nowadays it is mainly bred on farms in Europe and America. In captivity and in the wild the mink enjoys a reputation for having an exceptionally high libido. The beginning of the breeding season acts almost as a starting pistol for the male who immediately begins haranguing nearby females for sex. The randy little fellow tries repeatedly to mount the female while she, having learnt a few self-defence tricks by now, repels him with equal fervour. To the human observer the male mink appears to be an unrepentant rapist and a repeat offender; his excuse is that he is trying to whip himself and his girlfriend up into a sexual frenzy so that fertilisation will be success-ful. It is a defence that would be thrown out of court in the human world but nature is a more lenient judge and realises that the male mink's defence is valid. Without the degree of sexual arousal brought about by violent foreplay the female mink would probably not release her ripe eggs and the union would be sterile. For this reason the male mink refuses to copulate with the female until she becomes too weary to resist any further.

A SCREW WITH A DIFFERENCE

The penis of a pig is very similar to its characteristic curly tail. It is a stiff coil and when erect it looks like a corkscrew with an anti-clockwise twist. At about 45cm long, it fits perfectly into the cervix of the sow so that the two can remain love-locked for hours on end.

Another animal that has been relentlessly hunted and bred to make fashion accessories for humans is the crocodile; their tough and scaly skins are much sought after for handbags and shoes. Unlike the mink, however, the slaughter of crocodiles does not raise the same degree of outrage from humans, due no doubt to their fearsome reputation as man-eating animals. However, only one species is really a threat to man, the giant Estuarine or Salt-water Crocodile found in southern Asia and northern Australia. A fully grown specimen is a truly terrifying sight and usually measures about six metres in length at maturity. The largest crocodile ever recorded was found in India and measured an amazing ten metres in length. These creatures are very efficient predators as they have extremely powerful jaws with which they hold their prey. Their cone-shaped teeth, however, are not built for chewing and so they must swallow their meals in large lumps and the stones often found in their stomachs are thought to aid in digestion by grinding and crushing the food. Crocodiles have a natural advantage over their prey as they are extremely well adapted to water life with their broad tails which can propel them through the water at great speed. They can often spend up to five hours underwater without ever surfacing and their eyes, ears and nose are set high in their heads enabling them to remain almost totally submerged beneath the water but still watch what is going on above.

Considering their ferocious appearance and nature it comes as no great surprise to learn that their lovemaking is as brutal as their attacks on humans and other animals. The male crocodile is a notorious rapist and has been getting away with it for about 100 million years. The modern breeds; although smaller, remain substantially unchanged from the mighty crocs that roamed the earth during the Age of the Dinosaur. The male's sexual technique is just as primitive. When the urge comes upon him the male croc waddles stealthily up to the nearest female and grabs her with his powerful jaws so that she cannot escape. Brushing aside her vigorous objections, the ruthless male turns her on her back and slides on top, pinning her to the ground in the submissive missionary position. She is then forced to endure his unsolicited ardour and may even shed a few crocodile tears. Thankfully, the ordeal does not last long as the male's lust is easily satiated. He then walks calmly away from the scene of the crime, leaving the ravaged female flailing as she tries to regain her feet and dignity. Although this may seem like a case for laying criminal charges, this level of violence is justified as it is essential to provide the sexual stimulation required for a fertile union.

The male Grey Seal also tends to subscribe to the sexist slogan 'treat 'em mean to keep 'em keen'. Grey Seals mate on land, with the biggest and meanest bulls staying on shore for up to eight weeks. A lot of this time is spent sleeping and it is no wonder as they spend their entire waking time engaged in exhaustive copulation. The male keeps a harem of cows and services each of them in turn, sniffing the air for their special sex scent which lets him know they are in oestrous. Yet despite this sophisticated signalling system he still tries to mount her at every opportunity to make sure that he and he alone is the father of her offspring, even if she is not sexually ready. This is one male that will not take no for an answer, effortlessly brushing away the female's resistance. It looks like rape, in fact it is rape in human terms but paradoxically the cows are actually making a choice between partners. Their aggressive rejection of suitors means that only the strongest males fertilise them and thus they are assured of good genes for their young.

One of the most vile rapists in the natural world would have to be the parasitic wasp that lives inside the Green Vegetable Bug. It is amazing to think that an unassuming Vegetable Bug can actually house a hidden world of perversion and unsatiated sexual desire. In some species of this wasp, males are always born first as they develop more quickly than females for a very sinister reason. These callous males actually wait beside the female eggs until their virginal sisters hatch out and then rape them! The newly born females are still weak and can offer no resistance to their brothers' violent and incestuous attacks. Indeed, the males' horrifying appetite for sex seems to know no physical bounds and they continue to molest and rape until the very last female has hatched. It is some comfort, however, to learn that the females in other species of parasitic wasp have not taken this shocking behaviour lying down. In fact they deal out their own special brand of rough justice by eliminating the need for males altogether. Without male intervention the females lay eggs that hatch females only. They could be heading for a waspish world of women.

Then there are those animals who suddenly turn from being kind and considerate lovers into ruthless rapists. As we have seen in the ducks, rape can sometimes creep into the lives of the most well adjusted animals. Often however, it is a signal that the fabric of their society is fraying at the seams and this is the case with rats. These rodents, detested by most humans, must be given due praise for their incredible ability to reproduce in great numbers. Yet sometimes a sudden surge in the population can upset the balance of their society and it starts to disintegrate. At first the social disruptions are quite minor but the situation soon begins to deteriorate rapidly. As studies in large cities have proved time and time again, overcrowding brings out the worst in both humans and animals alike. Considering the Brown Rat's almost human ability to learn, remember and pass on knowledge, it is interesting to watch the disintegration of an overcrowded society of rats and note the similarities. Usually a spiralling wave of violence erupts with rape and murder becoming everyday occurrences until the evil element end up destroying themselves. Only then is law and order restored to a much reduced population.

Incest

The sexual behaviour of the Moth Mite, *Pyemotes herfsi*, reaches new heights of perversion. At first glance the male Moth Mite appears to have qualities of caring, sharing and sensitivity, especially when compared to other parasitic insects. From the moment he is born he helps his mother by acting as an obstetrician at the births of other Moth Mites. He is able to do this as they are born mature insects, having completed their development inside their mother. When the first signs of a young female emerge from the mother's sexual cavity her young son springs to her aid, grabbing his sister with his hind legs and pulling her out of the birth passage. However, he only does this with females, having an ulterior motive which is not hard to divine. Immediately the new moth mite appears in the world the male mates with her in a bizarre mixture of incest and child abuse. The whole process, both birth and mating, takes roughly four minutes after which the fertilised female goes in search of a Moth Caterpillar to act as her host. If she does not find one within a couple of days she will starve to death while her incestuous brother remains hovering around his mother's birth passage waiting for the arrival of the next baby sister. Even worse, while waiting he feeds himself by drilling a hole into the side of his mother's body and feeding on her juices!

Sadomasochism

It is often the case that those sexual practices deemed abnormal or abhorrent by human society occur naturally in the animal world. Although they seem deviant and cruel to humans they are there for that one basic reason: to ensure the survival of the species. Anything goes in nature. As long as the male and female find each other, copulate and produce offspring, no-one cares how they go about it. The ends more than justify the means but unfortunately there is a tendency among many people to judge animal life in human terms. Yet it is illogical to place moral labels on animal behaviour and call creatures good or bad according to human standards.

Sadomasochism is one such sexual practice found in nature. More commonly known as S&M, it is a sexual preference not unlike bondage, in that a master and servant style relationship is usually established between the two participants. One partner gains pleasure from inflicting physical pain (sadism) while the other suffers physical pain and humiliation to gain sexual gratification (masochism). In the human world this sort of sexual activity is generally regarded as perverse and deviant. The public perception of S&M is that of men and women in black leather wearing thigh high boots and wielding chains and whips. Most people are frightened or disgusted by the practice. Indeed the man from whom the word sadism derives, the Marquis de Sade, was imprisoned during the 18th century after he kidnapped a prostitute and submitted her to repeated beatings and other violent behaviour. While in prison he wrote several novels notorious for their themes of sex and cruelty.

Sadomasochists do not gain pleasure from the actual pain they inflict or undergo but rather the emotions provoked by the pain makes them sexually aroused. The moral majority has forced this sort of sexual practice underground but in nature there are some animals that use this violent behaviour as a way of ensuring sufficient sexual excitement for fertilisation of the egg(s) to occur. Sadomasochistic tendencies are part of the natural reproductive cycle which nature has established for the perpetuation of many species. When wild horses mate it is common for the stallion to bite the mare on the neck, who in return kicks him in the chest. Cats, after beginning their courtship by caterwauling, start copulating when the male bites the female in the neck. Turtles generally take sex slowly but occasionally a male will try to speed up the female's sexual response by snapping at her legs, slapping her face with his claws and striking her cloaca with the hard tip of his tail.

However, one of the most bizarre examples of sadomasochism occurring in the animal world can be found by examining the sex life of the

A male cat bites a female on the neck to sexually stimulate her.

Roman Snail (the edible variety) and the Common Slug. During the spring these animals become sexually active and meet up in pairs to mate. All of these land varieties are hermaphrodites, meaning that they have a set of both male and female genitalia, although the sex glands are located within the shell. The spermatozoa travel down from inside the shell through a complex system of channels before reaching the sexual opening.

Before the snails begin to copulate they must ensure that they are both from the same species. Firstly, the two almost glue themselves together at the head and begin rocking back and forth, arousing each other sufficiently to activate a special sac called the dart sac, in which a calcareous spicule known as the love dart is formed. The two snails or slugs both release this dart into their partner's flesh. This wound sexually excites the animals (although occasionally the dart pierces the lung of their partners, causing a fatal injury) and they insert their penises into each other's sexual cavity. The sperm is enclosed in an envelope called a spermatophore which eventually dissolves to release the sperm that will fertilise the eggs. Eggs are laid in early summer and they are buried in the ground for protection.

This sadomasochistic sex act is not exclusive to the Roman Snail. The African Naked Snail's foreplay is even more vicious than the Roman Snail as this variety carries a dozen love darts each up to three centimetres long. As zoologists are sceptical about an animal of the lower orders being able to feel pain, it has been suggested that these darts actually inject an aphrodisiac to stimulate a readiness to mate.

Violent reproductive behaviour is also found in the higher molluscs, of which cephalopods are a sub-division. This group can in turn be divided into two main orders: decapods which have ten arms (squids and cuttlefish) and octopoda which have eight arms (octopuses). These animals are the most intelligent of the invertebrates and there are more than a thousand varieties, from the tiny five centimetre specimen to the monstrous Giant

Sadomasochistic snails engaging in slimy sex.

Squid which weighs up to two tonnes. The sex life of these unique ocean dwelling creatures has fascinated man for many centuries; they were even studied by Aristotle and the sexual positions and foreplay of the cephalopods appear frequently in Ancient Greek art, literature and mythology.

Copulation between cephalopods is a complex procedure because unlike the snail, the sexes are actually separate instead of being combined in the one individual. The strange copulation ritual of the cephalopods has baffled naturalists for centuries. At first the male organ, known as the hectocotylus, which roughly translated means 'arm of one hundred suckers', was mistaken for a parasitic worm living inside the female. It was an understandable error as the arm is found severed from the male yet very much alive and mobile inside the female. How this strange reproductive method is carried out is best illustrated by the octopods.

When boy meets girl in the ocean depths, the male first arouses the female for some time by caressing her body with his hectocotylised arm.

While he is doing this, both sexes undergo some vibrant colour changes, often displaying a deep red colour as they bashfully get to know each other. After what humans would view as something of a petting session, the male reaches into his breathing funnel with his hectocotylus and pulls out several packages of semen from his mantle cavity and then shoves them into the female's mantle cavity. The female is nearly asphyxiated as the male arm is blocking her breathing funnel and she may violently resist the penetration of the hectocotylus which makes breathing so difficult for her. Battles may be waged between male and female, especially if the female is not yet on heat or has already been fertilised. On other occasions the male may be rejected if he proves exceptionally clumsy and blocks off too much of her breathing supply. However, if everything goes according to nature's plan, the packages of semen swell in the female's body and eventually burst so that the sperm is poured out over the eggs. A few females even have a special pouch where they hoard the male's semen until their eggs mature. When ready she then reaches into her own body and picks out the eggs one at a time, pressing them against the semen pouches and thus fertilising them.

Some crustaceans also have modified limbs which double as penises in the heat of the moment. Unfortunately sexual violence often accompanies copulation when the animal has a double purpose limb; perhaps he is compensating or covering up for not having 'the real thing'. Whatever the reason, when the male River Crayfish mates with a female the water often turns muddy with their struggle as the same sort of phallic violence occurs during their sex play as it does with the higher molluscs. In order to perform his sexual duties, the male must grip her with his claws and throw her onto her back otherwise he cannot fit his sex tool into her sexual cavity. The female often resists being so unceremoniously dumped on her back and frequently tries a few underwater self-defence techniques although, more often than not, to no avail.

It seems much easier for humans to accept sadomasochistic tendencies in lower animals than in higher creatures like the horse. Thus, to many people the fact that snakes indulge in S&M comes as no surprise. To those who fear snakes, and with good reason considering many venomous species can be fatal to humans, it is perhaps a relief to find yet another reason to revile them as their sex play is an awful spectacle. The male member is decidedly ugly as it is usually covered with spines, warts or hooks which allow it to lodge firmly in the female's sexual organ. Once embedded it may remain there for some time to guarantee that the sperm does fertilises the female's eggs. In the vipers and adders, two copulating snakes, if disturbed, cannot extricate themselves from the task at hand and are only able to lift their heads, hiss and strike at the intruder. Lizards too exhibit the same sort of behaviour and males sport the same seemingly cruel sex organ. In addition they also bite deep into the flesh of a female before they mate. Apparently this 'love bite' determines whether the female is sexually receptive. If she draws away then she is not ready but if she stays and endures the pain then the two mate.

HOW TO DRILL YOUR OWN VAGINA

Imagine meeting the woman of your dreams and discovering she does not have a vagina. For the male bedbug this is par for the course, as the blood-sucking female has no sexual opening. This would prove an insurmountable problem for humans but not for the resourceful bedbug. The male simply drills his own vagina. He even brings his own drilling equipment, his penis, which is large, curved and ends in a point. Thus he kills two birds with one stone by building a hole as he is having sex. The female's vagina soon heals over but it leaves a horrible scar. Presumably one could pick a virginal bedbug by her unscarred body.

Bondage

Bondage and discipline is closely related to sadomasochism even though sometimes it does not actually involve any physical abuse. It is a master and servant relationship. The slave is usually chained or tied up and endures all sorts of sexual humiliation which is meant to make all sexual inhibitions fall away and increase sexual excitement and pleasure. On the other hand the master is sexually gratified through feelings of power and control over the slave. As both master and servant are put in positions to which both are unaccustomed, sexual pleasure supposedly reaches new heights for them. Many animals practise bondage during courtship or copulation as it is the only way they know of having sex. To them it is completely natural, they have no hang-ups or inhibitions about it at all. Evolution has tried and tested their method of reproduction and found it to be the most successful so they stick with it, perhaps refining it every now and then to suit changing times and conditions.

The male water mite, for example, assumes the role of master in his sexual relations with female water mites. Feminists would cringe but unfortunately it is nearly always the female that assumes the servant role and becomes subservient. This is the case with the female water mite. The male actually pins her to the ground during sex with tiny hooks so that she can barely move. In addition, to drive home his dominance over the fairer sex he actually glues himself to the female so that she cannot escape even if she works her way free of the hooks. He then enters her with his penis or, in some species, with a maxillary palp. Some even use their legs as sex organs, the logistics of which are mind boggling to humans.

A unique method of mating among the insects is practised by the Damselfies. They are aptly named, as the damsel of this species is very

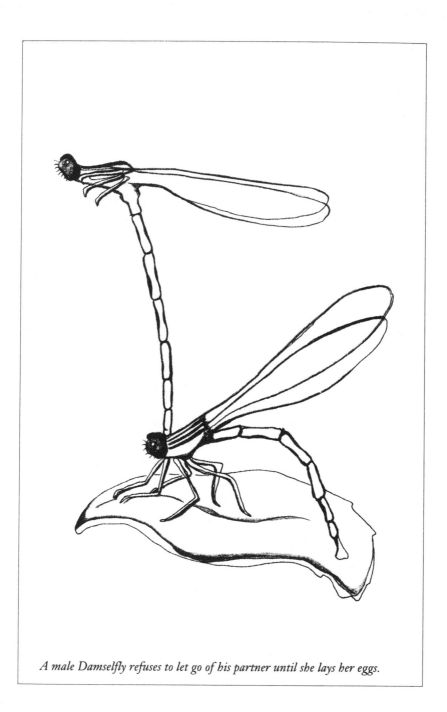

A male Damselfly refuses to let go of his partner until she lays her eggs.

often in distress although she is never rescued. When having sex the male transfers his sperm from glands at the end of the abdomen to an extra organ near the front of the body. He then hops on top of a female and grabs hold of her thorax with claspers located at the end of the abdomen. While in his vice-like grip the female twists herself around until her sexual opening touches that of the male and mating takes place.

Soldier crabs are not renowned for tender lovemaking either. As their name suggests they conduct their sex life with a military precision that leaves little room for love. Indeed, the way some males act one would think there was a full scale war taking place. Found in mangrove swamps, the diminutive male crab seizes the female with his giant front pincers when she walks by, taking his lover as a Prisoner-of-War. While holding her down in a vice-like grip as if she were the enemy instead of being his fiancee, he quickly builds an igloo out of sand with his free legs and dumps her in. Mating then takes place inside the prison of love until the male finally relents and releases the female.

Some spiders also indulge in a little bondage, usually to save their own skins from the ravenous appetite of the female who often mistakes her suitors for prey. Many male web spiders, for example, use their silk spinning skills to trap the female so that they are able to have sex with her and then depart without a scratch after the deed is done. Their approach is very smooth and slick. Oozing charm from every pore, the male spider slowly and cunningly tangles the female in a cocoon of silk, thus rendering her temporarily immobile. He then makes good his advantage and takes his time finding her vagina and placing his spermatophore inside. By the time the female works her way out of the male's silken trap he is safely out of sight.

Most amplexus, i.e. courtship in frogs, has nothing to do with bondage and discipline. Copulation is generally brief and involves the male jumping on the female's back, performing his sexual duty and then hopping off again. However, like most animals there are exceptions to the rule. The African Clawed Frog is one of them and even the name sounds ominous. Indeed this sense of foreboding is realised when the nature of its sex life is revealed. The males are complete chauvinists, wasting no thought on giving pleasure to their partners. When a male hops on top of a female he can never be sure how long copulation is actually going to take as he cannot leave until he makes sure the female has released her eggs. This African frog has only a limited amount of patience and become sexually frustrated very quickly if the female shows no signs of being ready to disperse her eggs. Suddenly he will climb off her, grab her firmly and spin her around like a top until she lapses into semi-consciousness. However, this spinning will have stimulated the release of the eggs and the male then climbs back on his helpless partner and mates with her.

The underwater world is no less kinky. The male Bullhead Fish actually

---

THERE'S MORE TO TURNIPS THAN MEETS THE EYE

One species of worm has developed vegetarian sex. The Turnip Eelworm lives in turnips and mates on the outside. When ready to copulate the female grows what looks like buds on her body. She then squirms up to the skin of the turnip and pushes her vagina through. Meanwhile the male slides around the exterior looking for love. When he spots her vagina poking enticingly from the turnip skin he immediately plunges his sex member in. Something to ponder when peeling your next turnip!

---

takes his female captive and does not let her go until he has had his way with her. Bullheads seem quite progressive fellows at first as they assume the roles normally designated to the females. They will build nests, guard the eggs and bring up the young in a role reversal not uncommon among fishes. However, appearances can be deceptive. When ready to mate the male lies in wait for a female in the small nest he has scooped out under a rock at the bottom of a stream. With his head poking out he waits for a pregnant female to swim by and when he spots her he will attempt to seduce her by planting love bites on her tail. This pleases the female and she usually swims into his nest for further hanky panky. At this point his whole demeanour changes for she is now his captive and slave and she will not be allowed to leave until she has deposited her eggs. Realising that she has been tricked the female lies listlessly on her back staring up at the ceiling. This does not stop the male who simply slides under and lies on his back as well. A battle of wills then ensues until the female, realising that she will never be released unless she unloads her precious cargo in his nest, finally spawns. Having got his own way the Bullhead male immediately expels the female from the nest and assumes the role of mother over the tiny eggs. While waiting for them to hatch he fans the water with his fins to increase the oxygen supply to the developing young. When they do finally hatch out he refuses to let them leave the nest prematurely, thus protecting from an almost certain fate with a predator.

Another animal that takes bondage to the extreme and makes its mate a prisoner of love is the Dysticid Beetle. Found in ponds, this beetle is a feisty little creature and a fierce and unrelenting predator on most other insects. Creatures of many talents, Dysticids are competent swimmers who are able to hang upside down using their feet to grip the surface of the water. Although most of the male's life is spent as a bachelor the time comes when he must look for a mate. At this point his skills diversify to include a remarkable talent for music. By drawing his hard leg across his scaly belly he makes a stridulatory sound which attracts the female. She is probably the first insect he has ever come across that he has not eaten and it is surprising that he can restrain himself. However, restraint does not bring courtesy. He immediately grabs the female with the suction caps on his feet and for the next few weeks she literally sticks by his side. The loving couple do everything together like Siamese twins; swimming, hunting, feeding and the all important copulation are all done as one. When the time comes for the female to lay her eggs the male beetle finally allows her to leave. He too must depart soon afterward as, in a final twist to his bizarre life, the offspring of his union become his predators and suddenly it is he who risks being eaten.

Bondage is popular among millipedes too. These tiny creatures possess what are called gonopods, or several legs which actually double as sex organs when called upon for duty. However, because the dual purpose legs are usually located in the middle and end parts of the millipede's body, the males have to roll themselves up in order to squeeze out enough sperm to fill their gonopods. They then go off in search of a female. Once they find the woman of their dreams the two joyful millipedes wind their bodies around each other as though they will never let each other go. The male then assumes a dominant sexual role and ties a knot around the front part of the female's body while he places the sperm into her sexual cavity.

Virgin birth

The idea that females can give birth without the introduction of male sperm is not new. Indeed, the stories in the Bible and Christian ideology rest on the notion that the Son of God was born of a virgin, the Virgin Mary. It would perhaps be a touch sacrilegious to link the birth of Christ with the birth of water fleas or plant lice but presumably they both occurred in the same manner, i.e. that the female was able to produce young without the participation of any males. The proper scientific name for this process is parthenogenesis, derived from the Greek meaning 'virgin birth'. Parthenogenesis refers to reproduction through the development of an unfertilised egg without the presence of male sperm. The theory of virgin birth in the Animal Kingdom was passionately debated during the 17th century when it was first discovered that plant lice or aphids were an exclusively female colony during the summer months. That females could conceive and give birth without ever touching a male was taken to ridiculous lengths during these heady times. What a blow to male pride to learn that the male sperm was dispensable in some species. Reports then began circulating that young girls had become pregnant by inhaling the morning air which was thought to be impregnated with certain germs or organic molecules. These more wild interpretations of parthenogenesis were quickly disproved and ridiculed and gradually the true picture emerged.

Virgin birth is the preferred method of reproduction for many small animals such as plant lice, water fleas, stick-insects, rotifers and roundworms. Some animals that favour virgin birth produce all-female young for most of the year while others like the Saw-Flies alternate between sexes; unfertilised eggs produce males while fertilised eggs produce females.

Solo propagation was first observed by two Dutch scientists and keen rose gardeners, van Leeuwenhoek and Swammerdam, during the 17th century. After cutting their roses one summer they noticed that the population of plant lice, or aphids, living on their roses was exclusively female. Aphids live off the sap of cultivated plants and spend their whole lives in this happy pursuit. Ants are usually not far behind as they love the sweet liquid called honeydew that the aphids produce. Meanwhile, from the other end of the aphid body a constant stream of offspring emerges. In the warm summer months one aphid can produce up to 25 daughters in a single day and these offspring are sexually mature and ready to reproduce in little more than a week. Some of these females are winged and fly away to spread the species further while the wingless variety remain and start to churn out new stock. All this reproductive activity, however, occurs without fertilisation by male sperm. Then suddenly during autumn winged male aphids are produced along with winged females. These new males pair up with the females and fly away to a nearby tree where the female produces her final batch of babies. The incestuous desire of the male then gets the better of him and he ignores his new found love and, shock, horror, has sex with his children instead. From each union a single egg is produced and from this egg an entirely new population of aphids emerges and the whole cycle begins again. This sexual practice may seem impersonal and highly immoral to humans and indeed it is little more than an assembly line. However, for the little aphid it is the most efficient method of reproduction. The manufacturing boom of aphids in summer is very necessary as the plant lice have many natural predators such as ants and ladybugs. Therefore the more off-spring the aphids produce the better their chance of surviving the winter. It also seems sensible to make the most of the abundance of food available during the summer months. By tapping the sap supply of plants the aphid also cuts down time and energy wasted on searching for food. The only disadvantage with reproducing by virgin birth is that if environmental conditions change or a new predator comes onto the scene then they face the very real possibility of being wiped out as they are all clones. However, never underestimate an aphid. At the end of summer these insects suddenly begin reproducing sexually, thereby introducing variation into the population so the forces of natural selection will continue to weed out the weaker strains in the colony.

Another tiny animal that uses virgin birth to produce copious numbers of clones is the water flea, *Daphnia*. Found in ponds and lakes it is usually referred to as a flea because of its habit of making its way across the surface of the water in jerky leaps and bounds. Water fleas feed on minuscule algae and are themselves devoured by fish and other water animals. With such a variety of hungry predators it is no wonder that the water flea has opted for the quickest possible way of increasing numbers. Like the aphids, the population of water fleas consists entirely of females during the warm spring and summer months. Thousands of eggs are produced without any help from males and are kept for several days in a brood pouch at the end of the water flea before emerging as adult females. A short period elapses before they grow to full size and then they too begin producing eggs. Indeed, their fecundity puts the breeding capabilities of the notorious rabbits and rats to shame. Some female water fleas have been observed laying batches of 30 eggs with only a two-day breather in between and each female is capable of laying up to twenty batches of eggs in her lifetime. Like aphids and other parthenogenetic species, water fleas are able to slow down and switch to sexual reproduction when conditions are no longer favourable. When this happens some of the eggs hatch as males who then fertilise the virgin population of females. For these newly awakened maidens this is the only real sexual encounter they will have. After laying two or three eggs, enclosed in a tough coat to withstand the winter, these water fleas usually revert to their old celibate ways and from their eggs spring the next parthenogenetic generation of females.

The mechanisms of parthenogenesis are similar to asexual reproduction in that a single parent produces clones leading to a rapid rise in numbers. Unlike asexual species, those animals who favour virgin birth are also able to introduce variation by sexual reproduction when times are tough. Thus the species continues to evolve through the process of natural selection. The main difference lies in the fact that these single parents are always female and always produce females when conditions are favourable. So much for being the fairer and weaker sex. These colonies of females are living proof that women can get along very nicely without men, thank you.

Males are not an essential part in the life of rotifers either. Otherwise known as wheel animalcules because of the two circles of cilia which resemble revolving wheels when they move about, rotifers are among the smallest and most widespread of the metazoans or multicellular organisms. Males are very seldom seen and for some groups of rotifers they are completely unknown. Some only lay eggs which develop into females and although a population explosion occurs their presence in the world is usually limited in this way. Those species that produce two different types of eggs, with one hatching females only while the other develops into a male or female, have a better chance of survival. The females that emerge from these eggs boast all the adult features except reproductive organs while the males emerge as sexually mature individuals.

Another common aquatic creature that favours solo sex is the gastrotrich. Both marine and freshwater species exist although the marine varieties are less known by scientists. Unlike the aphids and water fleas, the marine species are actually hermaphrodite but in one particular variety, the *Chaetonotoidea*, the male reproductive organs degenerate and all adults become females. In this way the tiny gastrotrichs have even more tricks up the proverbial sleeve than species that alternate between virgin birth and sexual reproduction. It seems incredible that in animals so small such a diversity of sexual practices can exist and yet examples of incest, transvestism and sexual reproduction can be found in most animals that opt for the purity and guaranteed numbers of virgin birth.

When parthenogenesis was first discovered it was thought by many serious naturalists and philosophers of the day that some species of mam-

---

THE CASE OF THE OVERGROWN VAGINA

The prize for the world's biggest sex organ, relatively speaking, would have to go the humble bumblebee eelworm. After mating, which results in the death of the male, the female undergoes an incredible transformation. Her vagina actually inflates until it is almost 20,000 times bigger than she is. At this point it takes on a life of its own. The female becomes superfluous and her body shrivels up and disintegrates. However, even her vagina is not long for this world. As soon as the eggs hatch and the new generation of worms emerge, it too passes away.

---

mals and other more advanced life forms also reproduced by virgin birth. These fanciful notions have since been disproved but on the other hand, virgin birth is not limited to the tiny aquatic organisms and terrestrial pests. Parthenogenesis is common among stick-insects, for instance, although they too alternate between virgin birth and sexual reproduction. Stick-insects and leaf-insects are often kept by small children as pets because of their unusual appearance which is designed to camouflage them from their natural predators. The stick-insect, as its name suggests, is very hard to distinguish from a pile of leaves and sticks and even when separated its body looks exactly like a bunch of sticks glued together to form an eight-legged animal. In some species a male is an extremely rare find. This is thought to be due in part to their slow and sluggish lifestyle which has no need for the rigours of sexual reproduction. They have developed such a good camouflage that to move around looking for a mate would instantly reveal them to their natural enemies. As long as a stick-insect stays put it is just another blot on the landscape. However, these creatures remain anything but still. During the warm weather months, a female stick-insect is capable of producing hundreds of eggs at the rate of two or three a day. These are casually dropped onto the ground where they remain for four to six months before hatching. Even then the young take another four to seven months to grow to maturity, their rate of growth depending largely on the weather. If it is unusually warm for the time of year they may take only a couple of months to reach full adulthood, at which point they are fully equipped for manic reproduction.

Among vertebrate animals, virgin birth does not appear to exist. Indeed, invertebrate animals really seem to enjoy a much more varied and exciting sex life than the staid lovemaking of the vertebrates. However, despite the sometimes unlimited sexual positions an insect, for example, is able to adopt, copulation among the invertebrates is usually so quick that it does not seem likely that either partner can derive much sexual pleasure from the encounter. On the other hand sex between vertebrate couples can last all night long with obvious signs and sounds of gratification from both sexes. Although there is no convincing evidence, some scientific circles believe that two species of lizard exist which make abortive attempts at virgin birth. The Chequered Whiptail Lizard found in Texas and the *Lacerta saxicola* of the Caucasus have been found in some areas with populations in which not a single male exists. In other areas both male and female flourish in both species. Scientists remain puzzled even today.

Homosexuality

Considered a heinous crime in some civilised countries with criminal penalties to match, homosexuality is almost as natural and common as heterosexual monogamy. Perhaps this is a slight overstatement but like many other sexual practices, homosexuality, i.e. having sex with a member of the same gender, occurs frequently in the natural world. In many higher animals, such as mammals and primates, homosexuality is a stage that many young males and females pass through before reaching sexual maturity. Perhaps this is due to the more relaxed reproductive timetables of some animals which give them time to experiment. It seems more likely, however, that they are merely practising on each other as no female would let a young male near her until she is sexually mature. As many breeders know, a female horse or cow shows her readiness to mate when she begins trying to mount others of her own sex in the male fashion. Male dolphins have also been observed making eyes at other males and ignoring the females.

However, there are many examples of mammals where homosexuality is not just a substitute for the missing member of the opposite sex. In the complex society of baboons, for instance, homosexuality is an accepted part of life and not an outlawed practice. It is thought by scientists that this is due to the complicated dominance rules among the gregarious apes. In order to demonstrate their acceptance of the dominant males and their submissive role among the baboon group the young males often offer themselves sexually to the dominant baboon. It is a gesture of humility that is rarely rejected by the leader of the pack. In the same way weaker females defer to stronger females in the group by allowing them to take their sexual pleasure with them. Both young females and males may benefit from their humility. In the case of a young male baboon who has

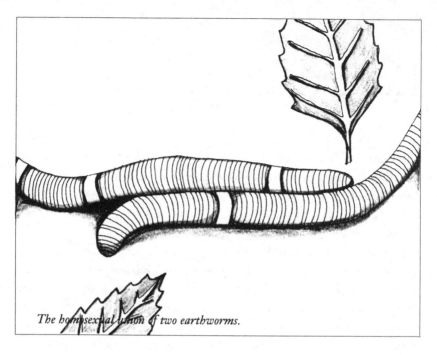

The homosexual union of two earthworms.

offered himself sexually to the superior male baboon, the dominant male will in return provide protection against the attacks of other apes. When the stronger of the two males is about to snatch food from the mouth of the weaker, a practice that is part of the law of the jungle, the lesser male frequently proposes sex and in return is allowed to keep the food.

Many hermaphrodite animals, or those which possess two sex organs, are homosexual in the strict sense of the word. Take the earthworm, one of Darwin's favourites, as a case in point. It is a fascinating animal and well deserved the attention Darwin gave it in his study *The Formation of Vegetable Mould through the Action of Earthworms.* They are natural ploughs, turning over soil as they move, changing dead plants into humus, mixing nitrogen and organic matter together in the soil and stirring up the soil particles so that oxygen and water can be spread evenly throughout. The appearance of earthworms was also a major evolutionary breakthrough as they were the first jointed animals. Every creature since can trace its ancestry back to the common earthworm, including humans. Instead of a tube the earthworm's body consists of several segments. It has a well-developed nervous system, a simple brain, a body cavity made up of a number of different chambers as well as muscle and blood vessels. Despite its complex structure the earthworm retains the amazing ability of some of its ancestors to regenerate if it is cut in two. However, the break must be somewhere near the middle and only one half will heal and survive. If too many segments are cut up the earthworm dies. Considering the number of natural predators the earthworm has, it is just as well it has some limited powers of regeneration to help replace the losses by heavy predation.

NO SLEEPING ON THE JOB

Imagine being caught in a loving embrace for almost half a year. A pair of Indian Pythons have been observed copulating for 180 days. Talk about suffocating love!

One of the most interesting features of the earthworm is the pale swelling in the middle of its body known as the *clitellum* which is Latin for saddle. From this bulge emerges the fertilised eggs. The earthworm has a distinctly homosexual union. It is a hermaphrodite and has testes at the rear end of its body and oviducts in the front. When it mates, however, the female half is still inactive and so what takes place is a strictly homosexual union. The two worms first place themselves in a sexual position, side by side, so that the head of one is touching the rear of its partner. The saddle in the middle secretes a 'love juice' which glues them together for the duration of their lovemaking. Each earthworm then discharges his sperm into pocket-like storage structures known as sperm receptacles but actual fertilisation does not occur for some time. The saddle must first secrete a substance which is passed by muscular contractions through the body of the earthworm, picking up the fertilised eggs along the way. Towards the end of its journey it hardens and changes into a closed cocoon which houses the eggs. This is then buried in the soil with enough food to nourish the young earthworms until they are ready to emerge as miniature copies of their parents.

Hermaphrodite slugs also engage in anal sex with each other. These land molluscs look like snails without shells although some may have a hard shell hidden just under their skin. During courtship both participants secrete copious amounts of slime, forming an edible trail which they both eat. In some species, such as the European Great Grey Slug and the American Black Slug, more than an hour is spent working up great quantities of slime before they suddenly wrap themselves around each other and throw themselves into the air with a rope of slime acting

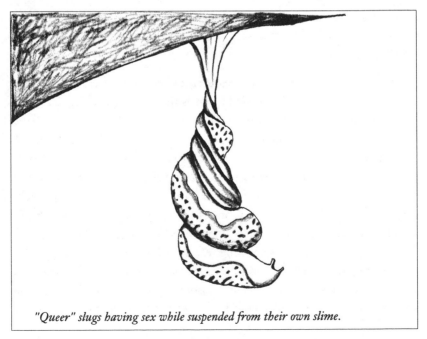

"Queer" slugs having sex while suspended from their own slime.

as a safety line. As they dangle from the slime both slugs whip out huge two-inch penises half their body size and wrap these around each other to exchange sperm. Then, after they have finished copulating, the penises are wound up again as they would impede movement if they were allowed to drag along the ground behind the slug. All of which goes to show that length is not necessarily an advantage.

Polyandry

The Animal Kingdom is on the whole a male dominated world and some species are clearly a case for women's liberation. Yet there is little room for change because nature has decreed a variety of mating styles to suit each individual species. Perhaps this is why polyandry, the practice of females having more than one mate at a time or in succession is so much rarer than its counter sexual style, polygamy. It is a classic example of role reversal where, after both sexes have mated, the male raises the young while the female goes off in search of her next sexual partner. In this aspect polyandrous females differ from promiscuous females, who may have sex with several males over a period but cannot escape their family responsibilities. The most well-known examples of polyandry can be found among birds like the Jacana, cuckoos, American Rhea and the Tasmanian Native Hen though some humans and insects also favour polyandry.

The development of polyandry in bird species is thought to have come about after a change in conditions set one member of a pair free from family duties. Historically this has been the male but in some cases the female has become liberated instead. Take the Jacana as a case in point. This large waterbird is found on the shores of lakes and big rivers. It is extremely well adapted to its environment having long legs, toes and flat claws which allow it to walk on floating vegetation without sinking. This gives the impression that the Jacana can walk on water and in some countries it is known as the Jesus Christ Bird for this reason. The female is generally larger than the male and more colourful too, thus breaking the rules of sexual dimorphism in the bird world. After all it is widely recognised that male birds usually boast the brilliant plumage and beautiful song while the females are plain and dull looking. This rule is turned on its head in the case of the Jacana where the female bird outshines the male in size and, to a certain extent, in colour. Both birds are generally black and maroon although the female displays bright yellow wings during courtship. In her relationships with male Jacanas, it is easy to see who wears the pants as the old saying goes.

A female Jacana will select and defend a large territory in which she keeps a harem of smaller and more inconspicuous males. During the breeding season she moves from one to the other, mating with each in turn and then leaving the male holding the baby so to speak. It is his duty to incubate the eggs and look after the chicks when they hatch. In the female Jacana's case the marsh environment has probably been the key to setting her free from domestic duties as it is a rich food source.

OH TO BE AMBIDEXTROUS

For the small fish known as the Four Eyed Anablep, its very existence depends on being able to tell left from right. The male's penis is either on his left or right side. The females may also have their sex organs on the left or right. So a male with a left penis must mate with a female with a right vagina and vice versa.

The Painted Snipe, so called because of its snipe-like build and bright colouring also favours a reversal of normal sexual behaviour. These small wading birds are found in the humid parts of Australia, Africa and South America and like the Jacana, the female is larger than the male and more brightly coloured. At mating time she is the aggressor and fights for sexual privileges with the males. Once she has laid her eggs she deserts the male, leaving him the task of incubation and care of the young. The Hemipode Quail are also thought to be polyandrous although little is known of their breeding activities in the wild.

In other bird species like the rhea and native hen, polyandry has assumed a slightly different appearance. The males are less submissive and instead play an active role in polyandrous mating. This variation is common in the human world and is usually referred to as 'wife swapping'. Two males, often related, take a wife and both have sex with her. It is a simple case of supply and demand where there is a far greater ratio of males to females. The American Rhea, which belongs to the same group as ostriches, is a colourful bird often found feeding on clover and lucerne with a herd of cattle. This bird has developed a mating system where females are passed around more than once as there are not quite enough to satisfy all the males. The Tasmanian Native Hen has also been observed fulfilling the law of supply and demand on that remote island.

Perhaps the most extreme example of polyandry is the female cuckoo. She mates with several males in one season but neither she nor the cock bird want anything to do with the eggs once they are laid. Thus, the female has developed a parasitic way of offloading her unwanted young on to other bird species. Cuckoos show none of those maternal feelings towards their offspring that make birds so endearing in the eyes of humans. Indeed, many naturalists have condemned the cuckoo for her laziness in not wanting to build her own nest or rear her young. Some have even pointed out that the species as a whole is so indolent that they even perch on the shoulders of herons during migration. Cuckoos are such poor fliers they would collapse from exhaustion if they had to make the entire journey unaided. While not all species of cuckoos are polyandrous, the most parasitic variety is recognised for this aberration. The female travels from territory to territory having sex with each male before stealing away to look for the nest of another bird in which to dump her offspring. Strange eggs in a nest are usually ignored or thrown over the side but the cuckoo has the ability to lay eggs remarkably similar in shape and colour to those already in the nest. Indeed, they are generally very successful in this subterfuge. Cuckoos' eggs are for the most part quite small and manage to go unnoticed in a sparrow's nest where the other eggs are of a diminutive size. The parents, even if they do recognise the egg as being an imposter, are often too weak to push it out of the nest and so resign themselves to brooding it along with their own. When the eggs hatch the demands of the chicks become intolerable and would become impossible were it not for the murderous habits of the new-born cuckoo. Although it seems like a helpless infant the young cuckoo actually pushes its stepbrothers and stepsisters out of the nest so that it is the sole recipient of food and attention. It then arouses the protective spirit in its parents who dote on it, feed it and rear it as if it were its own. If the cuckoo's egg is laid in a larger bird's nest, the young cuckoo chick need not slay his nestmates at so tender an age as the large parents are big and strong enough to feed one extra mouth without their own children having to suffer. The female cuckoo's lack of maternal instinct permits her to spend more time mating with males and in a good season she may lay and desert up to twenty eggs before flying on her way. Together, her polyandry and parasitism are a winning combination and serve to increase egg production and thus preserve the species.

Strange sex organs

Penises and vaginas come in as many different shapes and sizes as animals themselves. Given that there are over a million known species of animal life existing on earth, the range of sex organs is very varied and extensive. Most are in proportion to the animal's physical structure but as we know, nothing is ever completely ordered and uniform in nature. Indeed, there are quite a few surprises to be had in the organ loft! Many males, for instance, have evolved sex organs that cannot be classed in any other category except the bizarre. We have already seen the legs and arms that double as penises when called upon for duty and these must surely have painful consequences for the long suffering female. Yet this is just the tip of the iceberg so to speak. The list of weird and wonderful penises could go on *ad infinitum* but males are not alone in sporting peculiar organs. Females too boast some peculiar equipment. Some female worms, for example, become little more than inflated vaginas when they breed while others actually extend their vaginas to give a warm welcome to the penis.

Female threadworms are particularly strange creatures when it comes to their sexual organs. Although quite primitive animals, they have surprising similarities to higher orders with the two sexes being easily distinguished from each other. The female's vagina is located in the centre of her body while the male is equipped with a special pouch at the end of his body where he houses his hooked and fork-shaped penis. So far everything seems fairly normal. However, an element of the bizarre is introduced when the two come together. The way their sexual union takes place is far from the usual straightfoward insertion of the penis into the female's sexual opening. In one species, the Turnip Eelworm, for example, the female grows what looks like buds on her body. When ready to mate she brings herself close to the skin of the turnip which she inhabits. She then breaks through the turnip skin and pushes her vagina through the opening. The males then leave their turnip houses and slide around on the outside of the vegetable looking for a suitable bud into which they can insert their forked hooks. Although this may seem like an extremely strange sex ritual it actually makes sense as the worms are merely using their surrounding environment, in this case the turnip, in the most efficient way possible. When you pick up turnip with a hole in it, think of the little Eelworm.

BIGGER IS BETTER

The penis of the armadillo is about one-third its body length. Armadillos are also unique as each female gives birth to identical quadruplets. The four offspring come from a single fertilised egg that divides when development begins.

From the same group of worms comes the Bumblebee Eelworm that undergoes an incredible transformation after being fertilised. Once mating has occurred, which actually results in the death of the male, the female begins looking for queen Bumblebees to live in while she waits out winter. Once ensconced in her new home she undergoes a strange transformation. Her vagina begins to expand until it is fifteen to twenty thousand times bigger than her entire body. At this point her body becomes redundant until it hangs from the huge, inflated vagina like an insignificant thread. Finally her body disintegrates entirely and is cast off from the vagina. For a short time the vagina assumes a life of its own until the eggs hatch and the new generation of worms leave the Bumblebee.

One poor creature does not even possess a sexual opening. Although this would prove an insurmountable problem for humans, most people find it hard to work up any sympathy because the animal is one of the most repulsive insects known to humans: the bedbug. This blood sucking creature emits a foul odour and although it will live off any warm-blooded animal, it is particularly keen on human blood. Perhaps the one positive thing that can be said about the tiny insect is that it is very clean and does not transmit disease. Unlike the tick, whose greedy appetite can inflate it to the size of a golf ball, the bedbug stops feeding when it has had enough. At the point when the female reaches sexual maturity and an eager young male comes along he is more than a little taken aback to discover that his sweetheart lacks a vagina. But no self-respecting bedbug will let a small problem like that dampen his enthusiasm. He simply drills his own vagina. By tracing a more or less dotted line from the female's abdomen the male locates the perfect spot to begin gouging out his dream hole. The enterprising lad is even equipped with his own drilling equipment, a penis, which is large, curved and ends in a sharp point. In this way he can have sex on the job as the saying goes. Once his member has been inserted in the female he releases copious quantities of sperm which swim around in the female's blood until they reach special sacs. From these they make their way up to the ovaries and wait for the eggs to be released. The female's new vagina soon heals over but the event leaves a horrible scar. Although such a large quantity of sperm seems unnecessary, the female bedbug actually feeds on some of it when blood is scarce. Indeed, males have been known to drill holes and deposit semen in each other as an alternative food source when there is no blood available.

Despite the vampire-like diet of the bedbug it does have the decency to stop sucking while it copulates. The bed tick, in contrast, has no such scruples and instead makes a meal of sex. In this way the tick is even more repulsive than the bedbug. The male approaches the female while she is attached to her warm-blooded meal and forces his way in between her and her host. Despite being so rudely interrupted, the female shows no great signs of distress as the male busies himself with the task at hand. To begin with he starts dilating her vagina so he can fit in the packet of sperm he has been carrying round. Obviously the male bedtick is no great lover because during the course of sex the female never gives him a glance but merely continues feeding. The fact is, however, that she cannot afford not to. The blood, rich in nutrients, is essential for the successful fertilisation of her eggs and their subsequent development.

The female marine Bristleworm has an appetite to match that of the female bedtick although in a slightly different way. She actually devours the sex organ of her lover. Bristleworms are interesting animals from an evolutionary standpoint as they display primitive signs of courtship behaviour, which reach their peak in birds and mammals. At mating time they congregate in large numbers and the males put on a dancing show for the females, twisting their bodies in seemingly impossible contortions. Their performance drives the females into a state of wild sexual excitement and as this reaches its climax, they release their eggs. The males stop dancing instantly and spray the eggs with their sperm. However, in some species the female becomes so turned on by the erotic dancing of the male that she loses all control. In a frenzy of sexual excitement she leaps upon the unsuspecting male and bites off the top of his penis, in a kind of vicious underwater fellation. She then swallows the sperm which travels through her body and ultimately fertilises the eggs.

Females are also the dominant sexual players in other underwater species like the Deep-Sea Angler. These fish seem particularly bizarre to humans as we are used to thinking of males as being more powerful, larger and usually more beautiful. Yet the female Deep-Sea Angler is at least 20 times the size of her male suitors. These primitive fish live in the darkest depths of the ocean where there are only a few forms of life. Food is scarce and opportunities of meeting up with the opposite sex are slim. For this reason when a male spots a female ready to spawn he wastes no time courting her or coaxing her into a sexually receptive mood. Instead he simply attaches himself to her side and fertilises her eggs, never once leaving her. After some time he begins to grow out from the side of her body in a perpendicular direction. This strange arrangement is mutually beneficial as the male receives his food from the female's bloodstream and the female has a lover on call whenever she feels she needs one.

Some male sex organs are a source of wonder. The little barnacle, for instance, does not seem particularly interesting at first glance. The most common variety are the seashore Acorn Barnacles, shaped like little cones, that fix themselves firmly to rocks and usually appear in large numbers. Some estimates put their numbers as high as one billion over just one and a half kilometres of rocky shoreline. Originally they were classed as molluscs because they resembled the Limpet but today it is well known that barnacles are in fact crustaceans. Because of their sedentary lifestyle it was once thought that female barnacles merely released their eggs into the sea where they were randomly fertilised by the dispersal of male sperm. However, this has since been disproved. Although each individual is a hermaphrodite, self-fertilisation does not occur. Instead, the male barnacle has an elongated penis which he is able to extend to his nearest neighbour and fertilisation occurs in this way.

Fatal love

There are many examples of animals in the wild where the females have sex with a mate and then calmly eat him afterwards. This cannibalistic approach to love seems repulsive to humans but as we have seen there is always a reason in the natural world for even the most horrific behaviour. Often the impetus behind eating a partner after sexual intimacy is because of a condition known as protein hunger. After the male has performed his function, i.e. fertilising the female, he becomes superfluous in many species and, it is argued, would soon die anyway. Instead of wasting the wonderful nutrients in his body the female eats him. Thus, he acts as both father and food for the future offspring. While few females actually eat their mates some devour the sperm packet or spermatophore instead. The female grasshopper in particular considers the spermatophore a wonderful delicacy and it was probably her practice of eating the spermatophore which eventually led her to make a meal of the whole male instead.

The most famous example of sexual cannibalism is the Praying Mantis. These predatory insects derived their name from the manner in which they wait for their prey, with their forelimbs raised in a similar fashion to humans when they put their hands together in supplication. Praying Mantises are sinister looking creatures with amazing camouflage in both colour and shape. Their arms, although appearing to be lifted in prayer, are actually deadly weapons, that are able to cut small prey in half or hold them in an unrelenting grip while they are eaten alive. So adapted have they become to a predatory life that Praying Mantises have been known to add frogs, lizards and even small birds to their diet. Given their surprising hunting abilities it is no wonder that these accomplished killers treat their mates less than kindly. During the mating season, the male approaches the female with a spermatophore and the larger female throws her lethal arms around the male and accepts its placement in her sexual opening. She then turns around and falls on her lover and begins munching him for an after-sex snack. Sometimes the male has not even finished copulating before she begins nibbling away at him. Fortunately his sex drive is so strong he is able to continue even while being slowly eaten away. The female's ravenous appetite is the subject of some considerable controversy although most observers agree that she does eat the male on many occasions. It is still a matter of fierce debate.

The cannibal appetites of other species, however, leave absolutely no room for doubt. Scorpions, for example, display a tender and charming courtship to the world but this only lasts for a couple of hours and is only a cheap veneer of respectability. After lengthy dancing and caressing each

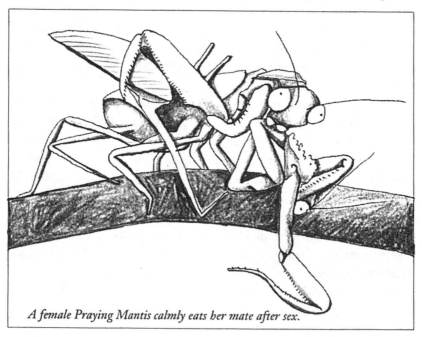

A female Praying Mantis calmly eats her mate after sex.

other, the female takes the initiative and leads the male off to have sex. Once she has ensured that fertilisation has been successful the female turns on her lover and makes him her next meal. Female Wheel-Web Spiders, *Argiope lobata*, have the same irresistible compulsion. The male expends so much energy having sex that he flops back exhausted and dies. The cold-hearted female does not even observe a polite period of mourning but jumps on his body straight away and begins feasting.

Tarantulas are not quite as bloodthirsty, although males must still be extremely cautious when making love overtures to females. The male is smaller than the female and is thus easily overpowered. This makes him a somewhat stealthy suitor as discussed earlier. The male Tarantula keeps his distance from the female at first to ascertain her mood. If she is receptive to his advances she will join him in a courtship dance which excites both sexes and prepares them for sex. Actual mating is a brief rough-and-tumble affair with limbs poking out in all directions. Once he has inserted his spermatophore the male does not linger but generally beats a quick retreat before the female changes her mind and decides to eat him after all.

The female Ant Lion is another accomplished murderess. The young of this fascinating insect build funnels in the sand and lurk at the bottom waiting for their prey to slide down into their perfectly constructed trap. If their victim tries to escape they throw loose sand at it, forcing it to lose its footing and slide back down again. When mature, ant lions gain large wings and the ability to fly, which they only do at night. The females have an insatiable appetite and are much feared predators although their bloodthirstiness only really appears when they have sex. Like the scorpion, the female turns ruthlessly on to her mate after sex, first murdering him and then devouring him. To the first count of murder will be added many others as she kills and eats every other male she can catch, adding new meaning to the term 'man-eater'. Golden Ground Beetles are another

The male Tarantula's dance makes the female receptive to lovemaking.

species who eat their lovers.

Often males duel over a female and in the process they sometimes wound each other, although nature has thrown up many safeguards to stop this happening. Usually the lesser animal realises when he has been outdone and slinks off, leaving the victor to carry away his bride. Many ornamental fish are extremely ferocious during the breeding season and the slightest provocation can start a fight over a female. Siamese Fighting Fish, as their name suggests, are particularly famous for their underwater duels. Most of these fights end with the characteristic gesture of submission at which point the winning male takes the spoils of war, namely the female, and lets the loser make good his escape. Their chivalrous behaviour is proof that not all bizarre sexual behaviour in the natural world is necessarily gruesome. Indeed, some of the most tender courtship rituals are found in the Labyrinth Fish. Another popular aquarium species actually kiss each other for up to half an hour before mating. This very human embrace has earned them the nickname, "Kissing Gourami". Perhaps this is why these colourful fish are so popular as pets. Not only are they beautiful to look at and easy to breed in captivity, they also imitate the romantic gestures of human lovers. Although kissing is generally a prelude to sex between male and female, two males may sometimes join at the lip to frighten rivals from their territory.

Age of consent

Most western countries have laws stating that a male or female is allowed to have relations with the opposite sex at either sixteen or eighteen. While it may seem a little heavy-handed to dictate the expression of sexuality in the highly individualistic human world, the laws of nature are usually even more rigid. If they are broken the lawbreaker is always caught and punishment follows soon after; generally the union is sterile. However, natural laws are broad enough to include the most bizarre sexual practices imaginable, of which child brides are just one. Reproduction before sexual maturity is scientifically called paedogenesis, from the Greek word *paidos*, meaning of a child. Sex at an even earlier age is known as polyembryony and we have only to turn to the incredibly varied world of insects to find examples of both. Indeed, no other group of animals has managed to develop so many different mating styles. Not only do they enjoy all the traditional forms of sex but have many more of their own. Take the Gall Midge for instance. These small flies, which look remarkably similar to mosquitoes, start to reproduce before they have grown up. This process begins when a mature female lays copious amounts of eggs which develop into larvae. The new larvae in turn produce eggs of their own which grow inside the larvae and eat the parent from the inside. Children producing children may continue for several generations without a single adult. Eventually they leave their original parent as an empty shell of her former self and turn into male and female adults. Sexual discovery is even earlier in the Chalcid Wasp as the eggs themselves breed. Chalcid Wasps are parasites that lay their eggs in the eggs of moths. When the moth egg hatches, the wasp becomes entrenched in the caterpillar's body. It then divides into clumps of cells which form embryos. These develop into adult wasps that eventually emerge from the dead caterpillar.

One of the most familiar child brides known to humans is the popular aquarium pet and textbook example, the axolotl. Found in Mexico, where they are considered a great delicacy, its name is the Mexican word for 'water sport'. The axolotl is in fact the larva of a salamander, an oversized baby that has never grown up. Axolotls become sexually mature but remain physically immature and instead of growing into a terrestrial form, they keep their wide fin down the back, their tail and the feathery external gills. Despite this immaturity, axolotls are still able to breed and produce

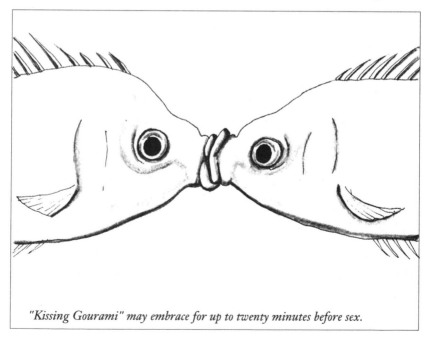

"Kissing Gourami" may embrace for up to twenty minutes before sex.

fertile offspring. Their stunted growth is thought to be caused by a deficiency in diet which prevents the production of a vital hormone, thyroxine, from the thyroid gland which controls metamorphosis. An essential ingredient in the composition of thryoxine is iodine and it is this mineral which is lacking in water. It is entirely possible that the axolotl's stunted growth is diet related.

OLD FASHIONED LOVE

One of the world's most ancient reptiles is the Tuatara lizard. It is the sole representative of a group of reptiles that flourished during the Age of the Dinosaurs and has survived almost unchanged for over 200 million years. Perhaps this is why it has one of the oldest ages of consent; tuataras do not breed until they reach about 20. They have simply not caught up with the times. They also have the longest incubation period of any reptiles as the eggs take up to 15 months to hatch.

Transvestism

In the human world sex change operations are a recent phenomenon; in nature they have been taking place for millions of years. The human operation, from man to woman or vice versa, is a drawn out process with many emotional and physical problems attached. Nature's operation is far simpler and much quicker. For instance, there are some male worms that, when they cannot find a mate, are not content just to live as parasites but change into females and mate with other males. Interestingly there are no known creatures who can change their sex from female to male. Quite why this is so remains a mystery.

The most popular example of transvestism in nature is that much loved bivalve, the oyster. Unlike the worm it does not change its sex because conditions are no longer favourable or it cannot find a mate. Instead, the changes occur on a fairly regular basis. The oyster is a hermaphrodite but as the eggs and sperm mature at different times there is always a rhythmic alteration between male and female. An individual oyster can be female one day, drawing in the sperm impregnated water through its gills to fertilise its ova. Within a week that same female becomes a male, releasing sperm so that its neighbouring female will be fertilised. In this way, the humble oyster enjoys the best of both worlds. By changing sex almost as frequently as the wind changes, oysters are able to reproduce at lightning speed. At one time scientists enthusiastically announced that a single oyster could produce ten million offspring a year when conditions were favourable. Since then the breeding of oysters has become much more established, and the estimates are more conservative. It is now thought that older oysters are able to produce up to one million offspring a year while the younger and less mature oysters produce a little less than this. Whatever the final figure may be it is still an admirable achievement.

Some hermaphrodite animals change sex because the testes mature before the ovaries or vice versa. The small sea slater, *Hemioniscuc balani*, for instance, is male when young and mobile but later becomes a female when it loses its ability to move about and becomes sedentary. They are parasitic by nature and usually fasten themselves to barnacles and make a meal from their tissues. While in the male mode, however, these slaters travel from one barnacle to the next, fertilising the sedentary females that live in them. Once it finds a barnacle free of females it gives up its nomadic lifestyle and its manhood and becomes a woman. Now it is her turn to sit and play the waiting game in the hope that a visiting male will come and fertilise her.

Transvestism can even be found among certain tropical fishes. The Cleaner Fish of the Great Barrier Reef in Australia for example, boast females that change into males on special occasions. So named because other fish allow the Cleaner Fish to remove parasites from their skin and even from inside their mouths, they open up shop near prominent pieces of coral or rock. Cleaner Fish generally run a group business in which eight or ten individuals have shares. Among this group there is only one male and he runs the show, ranking the rest of the group, who are all females, according to size. Each female is then given her own little territorial franchise to run. The largest and most dominant female has an extensive territory second in size only to the boss male. If he dies suddenly, she takes over the reins of the business and his territory and after a few days, she will actually turn into a male. Soon he/she will be fertilising all the females in the group and he/she will look and behave like a male. As sexual dimorphism is marked between the two sexes the female must accomplish quite a change. Females are blue and striped with black while the dominant male is bright yellow. When a female changes to male she adopts a patterned green, orange and yellow colour out of respect for the dead male's memory. It all sounds very fishy.

Couvade

Among both primitive and civilised peoples there is a strange custom where the male pretends to undergo confinement. When a woman becomes pregnant he will imitate her behaviour. He sleeps when she does, restricts his diet, tolerates all sorts of painful trials and tribulations and takes care of the infant when it is born. This tradition supposedly fosters a close link between father and child and in the animal world some amphibious species not only copy the actions of the pregnant female but actually experience them. The Nose Frogs, made famous by Darwin, leave no t's uncrossed nor i's undotted in their version of couvade. Found on the southern coast of Chile, these tiny frogs, *Rhinoderma darwini* , are famous for their child rearing traditions. When Darwin first observed them he noticed that the bellies of some specimens were swollen and that if slit open several tadpoles popped out. As a result they were assumed to be female but scientists were amazed that an amphibian should practise internal fertilisation whereby the young developed inside the body of the female. Imagine the uproar then when it was discovered that these 'females' were actually males. It seemed impossible to have found pregnant males and what is more, it was pronounced impossible. After further

---

MR MOM

The seahorse is the only animal where the male carries the burden of pregnancy. Role reversal is complete in this unique and progressive species of fish. When ready to breed the female inserts a nipple-like appendage into the male, releasing her eggs into a special pouch in the male's stomach. He then discharges sperm over them. Once fertilised the male's belly assumes its rounded shape. When the baby seahorses have grown sufficiently he releases the tiny offspring into the sea.

---

study it was realised that the male was actually an incubator for the eggs. Two weeks after the female lays her eggs, the male swallows as many as he can and stores them in a throat sac which extends from his chin to his thighs. The tiny spawn then grow into the tissue where they are nourished until they outgrow the tadpole stage and become tiny frogs. At this point they leave their father in the same way as they entered him — through the mouth. The Tree Frog also takes on the kids while still encased in their eggs. He has a somewhat easier time that the nose frog, however, as the eggs stick to his back where they complete their development. When ready to lead an independent life from their devoted parent, the father takes his burden down to a river or pond where the young are simply washed off to a life of their own.

Animal Kingdom

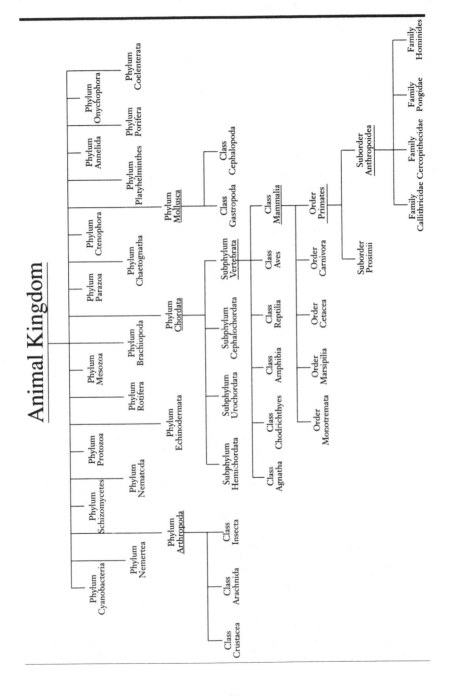

Glossary

amplexus
a mating embrace unique to amphibians and particularly common among frogs and toads.

carapace
that part of the exoskeleton covering the dorsal surface of an animal.

cloaca
end passage of the alimentary canal into which genital and excretory ducts lead.

dorsal
near the back of an animal.

epiglottis
a flap of tissue unique to mammals which covers the opening from the windpipe to the throat when swallowing.

genes
carriers of information which determine inherited characteristics. Located in a linear progression along the chromosomes in each cell nucleus.

gestation
period of pregnancy.

hectocotylus
arm or other appendage of an organism that doubles as a penis and fills with sperm before copulation. May snap off after sex or revert to its previous function. Found only in the *Cephalopoda*.

hemipenes
pair of penises that sometimes act as one during sex.

hermaphrodite   an animal that has both male and female reproductive organs.

larynx   voice box or vocal organ found in the windpipes of mammals.

mandibles   the lower jaw in vertebrates. A jaw-like appendage in invertebrates.

maxillary palps   large front legs found in some arachnids that double as a sperm-filled penis during sex.

micropyle   a special opening in insects through which the sperm travels after leaving the spermatheca.

oestrous cycle   the length of time a female mammal is able to be fertilised during the breeding season.

paedogenesis   used to describe animals that are able to reproduce before they reach sexual maturity.

parthenogenesis   or virgin birth. The development of an egg(s) without being fertilised.

pedipalp   a pair of appendages at the head of arachnids that is often modified for sex. May also be used as sense organ, or to help movement.

pheromone   a chemical that plays an important role in the sex lives of many animals, especially insects.

placenta a chord-like structure in mammals which passes food between mother and developing embryo. Also helps respiration.

polyembryony used to describe animals that are able to reproduce even at the embryonic stage of development.

sexual dimorphism physical differences between males and females from the same species.

spermatheca a body cavity used as storage space for sperm, which is used later for fertilisation when the ova are released.

spermatophore a packet containing sperm which may be inserted by a male into a female's sexual cavity or left on the ground for her to pick up.

spinneret a structure that produces and spins silk in arachnids.

stridulation the practice of producing noise by rubbing body parts together.

swim bladder a symmetrical sac found in fishes that fills with air, regulating the hydrostatic balance of the body.

syrinx the singing instrument in birds which controls and modifies song. Consists of muscle fibres which protect the vocal chords.

thorax the part of an animal behind the head. It often contains appendages used in movement. In vertebrates it contains the heart and lungs or gills, as well as the front pair of legs.

tymbal a drum-like structure found in some fishes that helps produce and resonate sound.

vulva the external part of a female's genitalia.

Bibliography

Barker, John and Grigg, Gordon, *A Field Guide to Australian Frogs*, Rigby Limited, 1977.

Bright, Michael, *Animal Language*, British Broadcasting Corporation, 1984.

Burns, Eugene, *The Sex Life of Wild Animals*, Fawcett Publications, 1956.

Burton, Robert, *The Mating Game*, Elsevier International Projects Ltd, Oxford, 1976.

Burton, Robert, *Animal Senses*, A.H. & A.W. Reed, 1973.

Burton, Robert, *The Language of Smell*, Routledge & Kegan Paul Ltd, 1976.

Clark, Michael, *Mammal Watching*, Severn House Naturalists Library, 1981.

Clyne, Densey, *Wildlife of Australia*, Reed Books Pty Ltd, 1988.

Clyne, Densey, *How to Attract Butterflies to Your Garden*, Reed Books Pty Ltd, 1990.

Darlington, C.D., *The Facts of Life*, George Allen & Unwin Ltd, 1953.

BIBLIOGRAPHY

Darwin, Charles. Abridged and introduced by Richard E Leakey, *The Illustrated Origin of Species*, Faber and Faber Ltd, 1979

Downer, John, *Supersense: Perception in the Animal World*, BBC Books, 1988.

Echternacht, Arthur C., *How Reptiles and Amphibians Live*, Elsevier Phaidon, 1977.

Encyclopedia of Reptiles, Amphibians and Other Cold-Blooded Animals, Octopus Books Limited, 1975.

Freedman, Hy, *Sex Link*, New England Library, 1977.

Frings, Hubert and Mable, *Animal Communication*, University of Oklahoma Press, 1964.

Guinness, *Remarkable Animals*, Guinness books, 1987.

Gooders, John, *The Great Book of Birds*, The Dial Press, 1975.

Gould, Stephen Jay, *The Panda's Thumb*, Penguin Books, 1980.

Larousse Encyclopedia of Animal Life, Hamlyn Publishing Group, 1967.

Lockley, Ronald M., *Whales, Dolphins & Porpoises*, David & Charles, 1979.

Macdonald, J.D., *Australian Birds: a popular guide to bird life*, Reed Books Pty Ltd, 1980.

BIBLIOGRAPHY

The Marshall Cavendish Illustrated Encyclopedia of Plants and Animals,
Marshall Cavendish Book Ltd, 1975.

Mash, Kaye, *How Invertebrates Live*, Elsevier Phaidon, 1975.

McFarland David, ed., *The Oxford Companion to Animal Behaviour*,
Oxford University Press, 1981.

Morgan, David (Supervising editor),. *Biological Science: the web of life*,
Australian Academy of Science, 1967.

Parsons, Alexandra, *Facts and Phalluses*, The Watermark Press, 1988.

Patterson, Colin, *Evolution*, University of Queensland Press, 1978.

Rowley, Ian, *Bird Life*, William Collins Australia Ltd, 1974.

Schwartz, Kit, *The Male Member*, St Martin's Press, 1985.

Street, Philip, *Animal Reproduction*, David & Charles, 1974.

Taylor, David, *The Ultimate Cat Book*, R. D. Press, 1989.

Tinbergen, Niko, *Animal Behaviour*, Time Life International, 1965.

Young, J.Z., *The Life of Vertebrates*, Oxford at the Clarendon Press, 1962.

Index

S